PAUL DANIELS

AND THE

STORY OF MAGIC

by the same author

FUNNY WAY TO BE A HERO
THE MAGIC OF LEWIS CARROLL
CALL THEM IRREPLACEABLE
GEORGE FORMBY: THE UKULELE MAN
'NEVER GIVE A SUCKER AN EVEN BREAK'
BODY MAGIC

PAUL DANIELS
AND THE
STORY OF MAGIC

John Fisher

JONATHAN CAPE
THIRTY-TWO BEDFORD SQUARE LONDON

First published 1987
Copyright © 1987 by John Fisher

Jonathan Cape Ltd, 32 Bedford Square, London WC1B 3EL

British Library Cataloguing in Publication Data

Fisher, John, 1945–
Paul Daniels and the story of magic.
1. Magic—History
I. Title
133.4′3′09   BF1589

ISBN 0 224 02492 2

Printed in Italy by New Interlitho SpA, Milan

for Larry Turnbull

Contents

8   CONTENTS

I

In the Beginning: a Cup and a Ball

If magicians were to be allowed signature tricks in the way that other entertainers acquire signature tunes, there can be no doubt that Paul Daniels's trick would be his dazzling manipulation of a small white ball and a shiny aluminium cup. Whenever you visit a theatre to see Paul perform, he will always open with this display. It invariably runs with Rolls-Royce smoothness – a special talisman of a trick guaranteed to reduce any audience to rapturous laughter and produce the stunned amazement for which it is intended. It is significant that this simple illusion should enjoy such special prominence within the act of the magician who redefined the face of magic for the British public, for it is the trick which possibly started the whole magic business thousands of years ago.

No one can pinpoint with certainty the identity of the first trick in the history of magic, who performed it, or where, but it is reasonable to suppose that it involved digital skill of some kind, that the sudden delight experienced by the caveman wizard in the random manipulation of some small object anticipated the realisation that such actions could be applied to a deceptive end, let alone predated the more contrived appliance of larger apparatus and machinery, however crude, to the same purpose. Not without reason did the word 'juggler' in its earliest form actually signify a conjuror as we understand the word, and not the skilled defier of gravity familiar from later usage.

In the more generally accepted version of the 'Cups and Balls' illusion, which has become regarded as the standard test of a magician's skill, there would appear to be no limit to the effects possible with three cups and three balls, as balls appear, disappear, reappear, congregate together under the cups, penetrate them, and even change colour, size and form in the process. For many years the myth persisted that a wall-painting discovered in a tomb at Beni Hasan in Egypt, dating from around 2200 BC, provided the first pictorial representation of a magical performance. This was almost certainly not so. Research and common sense have in recent years combined to suggest that the four enormous bowl-shaped objects depicted in the mural are pieces at play in some unknown game. Nevertheless, the passing similarity to upturned, if oversize, cups was enough to call the trick to mind, even though no balls were present in the picture! Even so, there does exist more positive evidence to suggest that the trick was popular throughout the Ancient World.

Seneca, the Latin philosopher and dramatist and one-time tutor to Nero, writing in the first century AD, compared the sleight-of-hand of the conjuror to the wiles of speech used by orators. 'Such quibbles are just as harmlessly deceptive as the juggler's cups and pebbles, in which it is the very trickery that pleases me. But show me how the trick is done, and I have lost my interest therein.' Writing around two centuries later, the Greek social reporter Alciphron gave a more vivid view of a typical performance of his day, bringing home the full versatility of the trick.

One thing I saw rendered me almost speechless and made me gape with surprise. A man came forward and placed on a three-legged table three small dishes, under which he concealed some little white round pebbles. These he placed one by one under the dishes, and then, I do not know how, made them appear altogether under one. At other times he made them disappear from beneath the dishes, and showed them in his mouth. Next, when he had swallowed them, he brought those who stood nearest him into the middle, and then pulled one stone from the nose, another from the ear, and another from the head of the man standing near him. Finally, he caused the stones to vanish from the sight of everyone.

Alciphron considered the anonymous wizard so devious that if he took him to his farm, he would 'never be able to catch him in his tricks. He would steal everything I had and strip my farm of all it contains.' As modern audiences are apt to remark in the presence of a magician, 'Keep your hands on your wallet!'

In spite of the negative value of the Egyptian wall-painting so long associated with the trick, there can be no more vivid proof of its overall popularity throughout history than the iconography it has attracted. Until the recent arrival of the rabbit in his top hat, the 'Cups and Balls' were the generally accepted symbol of the conjuror. The earliest known illustration of the trick is contained in a Planet Book of the fifteenth century. Such a work was intended to show the influence of heavenly bodies on children born under their aspect. The drawing in question, the work of one Joseph from Ulm in Germany in 1404, now contained in the University library at Tübingen, depicts the lives expected of those born under the planet Luna. The conjuror, cutting quite a dash with a swirling feather in his cap, is seated at a circular table holding one cup in each hand. There are three balls on the table. The illustration tells us little about the trick, but does throw considerable light on the social standing of the performer at the time. Also depicted as typical children of the Moon are fisherman, fowler, friar,

Note the conjuror and the company he keeps in this drawing by Joseph of Ulm.

miller, builder, and mercenary. It is not difficult to imagine the entertainer as a familiar, if not respected, member of the community. The most famous image of this kind is the painting 'The Juggler', by Hieronymus Bosch, now held by the Municipal Museum of St Germain-en-Laye. In the fifteenth century nothing had changed since Alciphron's day: one of the most memorable motifs within the canvas is that of the pickpocket, probably an accomplice of the conjuror, lifting the purse of a spectator totally distracted by the wonders paraded before her.

In later years, prints and engravings depicting the 'Cups and Balls' conjuror would proliferate, placing the image before a wider public, particularly in France during the nineteenth century. Caricaturists such as Daumier and Cham frequently incorporated the trick within their cartoons to make a political point. It was during this period that a more cultured performer than the standard strolling player could also be discerned as the prominent figure in more lavish fashion plates. There was reputedly a period in France when it became fashionable for the gentry to perform the trick among themselves. One French king even indulged in the pastime, a distinct forerunner of another Royal exponent – when Prince Charles was awarded membership of the Magic Circle in 1978, it was the 'Cups and Balls' which he selected for his audition piece.

That the 'Cups and Balls' performer became throughout history the most representative member of the wider fraternity of wonder-workers is underlined by a study of their names. One ancient Roman name for conjuror was *acetabularius*, a word coined from the Latin for wine-cup or goblet; the ancient Greeks reciprocated with *psephopaikteo*, alluding to the pebbles used and their movement under the cups. A French word for magician is *escamoteur*, derived from the word in France given to the cork ball traditionally used in the effect. Similarly, a German word is *Taschenspieler*, or 'pocket-player', with reference to the pocket-style apron the itinerant magician wore to carry and to enhance his tricks before conventional pockets became embodied in clothing in the mid-sixteenth century. Anyone who has seen Paul Daniels perform will realise that three objects share equal prominence – a cup, a ball and his pocket.

Daumier was one of several caricaturists who used the cup and ball trick to draw attention to political subterfuge.

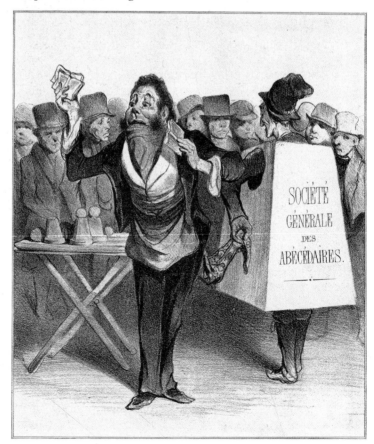

However closely you watch Paul, the ball is never where you think it is. The fruit salad at the end is an even greater surprise.

From country to country, the trick has assumed a succession of distinct national identities, while always remaining basically the same. The Egyptians will cause the balls to change into tiny chicks which skedaddle all over the table as soon as the cups are lifted; the Chinese, less squeamish, opt for baby mice. A European phase saw the fashionable production of hot roast potatoes. Since then the balls have changed into every conceivable kind of fruit or vegetable that will fit within the cup, not to mention full glasses of whisky. Due to the many variations it is impossible to say whether one nationality acquired the trick from another, or whether all those years ago it originated spontaneously in different places. Certainly it was only ever intended for intimate presentation – until, that is, Paul Daniels came along.

It is part of Paul's special talent that he can take the smallest of tricks and perform it in the largest of theatres without losing any of the intimacy the trick demanded in the first place. His achievement with the 'Cups and Balls' is all the more incredible, given his decision to follow the route pioneered by the Australian magician Al Wheatley, known as Chop Chop, and make the trick physically smaller still by discarding two of the cups and two of the balls. In reducing the effect to its bare bones, he becomes more able to emphasise the simple miracles that take place at his fingertips. As Paul explains, the ball can be in only one place at any one time – either in his hand, under the cup, or in his pocket. The member of the audience pressganged into assistance from the false security of his seat in the stalls has no chance of keeping track of the little white ball. In one amazing sequence Paul's tongue and hands go into overdrive without pause for breath as the ball keeps returning to the cup from his hand or his pocket, until the magician has to give in on behalf of the audience. 'Perhaps my speed is baffling you' is the understatement of his whole act. When – goggle-eyed, mouth agape, limbs akimbo – he goes into a superbly mimed impression of a television action replay, drawing out the words 'Where's the ball?' like a strand of toffee between his teeth, the spectator is still no wiser. There is no way he can win. When Paul says the ball is in the pocket, he will make sure it's under the cup, and vice versa. Obviously a lesson from magician to spectator is called for. To get the ball back under the cup is all a matter of flicking the ball in a certain way once it is in the pocket. And be careful not to put the ball in the wrong pocket. Paul lifts the cup to show why. You get a lemon! He has one further trick up his sleeve, 'And if you clap that, you'll go mad over the orange!' The second surprise, so soon after the first, is as arresting as fireworks over Manhattan.

2

A Magician in the Making

As the 1970s gathered momentum it soon became apparent that magic was on the verge of the kind of popularity not enjoyed since the heyday of hocus-pocus in the music halls, when the grand masters of illusion commanded a regal respect from their red-plush-seated audiences. The initial indications of this magicians' renaissance took place in America, first on the West Coast where Hollywood's Magic Castle, a private club for magicians and their aficionados, had already been gathering media attention for seven years as the decade began, and then on the East where on Broadway in 1974 at the Cort Theatre there opened a musical built around the role of a magician. Wisely the producers of 'The Magic Show' elected for an actual wizard to play the lead. His name was Doug Henning, his persona that of a counterculture flower child. Overnight the popular image of magic in America changed. No longer were the traditional white tie and tails *de rigueur*. When the young Canadian appeared on stage in skin-tight blue jeans and a whole kaleidoscope of technicolour tie-dyed T-shirts, the audience knew that there was no way whatsoever that he could conceal anything upon his person. When he then produced a live owl or a blazing bowl of fire, the effect was all the more awe-inspiring.

Meanwhile, in the razzle-dazzle capital of Las Vegas, the German illusionists Siegfried and Roy were building up their own reputation as magic's most dramatically exciting performers of today, with an act involving an exotic menagerie of lions, tigers, a leopard, a black panther, an elephant, an eagle, two crocodiles, a flock of flamingos, even a lepjag, a cross between an African leopard and a South American jaguar. They soon set a trend, to the extent that now the revue in Las Vegas without a featured magician is a rarity. However, their own position is secure. In Las Vegas itself they have become a tourist attraction second only to the casinos. In the wider world of magic their spectacle, panache and breathtaking speed all contribute to their undisputed position as the world's greatest illusionists in the grand style. Each night they lay their lives on the line for mystery in their death-defying feats and it is not difficult to see why season after season they are voted 'Entertainers of the

Left, Doug Henning brought a youthful enthusiasm to the old tricks. *Right*, Siegfried and Roy bring Las Vegas glamour and jungle danger to the world of stage illusion.

Year' in the gambling city against competition from the likes of Sinatra and Springsteen, Cosby and Rivers.

As magic made a comeback on the centre stage of American show business, it was inconceivable that a similar resurgence of interest could not assert itself in Britain. An indication that this might be so was the success accorded the 1976 Christmas Day edition of the BBC television show 'Parkinson'. At the time this long-running series, hosted by astute journalist and interviewer Michael Parkinson, was the nearest British equivalent to America's 'Tonight' show. For this special night no less than seventy minutes were devoted exclusively to magic. The programme featured the contrasting magic styles of three of the world's greatest magicians: Fred Kaps from Holland, Richiardi Junior from Peru, and Ricky Jay from America. It was sadly indicative at the time that none of them was British; it is even more sadly ironic that since the show aired the first two have departed from this world, leaving irreplaceable gaps at the top level of magic's performers. Both would figure in any discerning connoisseur's list of the six top magicians of the latter part of this century.

Kaps (1926–80) was the more versatile of the two. He brought a golden touch to every trick he performed, always transcending his material with a rare personal quality, a blend of authority and the ability to inspire wonder, which the esteemed magical historian Peter Warlock has cited as

Opposite, a souvenir in fond memory of Fred Kaps, one of the greatest all-round magicians of all time.

the closest modern parallel to the past master of British magic, David Devant. Kaps was able to switch conjuring styles more effectively than any magician in recent history, from cool precision in sleight-of-hand to elegance in manipulation, to a commercial approach to audience participation and the classics of magic, suggesting an elegant cross between Daniels himself and the Danish/American comedian Victor Borge. Just as Borge himself builds comic capital out of the tricks music and language can play on human beings, so Kaps, with a not dissimilar delivery, adopted a similar attitude to wizardry, his magic often appearing to assert its own control, 'Sorcerer's Apprentice'-style, over the magician. Salt would pour endlessly and unexpectedly from his fist; walking sticks would materialise in his hand when they were least required; smoke, candles, dollar bills and playing cards all led a life of their own. Kaps himself could be as bemused as his audience at this display of legerdemain on the rampage, for ever anxious that his frustration should not ruffle his suave exterior. In spite of the part he played, he may conceivably have been the greatest perfectionist the magic profession has ever known, bringing to every trick he attempted, however prosaic, the flawless perfection that Sinatra brings to a lyric: a combination of intelligence, importance, and technical concern. That he embodied within himself a film star's charisma also played no small part in his own success.

Much the same could be said of Aldo Richiardi (1923–85), who brought a Latin-American excitement to his presentation of large-scale stage illusions. It was watching an appearance by the Peruvian wizard on the Ed Sullivan television show in the late 1950s that first set Doug Henning on his eventual career. More obviously, Richiardi's dramatic approach to the presentation of an illusion has also inspired Henning's main competitor, David Copperfield. To Richiardi, presentation was everything. Most of the methods behind his repertoire of levitations, appearances, disappearances and transpositions were from the last century, yet he brought to his performance a dynamic style of movement and flair that suggested a distant cousin of Baryshnikov and Astaire, Ordóñez and

Magic's top photographer Irving Desfor captured Richiardi in this characteristic pose in 1973.

Marceau, all at the same time. When he had finished with a smaller prop, it was never placed down, always thrown flamboyantly away to be caught by a member of his well-disciplined company. No sword was ever plunged, no hoop ever passed, no box lid ever opened with swifter grace than by Richiardi. When he performed the classic suspension of a girl on a broomstick the complementary movement of his own body enhanced the actual weightlessness of the girl in a way no other magician has achieved. This mastery of movement makes it especially ironic that his death was the indirect result, through cardiac arrest, of a cut incurred during a swimming accident that led, by way of a diabetic condition, to the loss of one leg and the other foot.

In an interview by Peter Pit for *Genii* magazine shortly before his death, Richiardi was asked what he would most like people to remember him by. He replied, 'Probably for myself, my personality, because this is mine. I do not fake it. I just feel what I do. I do this with all my heart.' This was a quality Doug Henning had discerned. The younger star once described the maestro as 'The magician with the biggest heart: whenever you see him perform he just expands your heart and fills it with love.' Richiardi's highest compliment was paid by the difficult-to-please theatre critic John Simon. Describing Richiardi's New York season in 1978 he wrote, 'All too often we hear wishy-washy fans gush about "magic in the theatre"; here, at any rate, there is genuine theatre in the magic.'

Ricky Jay's position as the most original personality in modern American magic is underlined by his appearance: that of a hirsute, almost Old Testament figure clad in business suit and pink carnation with a cynical gleam in his eye. His style is a unique blend of wit, intelligence, dexterity and the bizarre. He is more likely to ask the volunteer in a card trick whether he was 'born under a picture of Balzac' than to emphasise that he has never met him before in his life; more anxious to treat you to a clockwork demonstration of the 'world-famous song-and-dance pig' than to risk boring you with another devilish display of sleight-of-hand. But amid references to subjects as diverse as thumb-fetishism, Ninja assassins, and the use of cards as weapons – Ricky is the foremost exponent of the feat of throwing playing cards impossible distances – his skill ultimately shines through, enhanced all the more by his unorthodox baroque showmanship.

The success of Richiardi, Fred Kaps and Ricky Jay with British audiences led television producers to ask where magic of this order and freshness had been in recent years. It had been there, but sadly British

The extraordinary Ricky Jay, (*left*) as he is, and (*right*) as he imagines himself to be.

RICKY JAY

agents and producers had made little, if any, attempt to go out of their way to find it. Now this success had created a demand. In America Henning had personified the boom and it soon became clear that there was scope for a native performer, maybe as unconventional in his approach as Henning was, to carry the banner of magic's renewed popularity with the British audience.

Slowly gaining prominence in the variety clubs and on commercial television during the 1970s was a young comedy performer who had been christened Newton Edward, after the discoverer of gravity, by his father Handel Daniels, himself as curiously christened after the composer of the 'Messiah'. Born on 6 April 1938, on South Bank, Cleveland, where his parents managed the local Hippodrome cinema, he had since changed his name to Paul and adopted the billing of 'The Unusualist'. In the context of the history of magic there was little unusual in what he did other than the brio and distinctive style of humour with which he performed it. In later years Paul has admitted that the title was a ploy purely to get around agents at a time when the aspirant performer with 'magician' on his letterhead found it the immediate passport to the 'out' tray of any prospective booking agent. This was the depressing state Paul found on the club circuit of industrial Britain in the late 1960s when he turned professional. It was a far cry from the heyday of the music halls when virtually every practitioner of the magic art was proudly proclaimed as a 'Monarch of Mystery' or a 'King' of something or other. But Paul knew that magic could still be made as entertaining for the modern audience as ever it was in a faded era of gilt and greasepaint, and cunningly sneaked his fresh, irreverent style upon managements and public unawares. A whole succession of mediocre performers, to the detriment of the few better ones, had defined magic in the eyes of producers as the last reserve of the untalented, an attitude summed up by the riddle, 'Why is being a Playboy bunny like being a magician?' 'It's almost like being in show business.' No one would do more to change that attitude in Britain than Paul Daniels.

Paul first became interested in magic on a rainy summer holiday spent at Helmsley in the Yorkshire Dales. He remembers with affection the landlady, Mrs Gillings, who lent him a book entitled *How to Entertain at Parties*. One particular chapter revealed an Aladdin's cave of card tricks, complete with full instructions. For a young boy who, amazing as it may now seem, was in his own words 'quiet, shy and bashful', the book represented a bewildering passport to the focus of attention among his school colleagues. That was when he knew he would become a magician. His first stage appearance took place at the local Methodist Youth Club, where he used manipulative skill to cause billiard balls to multiply at his fingertips and sheer cheeky effrontery to convince his audience that he could swallow goldfish, when in fact he was devouring sliced and shaped carrots. When he left school only his parents stood in the way of his turning professional, with the result that he endured spells as an

Above, the Australian illusionist Les Levante with his daughter Esme, herself a fine performer, and mascot. *Below*, Johnny Carson assists Milbourne Christopher in a mock spiritualist seance – Carson himself began in show business as a magician.

accountancy clerk in local government and as the proprietor of a mobile grocery store, in addition to two years National Service with the First Battalion of the Green Howards in Hong Kong, before magic became his sole means of livelihood.

It was a long haul to the major national impact which he made on Granada Television's 'Wheeltappers and Shunters Club' in February 1975. The setting for the breakthrough was appropriate, both the title and style of the show being typical of the traditional working man's social club in which the rising star had served his apprenticeship. Repeat appearances enabled him to consolidate his position with Granada, the British television company most famous for its twice-weekly soap opera 'Coronation Street'. It was inevitable that the BBC should register interest. In 1979 it recorded the first series of 'The Paul Daniels Magic Show'. It has been an annual event in the schedules ever since, the initial four shows in a series growing to ten. The boom in Britain had found its own man to wave the flag.

*

It is always fascinating to chart what might be termed the archaeology of influence upon a popular entertainer. However original a talent, a persona, subconsciously it will have absorbed the example of those who made the greatest impression during the owner's formative years. In the case of Paul Daniels the challenge is doubly intriguing in that such an analysis may be approached from the angle either of magic or of comedy. It is significant that when asked which magicians might have had such an effect in his early years, Paul will recall seeing the full evening illusion shows of the Australian Levante and the American Milbourne Christopher. Both attempted a straightforward presentational approach to magic in the grand style, as far removed from Paul's act today as is conceivable, but both made their greatest impact on audiences, not least the young Daniels, with their smallest trick. Levante (1892–1978) would release a small wooden cube from a ribbon, while Christopher (1914–84), to an engaging shaggy-dog patter story, would perform a sequence of trick knots with a single rope which culminated in an impression of 'Two Lazy Sailors Tying Two Figure Eights' with little more than a double flick of the wrist.

It was readily apparent on that first Granada appearance, as Paul demonstrated a series of fancy card shuffles, performed his 'Cup and Ball' routine, and transported a borrowed treasury note into a packet of Polo Mints or Lifesavers – an effect originated by Milbourne Christopher – that he needed no one to tell him that the size of the effect magic may produce on an audience bears no relationship to the size of the prop with which it is performed. Paul instinctively knew that no magician ever really became successful until he had developed that special quality which projects him as a personality independent of all his tricks put together. Informing that personality, in Paul's case, was a debt to the sturdy

Arnold de Bière and a younger Paul Daniels – partners in repartee.

tradition of the British music hall comedian.

The most refreshing aspect of his style when he first appeared on the scene was a razor-sharp sense of repartee, as irreverent as it was funny, as he baited the victims coaxed into helping with his experiments. No recent British magician had been as cutting in his approach, although the annals of magical history do reveal a possible antecedent in the person of Arnold de Bière (1878–1934), a successful variety performer of the early years of this century who himself scored best with small magic, principally the 'Egg and Bag Trick' and the 'Thumb Tie', in which solid hoops melted through his sturdily tied thumbs. A review of his performance at the Palace Theatre, Manchester, dated November 1910, states:

There is only one drawback to this artiste's show: i.e. he seems to get up an argument . . . this argument threatened to become a real 'row', the whole house being in an uproar for some minutes. I think this might be

avoided. At any rate, I go to see a magician, not to listen to a wordy
warfare.

No Daniels performance has ever reached such a vituperative climax,
although in the rough-and-ready atmosphere of the club circuit in his early
years it is not difficult to imagine Paul himself having to halt just such an
uproar before he could even begin his act. In the cut and thrust of such a
situation, his wit and audience skills became honed. Another review of de
Bière from December 1910 contained the advice, 'Woe betide the
individual who tries to get the better of him in repartee. The merry
answering retort, or confounding *bon mot*, are as penetrating as a rapier
point.'

While British audiences had long forgotten de Bière, they still had fond
memories of the aggressive attack of comedian Tommy Trinder and a
continuing relationship through television with his spiritual heir, Bruce
Forsyth, the two most successful compères of the long-running 'Sunday
Night at the London Palladium' television show. Forsyth first came into
his own during the audience participation sequence of 'Beat the Clock', the
game that each week dominated the central portion of the programme. The
young Daniels responded to him especially. The gangling compère
provided the yardstick for how far the cheeky magician could go, the
measure for the speed required for the comeback line to be effective.
Equally important in shaping his comic outlook was Eric Morecambe,
whose own rapid unscripted retorts to his partner Ernie Wise embodied a
sense of the absurd that Forsyth did not reach. When Daniels found
himself copying the short, sharp, staccato speech patterns of this beloved,
bespectacled clown he made the conscious decision to stop watching him,
until he became settled in his own style. Happily there are moments when
the spirit of Morecambe flickers to the fore in a Daniels performance,
especially when expressing agitated, mock-violent exasperation with an
audience volunteer. Paul may be unaware of them. At least he is certain
that when they do occur, they do so in respectful homage and not in
blatant imitation.

The ethos of one further comedian is seldom absent from a Daniels
performance. Paul shares with frenetic genius Ken Dodd, the most
effective 'live' comedian of his generation, the common experience of
months spent on a mobile grocery round. When Dodd confronts the
audience with the 'Hello, missus' of his act, he is back in his tradesman's
overall. Again, when Dodd's distinctive jaunty verbal rhythms surface in a
Daniels show, as from time to time they do, one is reminded that it was but
a short step for Paul from selling cornflakes to proffering playing cards.
Both demand a common touch if success at its widest possible level is to be
sustained. At a more fantastical level, the Daniels psyche will be
bombarded in the middle of a routine by the most inconsequential of
thoughts. 'Aren't plums cheap?' is a question that frequently asserts itself.

This is the quintessential world of Dodd at his most spasmodic.

Paul's comic genius prevents any two Daniels performances from being the same. A genuine spontaneity is fuelled by the interchange of what would be purely pleasantries in the hands of a less complete performer, his wit keenly tuned to their every response. Names, places, professions are all grist to this comic mill: 'What's your name?' 'Pat' 'Whatever you do don't ever wear your name on the front of your sweater'; 'Are you Japanese?' 'No' 'Oh, every time you laugh, you bow. Did you know that?'; 'What do you do for a living?' 'Printing' 'You don't look the type'. There was *one* occasion when he was totally lost for a word, but even then a prop saved him. Among magicians the 'Legs Table' has long been a standard comedy item. When two spindly chrome legs fall from the front of a table carried on by a girl assistant, momentary embarrassment is turned to comic advantage by a pair of shapely female wooden legs released from beneath the table top in the emergency. On the occasion in question Paul still had to cue that release when the audience volunteer at his side turned to him and said, 'Do you know what my job is? My job is making artificial legs!' The presence of just such a spectator at precisely that moment was a chance in a million. Paul had merely to look upstage at the girl: 'I can't wait to watch his face. Show him!'

What Paul has in common with both Dodd and Forsyth is a fingertip precision in the matter of audience control. It is bewildering enough from a magical point of view to see him cause two innocent members of the audience to stick fast to their equally innocent chairs, or to jump off them suffering from some phantom electric shock, merely by waving a paper handkerchief in front of them. Even more satisfying is his ability to involve the whole theatre audience verbally in a routine, whether orchestrating 'Gor-Blimey!' as the concerted response to a simple card trick or the whispered childlike asides – 'It isn't' 'It is' – to his magical version of 'The Three Bears', a minor miracle in which for one brief moment three unequal pieces of rope all become the same length before reverting to their earlier condition.

Any catalogue of the formative influences upon this distinctive talent must include mention of one single moment and one singular man. The latter was a gentleman named Ken Brooke, a performer sadly unknown to the general public, who came closest among magicians in the 1950s and 1960s to delivering the Daniels style before Paul registered it as his own. Ken earned his living from magic all his working life, but for most of that time withdrew from the spotlight of the commercial entertainer to the smaller and, for him, happier platform accorded the demonstrator of tricks who sells magic to other magicians. No magical dealer, though, ever went further out of his way to ensure that the items he sold were commercially viable. At any magicians' convention or trade fair he proved the inevitable centre of attention. One can recall him in his prime, spruce with slick black hair, his shirt-sleeves rolled up as far as they would go, his red braces

Left, we all have to start somehow! *Right*, Ken Brooke – conjuror, catalyst, and clown.

prominent, subjecting himself to a whirlwind of demonstration, the most memorable item of which was a version of the 'Three Card Trick' with giant cards entitled 'Chase the Ace'. His claim was that in spite of their size – these cards were gigantic – this was a trick for close-quarters. When taken to task by the inevitable know-all unable to reconcile close-quarter magic with props so large, Ken brusquely claimed that no matter what their dimensions they could be carried anywhere as easily as a handkerchief or a packet of cigarettes. So saying, he took the cards, slotted them through the gap between the back of his shirt and his braces, and slipped on his jacket. Point proved, collapse of know-all, and applause all round! It says a great deal for Ken's unsurpassed skills as a salesman that he probably sold as many copies of that trick to people who simply admired the cheeky audacity of using braces for that purpose as to those dedicated enough to work the routine into their own performances. One was always surprised, in fact, that he never carried a supply of red braces as well. Then he would have cleaned up! That said, he was a rare bird among dealers, putting the advancement of magic as both art and entertainment before any other consideration.

Ken Brooke, with his strident Yorkshire brogue, aggressive wit, and encyclopaedic grasp of everything important in both magic and comedy could, and should, himself have become a star. That he did not do so was a matter of personal choice, a vote for privacy and contentment away from the pressures of mainstream show business. Until Paul Daniels arrived on the scene, it is fair to say that no British magician performed with greater energy and gusto, with a more vibrant sense of humour and slapstick than Ken Brooke. Born in Leeds on 3 November 1920, he died on 26 February 1983.

This genuinely special person lives on in the influence he exerted upon a whole generation of British magical performers, not least Paul Daniels. No one had a sounder grasp of who was best in magic and what material was best for them. He always predicted Paul's rise to the top. He was also responsible for pointing him in the direction of an item entitled 'The Human Pump', one of the funniest sequences Paul has ever performed and the routine that provided the springboard to his major success on the 1984 'Royal Variety Performance' at London's Victoria Palace Theatre. For that special occasion the four volunteers called upon the stage by Paul were all champion sportsmen: athlete Sebastian Coe, boxer Henry Cooper, snooker player Steve Davis, and swimmer Duncan Goodhew. Their celebrity made the tableau that resulted at the end of this comedy of errors all the more absurdist: Cooper, his left forefinger in his ear, playing the hapless name part, while Davis pumped his right hand to release the milk, trapped by mistake against his head in an upturned can held by Coe, in a seemingly endless stream from a hole in his left elbow punctured by Paul, to be caught in a bucket through a funnel held by Goodhew. Paul would be the first to admit that the properties used in the sequence are some of the most elementary in magic, more the preserve of the basic children's entertainer than a magician by Royal Appointment, and at first he needed some persuasion to adopt the routine. He would also be ready to confess that few items have ever given him greater personal pleasure to perform and had such a positive comic effect upon audiences of all ages.

While Ken Brooke possibly taught Paul Daniels more about comedy applied to magic than any other single individual, by Paul's own admission one single event taught him more about the actual practice of comedy than all the joke books put together. Significantly it occurred on his very last day with the mobile grocery store. One character was always coming on board to size up the difference in price between Paul and his major competitor Andy, letting the whole neighbourhood know at the top of her voice when the rival concern had a better deal. On the day in question her value assessment had been totally scathing of Paul, but fortunately he did have one line exclusive to him, namely home-made cakes. Having dismissed the rest of his produce, she turned and said, 'But I'll have one of those custard tarts.'

Paul could not resist the temptation.

'Do you want it in your bag or in your face?'

'You wouldn't dare!' The Keystone Cop instinct got the better of Paul. 'Oh, you bugger,' she cried, 'now you'll have to give me a lift home.'

Paul had to agree. So there he was, driving his bus with the North-east's answer to Hilda Ogden in the back. The snag was there was still another custard tart.

Appropriately armed, she comes up behind him. 'Now when you stop you're going to get this in your face!'

There was no way he could avoid stopping. It was a very busy round with a seemingly infinite number of traffic lights, and Paul could not keep from laughing. He knew full well that he too was going to get the custard pie treatment. The sheer anticipation proved even funnier than the actual deed. The bus stopped and they sat there laughing, a couple of custard twins together. On the threshold of his professional career, the tables had been turned.

Today Paul's handling of volunteer assistants is calculated with a shrewd understanding of slapstick psychology, the magical fate in store for them skilfully telegraphed for maximum laughter without destroying the ultimate element of surprise. As personal possessions disappear, items of clothing become mutilated, and the threat of torture looms – whether in the shape of sword, saw or guillotine – the spirit of fun is never absent. As Paul learnt all those years ago and engagingly conveys to his audience today, far worse can happen to you than receiving the magical equivalent of a custard pie in the face.

Since Paul was not the first to realise the advantages of the marriage between comedy and magic, it is proper that in an historically based celebration of his own talent, some of the more successful of his forebears in the area where magician's wand and jester's cap and bells are interchangeable should be the next to attract our attention.

3

Funny Way to be a Magician

The Man Who Made Ice Famous

Since the middle of this century audiences in America, France and Britain have been consistently amused by their own comic hero with delusions of deception: the brash, slapdash effrontery of Carl Ballantine; the diffident, spasmodic pathos of Mac Ronay; the nervous, bumbling bewilderment of the late Tommy Cooper. Each in his own way has guyed the self-importance of every second-rate prestidigitator who can pull anything out of a hat but his own personal triumph. Today, however, few people realise that the role of the burlesque man of magic was pioneered at headliner level almost half a century earlier by an American, Frank Van Hoven.

Left, Carl Ballantine, the frantic face of comedy mayhem, and (*right*) Mac Ronay, magic's greatest droll.

VAN HOVEN
THE DIPPY MAD MAGICIAN

Left, Frank Van Hoven, pioneer of magical burlesque, and (*right*) Tommy Cooper, Britain's beloved fez-capped zany.

Born on 5 February 1886, Van Hoven began his working life as a fairground peanut seller whose aspirations towards juggling as a more permanent career were redirected to all things magical at the suggestion of the legendary illusionist, Dante. His ambitions to be a magician in the grand manner were soon undermined by insecurity and lack of talent. In desperation he begged the booking agent of the Majestic Theatre in Chicago for an engagement. About to throw him out for impudence, the agent, perhaps taking pity on Van Hoven's poverty-stricken appearance, relented enough to give him a nickel, with the instruction to take a note to a performer he was booking as an emergency replacement. The note was never delivered: the nickel was spent on urgent nourishment, enough for Van Hoven to reason, 'Why shouldn't I fill the gap at the Majestic?' The ruse came off. The management did not suspect their wizard was not the bona-fide substitute.

Never having appeared in a theatre of such importance in his life, Van Hoven was nervous to the point of distraction, but he had to go on. His suit was threadbare, redeemed, if at all, by its owner improvising creases down the trousers with pins! Eventually the stage manager had literally to push him on. The response was sustained laughter for the whole act. When he came off the manager asked him to state his terms. Van Hoven replied, 'Fifteen dollars a week', but the manager would not hear of less than seventy-five, with a promise of more if the audience kept laughing. Within a short time Van Hoven was at the pinnacle of vaudeville success, where he stayed until his death in Birmingham, England, in 1929.

Everything might have gone wrong that night in Chicago, but Van Hoven was astute enough to realise that for his burlesque humour to score consistently, it should be seen to play against some level of competence. For that reason he would always begin his act with one item performed in absolute seriousness, the classic 'Rice Bowl' trick in which rice between two inverted bowls multiplies to overflowing, before changing to water. His credentials as a magician established, the scene was securely set for what followed. A prop kennel was dismantled, but would not fit together again. 'Let the dog die!' he would yell. A large cloth was held with both hands over a small bell. The bell rang: it was not too difficult to see that a third hand was involved and that one of those hands – holding the cloth – was not all it should be. Darting off-stage, he would come back with a large Navaho blanket. He would display this on both sides and, as the drum rolled, throw it down on the stage. When he picked it up there was one small, sad, sick feather flower. '*Somebody* must like it,' he would literally cry in a delivery born of comic frustration.

Another cloth was used as cover to produce a huge bowl of water. From this point upheaval ensued right until the final curtain. 'I must have a boy' became a catch-phrase for Van Hoven, the cue for three sullen urchins of

Van Hoven's name became literally synonymous with ice.

WHO SAID ICE?

assorted size to come out of the audience. One boy is given the bowl of water, another a candlestick with lighted candle, the third a massive block of real ice. A handkerchief is borrowed which Van Hoven will now attempt to shoot through the water into the centre of the block of ice. Firing impossible instructions at the bewildered assistants with machine-gun speed, he keeps changing his mind as well as his position on stage in order to get the several articles into correct line. Confusion reigns, but nothing seems to happen. By the end the stage is awash with water slopped from the bowl, while the ice – 'Give him the candle and you hold the ice' – slithers from the grasp of one boy to the other. The pressure builds for the trick to reach a successful conclusion. Magician and boys are recruited to the common cause of averting disaster as props, tables, chairs are upset in the traffic to and fro across the stage. By the end of the act Van Hoven is dishevelled and deep in despair. His voice almost gone, he remonstrates that the boys 'do not seem to understand the trick. I won't be able to do it.' Anarchy triumphs, nothing has happened to the now-forgotten handkerchief, the fat boy drops the ice and Van Hoven, falling over it, slides inexorably into the prompt-side wings. There are people who say that nothing funnier ever occurred on the vaudeville stage.

Van Hoven's original billing was 'The Dippy Mad Magician', but he became known in time simply as 'The Man Who Made Ice Famous'. In retrospect we should salute not only his originality, but the timelessness of a concept which he did more than anyone to establish. As long as comedy and magic thrive together, tricks will continue to go gloriously wrong to the delight of audiences unashamed of the belly-laugh.

The Human Hairpin

While the burlesque magician with his catastrophic conjuring has a sincere place in the affection of the public (a case of the Pagliacci syndrome applied to prestidigitation), another less obvious kind of comedy wizard must not fail to claim our attention. Here the ambivalent mask of comedy and tragedy, smiling yet groaning at the same time, changes the emphasis: now one has to imagine joy superimposed on cunning or vice versa. It *is* possible to reduce audiences to hysterics and amazement at the same time. This rare aspect of magical performance has been brought to heights of sophistication and popularity by Paul Daniels himself, but Paul is only the latest in a select line that extends back to the headier days of the music hall.

Of all Paul's predecessors to achieve success at that time, it is hard to believe that any were intrinsically funnier than Carlton. It is also impossible to imagine that audiences today would not have laughed at the outrageous eccentricity of his appearance before a word had been spoken, a single manipulation ventured.

His real name was Arthur Carlton Philps. He was born in Holloway in

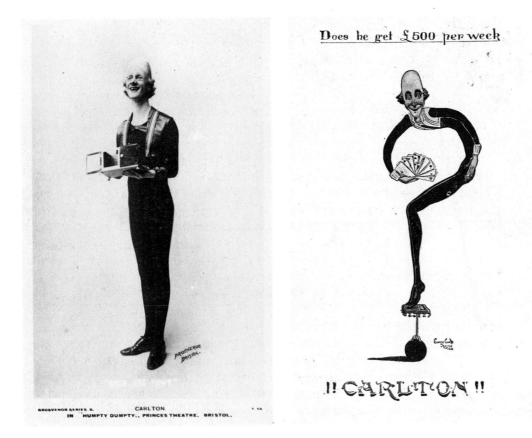

!! CARLTON !!

GROSVENOR SERIES B. CARLTON Y 16
IN 'HUMPTY DUMPTY., PRINCES THEATRE, BRISTOL.

Left, Carlton with his 'Sliding Die Box'. *Right*, did he get £500 per week? Yes, in 1907!

1881 and as a young telegraph messenger on the streets of London was the first to suggest to the postal authorities that distance could be covered more profitably by bicycle. For this resounding innovation he received three shillings and sixpence extra for the upkeep of his machine. However, conjuring was his first love and it was not long before his creative mind turned its attention from postal problems to the presentation of magic. Thinking that the public was openly suspicious of traditional evening-dress and its 'up the sleeve' connotations, he decided to wear skin-hugging black tights so that everyone could see that concealment was impossible. Not surprisingly, the first time he set foot on stage in this revolutionary attire, the audience dissolved into laughter. Carlton instantly grasped his opportunity in the cause of comedy. Naturally tall, he added elevators to his shoes and a huge domed bald wig to his head, raising his height from six foot two to almost seven foot. Pictures today suggest an elongated hybrid of the legendary clown Grock and the wonderful British comedy veteran Max Wall in his incarnation as the grotesque Professor Walloffski. His gawky appearance, accentuated by the curious twist of his knees and elbows and a knack of being able to stretch the muscles of his knees, hips, chest and throat to give added inches still, produced one of the most original comic creations of the music hall.

Carlton's own words, delivered in a piercing falsetto voice from which he occasionally lapsed, whispering, into a sort of disembodied commentary on his own actions, give the most vivid picture of his appearance. A favourite exchange involved overhearing mother and child in the front stalls.

'Oh, Mummy, I know how it's done – I can see the wires.'

'Quiet, dear. Those are not wires – they are his legs.'

In the same way, another inquisitive child was heard to comment, 'Oh, Mummy, is it a man or a pair of scissors?' while Carlton himself was known to inquire confidentially of a lady sitting in the front row, 'How would you like me for a hairpin?' In time his most famous billing became 'The Human Hairpin', although he was also known for a while as 'The Human Match Stick'.

He was as much a master of the throwaway line as he was of card manipulation, at which he excelled: 'Is there no limit to the man's cleverness?' Like Paul Daniels today, he could hold an audience spellbound with no more than a pack of cards, running through a technical catalogue of fans, waterfall shuffles, productions, front changes, back and front palming, then finally vanishing the whole pack and producing the cards in a string from his mouth, 'Oh, what a fantastic performer; and he carries all his own scenery.' Then, on the applause, 'Thank you. I deserve it. I have now great pleasure in presenting myself with a medal.'

He would count out twelve cards and magically send them along his sleeve into his pocket. 'I want you to imagine my left hand is Manchester Station, my sleeve the L. & N.W. Main Line and my pocket Euston. It wants a lot of imagination!' As the various cards arrive one by one his remarks build for their own cumulative effect: 'Marvellous.' 'Isn't he graceful?' 'Wonder if he's married?' 'I performed this trick before the Prince of Wales – was King.' 'Sometimes I get applauded for this trick.' And then when he does: 'Thank you – that's a friend of mine.' His most

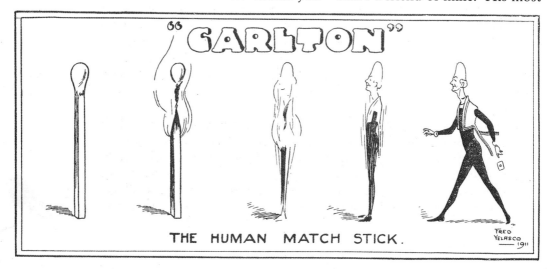

THE HUMAN MATCH STICK.

impressive skill is reserved for the single-handed vanish of five individual cards, showing the back and the front of the hand after each disappearance, then re-producing them one at a time at his fingertips. At one point he hoaxes the audience. The comment 'By the kindness of the management all these tricks are fully explained on the back of your programmes' causes much inquisitive rustling of paper and the added remark, 'Look at them all looking at their programmes – funny! I shall now present myself with another medal!'

Once established in his career, Carlton would always close his performance with the trick known as 'The Sliding Die Box'. The illusion in question falls into a category known among magicians as 'sucker' tricks. Ostensibly the magician seems not at all worried about exposing the method involved, until the tables are turned and the audience realises that it has been fooled regardless. On a recent edition of his television show Paul Daniels obtained much mileage from the basic presentation of this item in the presence of Lester, the irreverent dummy of the stunning American ventriloquist Willie Tyler. Carlton had been the first, however, to take what was even then a relatively hackneyed trick and milk it for the slightest comic possibility, a presentation that became one of the most copied in magic.

Having finished his card manipulation, Carlton somewhat breathlessly addressed the audience. 'Properly speaking that ends my act, but if you applaud very, very loudly I shall come back and do the trick you see on the chair over there. Between ourselves, I've just got to do it, because it's in my contract. Still, I like the management to hear the applause – it does me a bit of good.'

The applause swells over the footlights and Carlton returns, mincing and smirking in his contrived glory, to pick up the box in question. It is divided into two compartments, each having a front and a back door. A large die is placed in one of the compartments and all the doors are closed. The box is then obviously tilted and the audience hears the die slide from one compartment to the other. Carlton opens the first compartment. It is empty. The audience shouts for him to open the other side. The box is tilted, the die slides back, and the other compartment is opened. Again no die. This could be kept up all night as Carlton works the crowd into a frenzy of bluff and counterbluff. 'Open all f-o-w-e-r,' shouts an earthy voice from the back of the auditorium. Suffice to say, Carlton eventually gives in and all four doors to both compartments are opened. The die is nowhere to be seen.

The showmanship of his presentation is not yet exhausted though. With the audience applauding he leaves the stage, only seconds later to project the upper half of his elongated body from behind the proscenium arch, laughing mockingly at the crowd. Seconds later again, the same image appears on the other side of the stage. Finally, just as the front tabs fall, his head appears from beneath the rear curtain, and in uncharacteristically

gruff tones he echoes the rustic cry of his audience stooge, 'Open all
f-o-w-e-r.' The place would be in uproar.

For several years his act also embraced a display of mock-hypnotism for
which he employed a team of so-called 'Satellites' who included within
their number a fat man and a dwarf. Carlton never lost an opportunity to
overstress his own grotesque appearance. Sadly, his last days were not
happy ones. From being a worldwide headliner who once topped the bill
in five leading central London music halls in the same week, he became
reduced to poverty. As music halls went out of fashion, he put on weight
and his image was destroyed. The London *Evening News* for 10
September 1938 carried the ironic headline: ' "The Human Hairpin" is
now 17½-Stoney Broke.' At his peak he had weighed just nine stone. The
antithesis of his earlier spindly self, he played with the idea of performing
his old act within a Micawber characterisation, but while the tricks were
there, the real magic had drifted away. He died on 27 June 1942, but one
has a funny feeling that had his earlier self been alive today he would be a
star still.

'Where's he gone to now, Mummy? He's disappeared.'

'Hush, my dear. He's only turning sideways.'

The Magical Comedian

If during the 1920s and 1930s the billing 'The Magical Comedian'
belonged on a sheer copyright basis to one performer and no other, then
that performer was the Englishman Fred Culpitt. Culpitt's behind-the-
scenes talent as an inventor of magical effects – his production of a girl so
large from a doll's house so small must be one of the most often performed
illusions of all time – was matched by his prowess as a light comedian with
a dry line in self-deprecation. 'Some men are born to greatness, but others'
– here he would tap his considerable girth – 'have it thrust upon them!'
When he presented the 'Doll's House' illusion he would preface the effect
by emphasising that it was just an ordinary child's toy, taking out
examples of the miniature furniture within. He would then remove the
chimney. 'Anybody want the flu?' Nothing was sacrosanct. When he
embarked upon a comedy mind-reading sequence he made it clear exactly
where he stood. 'I want to show you some thought-reading or, in other
words, poking your nose into other people's business.' He developed what
may be the definitive so-called 'sucker' trick, in which the audience is led
up the garden path of an apparent explanation only to have its illusions
shattered still further at the last moment. Tucking a silk handkerchief into
his fist he would transform it into an egg. Explaining that the egg was
hollow, he showed the hole on the other side into which he had pushed the
silk. Turning the egg back, he cracked it in a glass – yolk, white, shell, but
no silk handkerchief!

Who could resist the appeal of such a smile on a theatre marquee?

If one trick encapsulated the comic ambience of this jolly, portly individual it would be his 'Bathing Belle' mystery. A large poster depicted the lady in question at the seaside wearing a bathing costume and a spotted bathrobe. Fred would roll the poster into a tube, and then from one end pull the robe. When he unrolled the poster, the lady was wearing just the bathing costume. Again the poster was rolled, and this time the costume was produced. With voyeuristic relish Fred would look through the tube like a telescope – 'This looks good' – only to be confronted by his embarrassed girl assistant (in actual fact his wife) known professionally as Miss Jan Glenrose. Traditional cross-talk ensued as she forbade the magician to unroll the picture. Eventually the poster was opened to reveal the girl up to her neck in the waves. 'Sorry, gents,' said Fred, 'but I'm afraid the tide's come in.'

For a brief time he performed a pastiche Oriental act billed as 'Chow Fat and Charm Ing', raising great laughs as he attempted the production to end all productions from a giant scarf, only to produce nothing more impressive than his own slipper. In 1909 he had toured in Australia on the same bill as the most successful of all the serious acts of this kind, Chung Ling Soo, Culpitt following the make-believe Chinaman two acts later with a contribution entitled 'A Chinese Travesty'. The centre-piece of this act was a gaudily draped table which turned out to be nothing more glamorous than a soap box. Soo, anxious to help the younger performer, offered him a richly embroidered banner decorated with Chinese symbols to use instead of his makeshift cloth. Little did Culpitt know at the time that Soo was poking his own gentle fun at the Englishman. Only when Fred was playing Liverpool or Limehouse with a fair representation of actual Chinese in the audience was the banner revealed for what it really was – indication that Culpitt was a fully paid-up member of the Foochow Undertakers' Union.

One of Culpitt's favourite tricks was a version of the 'Vanishing Walking Stick'. He would wrap the cane in a newspaper, tap the parcel against the stage, then – 'You don't want to see any more of that' – crumple the paper. The cane had vanished! The secret was simple. Few British theatres worthy of their music hall past are without what is known as 'The Culpitt Hole'. His first task on visiting a new venue was to bribe a friendly stagehand to drill a small hole in the boards. In the course of his routine he would rest paper and cane momentarily above the gap. The stick fell below, leaving the paper shell intact for the eventual vanish. On one occasion it is said that the cane fell on to the head of another performer below stage. Unaware of Culpitt's ruse, and not realising the stage was above, he grabbed a chair, stood on it and pushed the cane back up through the hole at the very moment Culpitt produced a duplicate stick from the back of his coat collar. Against the grain as the incident was, it is doubtful if 'The Magical Comedian' ever scored a heartier laugh.

On at least one other occasion Culpitt's routine apparently departed

Fred Culpitt was versatile in the spelling of his name as well as in the tricks he performed.

from the rehearsed norm. As he made one of his favourite comic asides – 'There's a lot of twisting going on in this show' – his rotund body became elongated, while his assistant's head dematerialised. What made the occasion memorable, as well as the disaster forgivable, was the fact that this was the first regular television programme to be transmitted by the BBC, from Alexandra Palace on 1 October 1936. A fault had developed in the water-cooling system essential for keeping the transmitting equipment at the right temperature. Nevertheless, Culpitt was secure in the history books as a pioneer of magic in a medium where half a century later Paul Daniels would achieve his greatest success. Sadly, he died at the age of sixty-seven in 1944, by which time hostilities had artificially stunted the advancement of television, with the result that performers like him were unable to appreciate the vistas which it would one day open up.

The Humorous Trickster

It is doubtful if any entertainer provides a closer parallel to Paul Daniels than Emil Jarrow, a star of the American vaudeville stage during the first part of this century. It is not just that Jarrow (as he was usually billed) was extremely funny; nor that his rapport with the participants whom he inveigled into helping was free-wheeling and spontaneous, with no attempt at comic make-up or characterisation; he could, in addition, captivate the largest audience with the minimum of props. Paul Daniels is able to cause as much, and usually more, mystery and entertainment with a cup and a ball, some cards, three ropes, and a borrowed treasury note that finds its way into the centre of a walnut within the centre of an egg within the centre of an orange, as most of the grand masters of stage illusion have been able to achieve with truckloads of heavy equipment. The fact that he may be performing at the London Palladium or even New York's Radio City Music Hall makes no difference. The audience contact is as sharp and vital as an electric filament. This went for Jarrow too.

With the possible exception of Carlton and Nate Leipzig (a more restrained contemporary of Jarrow who featured an act using exclusively thimbles and cards, with greater emphasis on mystery than comedy) no two magicians have been able to create a greater sensation with material that most magicians would consider totally unsuitable for audiences so large. According to Dai Vernon, the elder statesman of American magic, who resides now at Hollywood's Magic Castle after a lifetime as confidant of every major American magician of note, Frank Van Hoven and Jarrow were the two top-salaried magical performers on the American 'Big Time'. He presumably excludes from this consideration Houdini at the height of his fame, but nevertheless it underlines how high a premium managements placed even then on hilarity before mystery.

Depending upon which account you read, the man who billed himself variously as 'The Merry Magician' and 'The Humorous Trickster' was born in Holland or Germany in 1874 or 1875. The style of his humour, enforced by a heavy Dutch/Jewish accent in the manner of the famous comedy team Weber and Fields, which openly parodied the speech of new immigrants to America, suggests the former birthplace. There is less doubt about his arrival in the USA in 1891. While in Europe he had become attached to Buffalo Bill's Wild West Show as a strongman, having got the job by lifting with one arm a lancer weighing over 200 pounds who dropped dead from his horse during a performance. To the young Emil the body was little more than a sack of grain to be tossed over his shoulder and carried out of the arena. With Buffalo Bill providing his passport to the New World, Jarrow was set to continue his Herculean success until the stage of a Chicago theatre collapsed beneath him and broke his leg in the process. He then decided to turn to safer ways of entertaining the public, first by juggling and then by magic, eventually becoming a major attraction on the prestigious Hammerstein and Keith circuits and appearing in many productions of the legendary Florenz Ziegfeld.

To appreciate the impact of his comedy style, one has to understand the audience at which it was aimed. Many of his lines sound banal and crude today, but delivered in that strong Dutch accent they represented the struggle that faced all immigrants in learning the English language. When, say, 'underwear' was confused with 'under where?' the pressure of their task became released through humour. At the same time the smaller, more educated part of the vaudeville audience, who might have resented the banality even then, would forgive anything of this quaint little man with the pixie-style demeanour because of the sheer skill that could be, and was, the only solution for the intelligent mysteries he perpetrated.

Jarrow would start his act by limping on stage saying, 'The kid's clever, but he's got bum feet.' Then he would turn to the drummer to lay the groundwork for what would become a running gag. 'Hit it, George,' he would demand in his strong guttural accent, the response being a cymbal crash, followed by laughter. 'Hit it again' would produce a second crash, followed by laughter. He would then turn to the orchestra leader, 'Go ahead, kid, fiddle.' More laughter. 'Hit it, George.' 'Hit it again.' And so on. He would eventually engage the leader in conversation. 'Tell me, Mr Leader, why is an unripe tomato [pronounced tomater] like an old maid?' 'Why?' 'Because it's hard to mate her! Hit it George!' All his asides and ad-libs, not to mention magical climaxes, would be punctuated in this fashion.

At the height of his fame Jarrow was invited to appear in London. He accepted, but had grave misgivings about how the English would react to his style of comedy. He confided his fears to Frank Tinney, a black-face comedian, who tried to put his colleague at ease. 'Jarrow, you open on a Tuesday. If the act fails to register, don't worry. Come right back. There's a boat that sails Wednesday.'

Jarrow came to London and on his opening night at the Palace Theatre went through his routine. Nervous as he was, he had not accounted for the hauteur of the orchestra leader. He got to the point where he asked about the unripe tomato. 'Tell me,' replied the superior musician, 'why *is* an old maid like an unripe *tomahto*?' Jarrow stared at the audience, exclaimed, 'Well, the boat sails Wednesday', and stomped off-stage! Disciplined by the management for being disrespectful towards the musician, Jarrow pointed out that his contract stipulated that he had to perform the act exactly as he did in America. The result was that the theatre had to substitute another person in place of the leader during this gag!

In spite of this initial set-back, Jarrow was a greater success in London than he had ever imagined. When he returned to Broadway he had with him a pile of favourable press reviews as well as the feeling that he should be paid more. He was already one of the most highly paid acts in vaudeville, but after much argument Jarrow got his way, on condition that he include an assistant in his act. He agreed, but had no intention of sharing the stage with anyone, giving rise to what would become another running gag. When the booking agent went to watch the revised act, he was surprised to see Jarrow alone on stage. When tackled afterwards, there was only one way the magician could wriggle out of his predicament. He explained that his partner was ill and, when asked what his name was, called out the first one that came into his head, 'Johnson.' From that day he would open his act, 'I'm very sorry. My partner Johnson is sick, but I'll perform his tricks too, just as if he were here in person!' He would then proceed to tear a giant paper tree or a ladder from a rolled-up newspaper. While visually effective, this was the weakest part of his show magically. This Jarrow knew. 'I have a lot of "noive" to come out in front of such an intelligent audience and do such a lousy trick. But that's one of Johnson's. Hit it, George! Hit it again!' The invisible Johnson thrived for the whole tour on the Keith circuit.

Magically Jarrow never intended the newspaper trick as anything more than a curtain raiser. In the same vein would be his sequence of card manipulation, essentially the lead-in for him to perform the strongman's feat of tearing a full pack first in halves, and then in quarters, a stunning demonstration of digital strength rather than a baffling mystery. The magic became serious when Jarrow asked for the lights of the auditorium to be raised. Looking towards the back of the theatre, he would ask a gentleman to stand, remove a small coin from his pocket, and hold it clenched tight in his left hand. So that everyone could see, the spectator was asked to stand in the aisle. Jarrow would ask him to name the coin. 'Boy, you don't take chances, do you?' was his usual comeback line. He would extract every ounce of comedy out of positioning the man to the best advantage of the rest of the audience, until he had him standing right down by the steps to the stage. All the while Jarrow kept asking the man whether he still had the penny (or whatever). 'Open your hand. Be sure. Close your hand. Come a little closer. Hold it tightly. Do you still have the penny? Open your hand. Make sure. Close your hand. Hold tightly. You still have the penny? Would you bet your life on it? Would you bet a nickel? What, you'd bet your life, but you wouldn't bet a nickel! Would you bet a drink? For the house? Hit it, George!' Jarrow would ask to see the coin again. When the man opened his hand the next time, he would have a nickel, Jarrow would have the penny. The dexterity with which Jarrow made his switch was so exquisitely executed that the audience had no idea that the magician had even touched the spectator's hand. Such is the power of magic in the hands of a showman that the next day they would be telling their friends how the magician changed the coin while the man stood at the back of the theatre.

Sometimes Jarrow would invite the man on-stage to supervise a trick that happened in his, Jarrow's, hands. The magician would pull back his sleeves, leaving both arms bare. He would then ask the spectator to break open a cigarette and place the loose tobacco on his upturned left palm,

Emil Jarrow – rope magic expert – but his tongue never got tied in knots.

together with the rolled-up cigarette paper. Slowly he would close and turn over his hand at the same time. Mysteriously the whole cigarette rose restored from his fist, not a grain of loose tobacco, nor a shred of torn cigarette paper to be seen. 'How is it done?' Jarrow would ask. 'None of your business!' was his own quick-fire reply.

As a diversion before his magical *pièce de résistance* Jarrow would perform the juggling feat based on inertia, where four eggs positioned on a tray over four glasses of water are caught without breaking in the glasses when the tray is knocked away. For this he would have a confederate in the gallery keep interrupting him, 'Them ain't real eggs.' Jarrow ignored him until the end of the sequence, when he challenged the man to come on to the stage. The magician placed a glass on his outstretched hand and broke one of the eggs into it, then held the glass up to show the egg. However, the glass had no bottom! 'Hit it, George! Hit it again!'

Jarrow then came to the trick which he claimed as his own invention, which alone would have made his reputation and stands as the forerunner of a similar trick in Paul Daniels's own repertoire today. He would borrow three notes of different denominations from his audience. Sometimes he would have their numbers noted. In those days, however, when paper money was larger and more brightly coloured, it was not always necessary to do this to confirm the climax of the effect. As the money was volunteered, he would tell a story about Heaven and the angels. He would explain that a hundred years on earth was only a minute in Heaven. Looking up to the balcony he would then ask, 'Has anyone up there in Heaven a hundred-dollar bill?' 'Yes, in a minute.'

The plot of the trick was simple. The money would be folded and given to an audience member to hold through a borrowed handkerchief. When Jarrow suddenly pulled the latter away, the money had vanished. Taking a previously examined lemon back from the custody of the audience, he would now cut it open at his fingertips. This was the one moment in his act when no jokes were allowed. The dramatic revelation of the three notes drenched in lemon juice in the centre of the fruit was presented in total seriousness, emphasised by the rigid beam of the spotlight now pinned on him. Not that this had always been so. He once confided to Dai Vernon that in his early days he would cut open the lemon and say, 'This reminds me of a synagogue when you see the juice come out.' There were some moments when even Jarrow came to concede that the mystery was more important than the laughter.

Jarrow died in 1959, having seen vaudeville, the institution in which he flourished for so long, fall into decline. In his latter years he concentrated on nightclub and private engagements. Here he had the last laugh on his magician colleagues who had featured in larger shows and were less flexible in adapting to more intimate surroundings. Always Jarrow had known that 'small is beautiful'. It certainly never held him back. When the 'Sawing a Woman' craze was at its height, Jarrow found himself booked to play a theatre opposite one where illusionist Horace Goldin was billed. Around Goldin's theatre were blazoned in lights the words 'See Goldin Saw a Woman in Half'. But Jarrow played to bigger business. Around his own theatre he retaliated in glaring neon for the whole world to see: 'See Jarrow Saw a Lemon in Half'.

One of the Better, Cheaper Acts

That billing may be the best ever coined for publicity purposes by a vaudevillian, encapsulating with perfection the subtle false modesty of the persona of its genuinely modest creator, Jay Marshall. He is the last in a select line of debonair deceptionists who became prominent interweaving hocus-pocus with light comedy in America around the middle of the century, and which included Roy Benson, Fred Keating and Russell Swann.

James Ward Marshall was born on 29 August 1919 in Abington, Massachusetts. After holding out against the attempts of his family to urge him into a more conventional livelihood, Jay embarked upon a show-business career that became distinguished during the 1950s and 1960s by a record fourteen appearances on the celebrated Ed Sullivan television show. When the Sullivan Show went on tour, but the host had to stay in New York, Marshall was the obvious choice to step into his shoes. In his own right he played repeat engagements at the London Palladium, the New York Palace, and Radio City Music Hall, as well as appearing in the Golden Jubilee Edition of the 'Ziegfeld Follies'.

Whatever the implications of his billing, once established Jay played nothing but the best. However, for a long time a story went the rounds that at the peak of his career his cronies at the Lambs Club in New York were perusing the 'calls' in the latest edition of *Variety* when they discovered that the following week their headliner friend was playing a second-division date at a small venue in Hartford, Connecticut, an engagement totally inconsistent with his current status. They could not believe that his career was on the slide so abruptly. Their anxiety was curtailed minutes later when Jay himself entered the room. The excuse was matter-of-fact. 'I just wanted a week to play in a new suit.'

Marshall today takes pains to point out that the story is apocryphal as far as his own involvement is concerned, but that it was first recounted by himself of a fellow performer, Judson Cole, who also brought comedy to magic in his own distinctive way. Whatever the origin, it pinpoints the attention to detail that will be paid by the conscientious show-business professional, of which Marshall remains a shining example. When he was engaged to host a BBC television special in 1977, he made a special journey across London the day before the recording to a band-call for another show with the same orchestra to hand over his own musical requirements.

Jay Marshall – magic's greatest ambassador of knowledge and fun – with Lefty.

They amounted to a single rimshot, an instruction that could as easily have been given the following day. The tongue-in-cheek side of Jay Marshall was perfectly aware of that, but the more serious side, not revealed to the laughing musicians, knew that now there was one less detail to worry about for the next twenty-four hours.

In appearance Jay gives an accurate impression of his true self, the courteous, leisurely, articulate Anglophile, who might as easily pass for a college professor or corporation president, if one did not know his actual vocation. Beneath this, however, lurks a skilfully honed sense of the ridiculous that owes much to great American humorists such as Benchley and Perelman in its off-beat approach to words. He will introduce a trick as 'the encore to my act – not the act I'm doing currently – when I was doing the other act, they never called me back for this encore, so this is practically new'. Or he may preface his act with the apology, 'I have a little routine that's called the triumph of industry over talent or nothing spread thin. It introduces a new style of comedy: just intellectual nods and deep breathing.' Bringing lines like these to life shows a sense of timing on a level with the definitive monologue comedians, Jack Benny and George Burns. As he stares at a knot in a handkerchief waiting for it to untie itself, his look of impatience hangs in the air almost defying the audience not to laugh: 'Oh, come on.' The knot unties, the audience laughs even more. Attempting to replace the handkerchief in his top pocket while continuing to talk to the crowd, his hand persists in sliding over the opening, until, that is, he looks down. 'Thought it healed up on me,' he adds wryly. One begins to realise the importance of knowing one's way about a suit.

Nowhere do Jay Marshall's magic and comedy talents achieve a happier liaison than in his performance of the 'Chinese Linking Rings'. The visual impact of his comedy comes rushing to mind: Jay getting his nose caught as he painfully pulls a ring away from his shoulders and up over his head; sighing with mock ecstasy as he sniffs the blooming rose, one of many designs – others are a swing, a globe, and a butterfly – he makes from the rings; announcing that he will link all the other rings on one 'in one simple dextrous move like this', then hurling himself into a frenzy of jangling discord to achieve it; the beaming complacency of his smile when he does. Alongside the laughter, however, the audience can only be dazzled by the skill of his technique. No sooner has the ring been pulled off his head than without hesitation it is thrown up in the air to link itself of its own accord on to the top of the chain in Marshall's hand on its way down. Overlapping two separate rings, he inserts a finger in the overlap to create the illusion that the rings are linked; he then changes finger for thumb, takes the thumb away, and to the amused surprise of the audience they *are* linked! That 'simple dextrous move' looks impossibly chaotic to an observer, but has been rehearsed to the 'nth' degree for its complexity to achieve the desired result in the same way at every performance.

Few magicians have devoted more time than Jay Marshall to the practical study of what are known as the allied arts of magic, an area in which he has inherited the spiritual mantle of the brilliant French magician, Félicien Trewey (1848–1920), who dazzled audiences in Paris, London and New York with an act that became known as 'The One-Man Variety Entertainment', such was his versatility. Jay too is an accomplished performer of hand shadows; an expert in Chapeaugraphy, the skill of transforming a simple ring of felt into a succession of different hats; and in Troublewit, that of transforming a sheet of pleated paper into a succession of different shapes. He is a qualified Professor of Punch and Judy, as well as a veritable encyclopaedia of impromptu magic. It is nothing for Jay, when sitting in a restaurant, to transform his plate into a rotating

MONS. TREWEY.

JUGGLER, SHADOWGRAPHIST, AND—WELL, EVERYTHING.

Trewey – vaudevillian 'jack of all trades'.

grindstone against which to sharpen his knife, to prove that the bread rolls are made of rubber by bouncing them on the floor, and then to lift the serviette he has spread over his plate to reveal his shoes.

Not surprisingly his talents also embrace ventriloquism. Discovering that it was not practical to carry around a conventional dummy while on army service as a USO entertainer during the Second World War, he turned to a device known as 'The Talking Hand', represented as early as 1755 in an engraving by William Hogarth entitled 'An Election Entertainment'. Rather than paint the features on the hand, Jay stuck two beads for eyes on a glove and, with two further fingers from another glove for ears, created a rabbit that can talk whenever Jay's thumb and forefinger allow. Originally the puppet was made of khaki, but once hostilities were over it soon became snowy white. This 'very lucky young man has a wife and a cigarette lighter and both work'. His name is Lefty: 'You may have seen him on television, but that money's all been spent.' The intimacy Marshall achieves in his dialogue with this small, simple creature becomes all the more remarkable when projected in the largest theatres. Over the years every word and action has been honed for maximum economy of effect, what began as a twelve-minute routine having been imperceptibly cut down to six minutes. Nothing has been added, only the very best left in.

The banter between man and beast is traditional, but the charm as Jay cajoles the slightly irascible bunny into song is immense:

JAY: Sing 'If I had my way!'
LEFTY: If I had my way, I wouldn't sing.
JAY: Don't say that. Are you ready?
LEFTY: All set.
JAY: Go ahead.
LEFTY: Throw it into me.

Lefty remains arguably the most appealing ventriloquial creation since Edgar Bergen breathed manipulative life into Charlie McCarthy and Señor Wences gave audiences a glimpse of that disembodied head in a box: ' "S'all right?" "S'all right!" ' Nor is it difficult to see the influence Marshall must have exerted on Muppet creator Jim Henson in his formative years. In the curious miscegenation of puppetry, it is hard not to see Lefty as a not too distant relative of Kermit the Frog, however great the leap from white mammal to green reptile may be in strict biological terms.

Jay Marshall is now retired and living in Chicago where, with his wife Frances, he helps to run a prosperous magical retail business and presides over one of the greatest private collections of magical books in the world. From time to time he will be invited away to perform for a convention of magicians who recognise in him one of the greatest ambassadors their profession has ever had. It is extremely seldom that he refuses. As Lefty would say, 'Well, *goody* for you!' Besides, the standing ovations keep him young.

Jay with his wife Frances Ireland Marshall, the first lady of magic.

4

A Magical Crusade

'Nobody Wins in the Bunco Booth'

When Paul performs with cup and ball on stage or television he imparts to his presentation a respectability the trick did not always have. It is as well to be reminded that in earlier times magicians hobnobbed with rogues and vagabonds and on occasion could not be distinguished from the company they kept. The professional presentation of magic as we know it today began at the shows presented at fairs and market places by itinerant performers. It took a considerable time to work its way up the social scale into the genteel drawing-rooms of the early nineteenth century and the theatres, music halls and cabarets of more recent years. The 'Cups and Balls' illusion is significant here, because technically it is a close relation of the classic fairground swindle with three walnut shells and a pea. The only

An 1839 print depicting thimble-rigging, the original three-shell game.

Published by T. McLean, 26 Haymarket Street, 5th June 1839. THE THIMBLE RIG Lith. A. Ducôte.

real difference is that when you can't keep track of the balls, you gain in enjoyment; when you can't keep track of the pea, you lose financially. In another form thimbles were substituted for shells; hence the phrase 'thimble-rigging'. And yet the result was always the same. You laid your bet on where you thought the pea would be found. You never won, unless you were an accomplice or 'shill' of the manipulator.

It was to present traditional carnival flim-flam of this kind in the context for which it was first devised, while at the same time educating the public to its pitfalls, that the 'Bunco Booth' was devised for 'The Paul Daniels Magic Show'. It derived its name from an early American term for defrauding at cards, and as a regular item has proved one of the most popular on the programme over the years, allowing Paul full rein for both digital dexterity and cheeky repartee. 'Nobody Wins in the Bunco Booth' and 'Heads I Win, Tails You Lose' are two slogans that have hopefully prevented more than one otherwise unsuspecting member of the public from being conned on a race course, at a fairground, or even on a street corner.

Today grafters can still be seen working the most famous of these swindles, the three-card trick, on London's Oxford Street. In one of his favourite demonstrations Paul shows how there is no way you can ever beat this fraud, and leaves you totally baffled in the process. But you should not need to know *how* it is done to ensure that you never take part in it. Even when Paul openly bends the corner of the Queen, traditionally the odd card out, in 'Find the Lady' style, and invites you to place your hand on the very card with the dog-ear, you still lose. The Queen is no longer bent; the crimp is now in one of the other cards. The old-time Mississippi riverboat gambler, a guise in which Paul has recently continued his Bunco crusade, would recite a short rhyme as he enticed the sucker to his lair: 'A little game from Hankey Poo, the black for me, the red for you – all you really have to do is keep your eye on the lady – ten gets you twenty, twenty gets you forty – here we go – keep your eye on the lady.' Since those days specialist card magicians such as Dai Vernon and the late John Scarne have subtly embellished the basic premise of the original game to the point where they could doubtless turn the tables on the Mississippi operators themselves. The Queen can be actually pinned to the table, but still it is not the Queen!

The most extreme lengths taken by Paul in the 'Bunco Booth' to prove how gullible the public can be involved his attempt to give away a Rolls-Royce complete with champagne and a night on the town with Debbie McGee. Five keys were shown. It was demonstrated how none of them could open the locked door of the car. The only key that would do so was in Paul's possession. All six keys, looking alike in every other respect, were displayed on a turntable and spun so that their relative positions were unknown to the committee taking part. In turn each member of the committee chose a key, only to discover that it would not possibly open

There are some Mugs

AT STAINES

Left, an umbrella provided a favourite working surface for race-course tricksters. *Right*, 'Nobody Wins in the Bunco Booth!'

the car and that he would have to be content with a toy model of a Rolls-Royce instead. The procedure differed only in the case of the fifth and last man. Having made his choice of one key from the remaining two, he was given the chance by Paul of exchanging it for one of two envelopes. Paul explained that one contained a slip of paper, the other Paul's personal cheque for £10,000. The spectator decided to take the risk. Paul tied the key he had chosen, and was now prepared to trade, to a ribbon to identify it at a later stage. The man then opened the envelope of his choice to discover a message that read, 'I'm the loser, but I'm a good sport. Notice how I smile.' As a relieved Paul first opened the other envelope to reveal his cheque, and then applied the beribboned key to open the car, it is doubtful whether in real life that smile would have been so apparent.

On another occasion Paul adapted the conventions of the television quiz to the Bunco theme. Everything was improvised. A girl from the audience was teased into playing the contestant, while a man was asked to provide the prize, in this case a ten-pound note. He was also asked to contribute the answer, on this occasion a chosen card, say 'the six of clubs'. Both were placed openly in envelopes: the first, marked 'The Prize: £10', was clipped to the girl's blouse, and the second, marked 'The Answer: six of clubs',

Opposite, discovered by Cyril Bertram Mills, the incomparable Borra soon became European circus's biggest star.

was clipped to the man's lapel. The object of the game was for the girl to get three correct answers in a row by always answering 'the six of clubs':

PAUL: We've been doing this all week in rehearsal – you feel pretty stupid when you get it wrong, don't you?

GIRL: The six of clubs.

PAUL: How many have you answered right so far?

GIRL: The six of clubs.

PAUL: That's two in a row. Now, for the third and final question: if you get the third answer right, what do you want, the six of clubs or the money?

GIRL: The six of clubs.

PAUL: That means you've won, but you prefer the six of clubs!

The sudden realisation by the girl that on the last question she has been utterly bamboozled provided the magician with one of his loudest laughs, one it was difficult for Paul not to contribute to with devious glee himself. In real life, of course, an argument would have ensued, but, as in real life, the professional swindler has always covered his tracks. Paul opens the envelope marked 'The Prize' to take out not the money, but the six of clubs, exactly what the girl asked for. Back in the other envelope, in place of the card, is the original ten-pound note!

Today the link between conjuror and vagabond is underlined by the professional stage pickpocket. The undisputed leader in this field is Borra. While not a magician *per se* – the key to Borra's skill is that the audience *does* see how it is done while his unsuspecting victims haven't a clue – nevertheless his showmanship, charisma, and dexterity qualify him as a very special honorary member of the magic profession. It is inconceivable that this book should not celebrate his fame.

Born Borislav Milojkowic in Yugoslavia on 26 April 1921, he became an Austrian citizen after the Second World War, and attained his greatest fame in Britain as the star attraction with Bertram Mills Circus in the 1950s. Audiences of over 5,000 were mesmerised and reduced to hysterics at the same time as he spirited away watches and wallets, braces and ties, with disarming bonhomie. The moment when he snaps the spectacles off an audience volunteer and places them on his own nose without – hard as it is to believe – the spectator realising, remains one of the most hilarious of contemporary show business. Such is his renown – he must be the highest paid of all European circus and cabaret entertainers – that a street has been named after him in his home town of Graz. It seems impossible that he will ever be surpassed in his own area of specialisation, or in the degree of genuine warmth and humanity he radiates both on and off stage. And if suddenly you discover that your watch has flown or your car key has walked, remember that, like the Bunco Booth, it's only for fun and the likelihood of your becoming a victim in reality is that much less as a result.

Extra-sensory Deception

There is another area where Paul conducts a personal crusade as rigorous as that against the sharp practice of the 'Bunco Booth'. Following in the footsteps of John Nevil Maskelyne and Houdini, his campaign to denounce all so-called psychic achievement which his magical knowledge tells him can be attributed to deception and fraud, and not to genuine practice, led to the inclusion in his television show of the item known as 'Under Laboratory Conditions'. The three words are self-explanatory. Under the severe scrutiny of an overhead television camera and test conditions imposed by members of the audience chosen at random to participate in the experiments, Paul was able to reveal the total naïvety of the scientific process in the investigation of alleged psychics. The unscrupulous shenanigans of spoon-benders, surgeons performing blood-less operations, musical mediums, and fortune-tellers, impelled by greed to raise false hopes in less rational individuals, are all grist to his mill as he demonstrates – in deference to the magician's code, without revealing exactly how – what it is possible to achieve by sleight-of-hand and the other established techniques of hocus-pocus. Uri Geller's claim to be able to bend spoons and keys with his mind becomes totally insignificant when held up against Paul's ability to cause watch-hands to move, a nut and bolt to become unthreaded, modelling clay to cut itself, and – far more usefully – blank keys to assume a chosen shape without any apparent human agency. Paul can also guarantee success every time! However, the most talked-about experiment by Paul in this area referred back to a phenomenon that preceded Geller by several years.

In the 1960s an American, Ted Serios, caused a minor sensation when he claimed he was able to project his thoughts on to photographic film. These claims became largely discredited after the publication of a now-famous article in the October 1967 issue of the magazine *Popular Photography* by the magician and then photographic journalist Charles Reynolds in the company of magical colleague David B. Eisendrath, Junior. They drew attention to the simple small paper tube, described farcically by Serios as a 'gizmo', which it was necessary for him to hold close to the camera in order to focus his mental picture. Serios's talents obviously amounted to little more than the manipulative ability to introduce secretly into this miniature telescope a transparency of the image he wished to project. In Paul Daniels's version of the experiment no gizmo was necessary. A representative of the Polaroid photographic company was requested to bring factory-fresh to the studio the simplest camera in the Polaroid range and a sealed packet of film. Vouching for these objects before the camera, she was asked to open and load the film while Paul turned to his other three independent guests. All were prominent celebrities and well used to the sound of the photographer's click, but not with the results that Paul would now demonstrate.

Actress Jill Gascoine was asked to think of a colour. Songwriter Tim Rice was asked to imagine his name up in lights on a theatre façade. Artist and entertainer Rolf Harris was asked to think of a popular view of London. Without a gizmo in sight, each in turn was then asked lightly to touch the lens of the camera, with their fingertips. Each time the Polaroid representative snapped away and handed the photograph subsequently delivered directly into the custody of the celebrity involved. At no time in fact did Paul touch the camera, let alone the prints. By the time Rolf had been subjected to this treatment, Jill's own print had developed. This was the least successful, revealing a striped rainbow effect rather than her specific colour. As Paul explained, his instruction to her not to think of any other colours had doubtless caused confusion in her brain to the point that it was impossible to think of anything but all of them. There could, however, be no doubt about the result of both Tim's and Rolf's part in the experiment. Never did the name of Tim Rice glare or the statue of Nelson atop his column rear so magnificently, even if the latter was shrouded somewhat by a mist that could have been either fog or puzzled uncertainty in the Harris mind. The sequence concluded with the Polaroid official taking both camera and film back to her headquarters to test them still further under her own laboratory conditions.

*

Ruthless as Paul Daniels is in his opposition to the unprincipled end of the psychic business, where unsuspecting, if naïve, human beings become pawns in a game of mercenary and egotistical greed, he would be the first to champion the entertainer who channels the same techniques for purely entertainment purposes, often leaving the matter of his psychic ability to the audience to decide for itself. The most successful performer of this kind in the history of magic was the American mentalist Joseph Dunninger. He was born on the Lower East Side of New York on 28 April 1892, by remarkable coincidence the very year the word 'telepathy' was first coined by F. W. H. Myers, an English philosopher interested in psychic research.

The son of a German immigrant tailor, Dunninger started in show business as a boy magician, working by day first as messenger and then as clerk in a department store. In those early years he saw the shows of many leading magicians, but none would have the impact of the performance by Mr and Mrs John T. Fay, who at the turn of the century presented a question-and-answer act in the fortune-telling category based on that of John's mother, Anna Eva Fay, the greatest stage psychic of the early vaudeville period. They pointed the way for Dunninger, with one major variation. He was determined to present his own mental magic alone, without an assistant. He devised a presentation based on reporting the findings of a supposed scientific investigation and in 1920 found himself giving a performance to the Press Club in Boston as the president of the

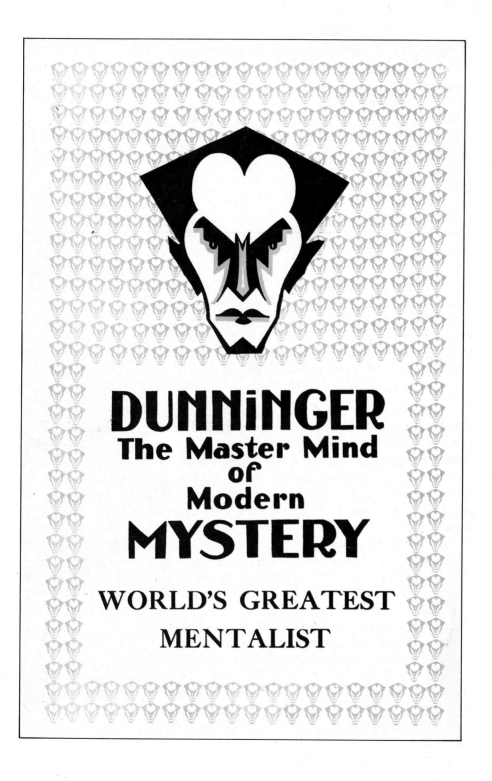

DUNNiNGER
The Master Mind
of
Modern
MYSTERY

WORLD'S GREATEST

MENTALIST

This stunning image of Dunninger is more than it seems. Look carefully at those eyes again.

so-called 'American Psychical Society'. The *Boston Post* covered the appearance in detail. After an introduction emphasising the potential advantage of telepathy to mankind, Dunninger distributed squares of paper among the audience, asking the spectators to write words or numbers, names or dates upon them. When all the pieces were folded and secure in the pockets of the crowd, a volunteer was asked to collect five of the folded papers in an envelope:

> which the collector did with the assistance of the professor [Dunninger], who tucked them deeply into the envelope, which he then threw carelessly on the floor (flap side up) and asked the collector to put his foot on it and keep it there. The professor then walked perhaps thirty feet back from the audience and sat down behind a table which concealed from us all there was of him below his elbows. He explained he could read human minds more readily when our mentalities were on the same level as his own. To the complete flabbergastation of all present, he easily read exactly what each of the five had written on their scraps of paper. This all the five admitted, and loud applause followed each demonstration.

As the performer became more confident, he would conclude by asking the last spectator, 'Are you thinking of the word "amazing"? Is it in reference to me? Thank you very much.'

His presence was his greatest asset. Tall and broad-shouldered, wearing flamboyant clothes, he dominated a stage. Prominent American journalist Maurice Zolotow likened him to Al Jolson, no less, in his ability to hold an audience by the sheer force of his personality. So assured was he that when magic shops started without authorisation to advertise for sale the method he used to perform his envelope test, he resorted to the most brazen ploy to allay suspicion. In an article in the November 1927 issue of *Science and Invention* he wrote, 'Many dealers in magical equipment are charging exorbitant prices for this effect, claiming it is the method employed by me in my performances on the Keith circuit. To prove it is not, I am disclosing the system herewith.' He then gave in accurate detail the actual method he continued to use for the rest of his career! Illustrations showing the precise technique only added to the effrontery. Readers believed, and magicians who did know his secret could only wonder at his audacity. To further protect himself he issued a standard challenge, at one point amounting to $10,000, to anyone who could prove he used stooges or confederates in his act. He always knew his money was safe.

Had they ever offered a Nobel Prize for publicity, he would, after Houdini, have been its recipient. Ever one to turn a situation to his advantage in this way, he was once charged in New York on a car parking offence. When the misdemeanour hit the press, Dunninger was reported as reading the magistrate's mind: 'Don't park your car near theatres during

Dunninger attempts to read a secret message sealed within a cloth bag.

the rush hour.' When the magistrate then challenged Dunninger to tell him the sentence he was about to pass, the mind-reader replied, 'Yes, five dollars or two days in jail'. Dunninger could well afford to pay the fine. On another occasion he parked his car near his home at 147th Street and Third Avenue. When he returned, the car had gone. He reported the theft to the local precinct where he was greeted with cynicism: 'Why don't *you* tell *us* who stole it and where it is?' The showman began to concentrate. 'I don't know who stole it,' he admitted, 'but I think you will find it in Yorkville.' Eventually the car was found in this very district of Manhattan, smashed against a pillar of the elevated railway. Suspicions that Dunninger might have planted it himself were allayed by the fact that inside the car the police found one Robert Cunningham, a professional car thief.

Dunninger was the first magician of any kind to make full use of the mechanised media, pioneering the success in Britain of mental performers such as The Piddingtons, Bayard and Marion, Chan Canasta, and David Berglas. He graduated from vaudeville to specialising in astronomically well-paid private engagements for the élite of American society, but it was not until 1943 that his name truly became a household word. He had attempted radio once before in 1929, but his concept of a series of 'Ghost Hours' failed to capture the public imagination. When, fourteen years later, he began broadcasting over the NBC Blue Network as 'Dunninger, the Master Mind' the response was different. In 1948 he transferred his radio popularity to television, where he had the rare distinction of starring in a series for all three major American networks.

A feature of both his radio and television shows were the so-called 'Brain Busters', where his telepathic experiments were subjected to a dimension not previously allowed within the confines of a vaudeville stage. Dunninger, safe within the studio, tuned into the thoughts of his guests as they ploughed beneath the waves in a submarine, speeded overhead in an aeroplane, or parachuted to the ground from a tower at Coney Island. On one show he opened a safe at the National Jewellery Exchange via the thoughts of two guards, each of whom knew one half of the combination; on another he wrote in advance the name, address and postmark of a letter selected at random by the New York Postmaster from one sack among hundreds on a passing conveyor belt at the head post office. Each week the growing ingenuity of the tests grabbed bigger headlines in the press, thus ensuring larger audiences for the programme next time around. Throughout his career he made mileage of the fact that he had read the minds of virtually every famous person of the day. Harry Truman, Franklin D. Roosevelt, Thomas Edison, Pope Pius XII, the Duke of Windsor, Jack Benny, Barbara Hutton, Babe Ruth, Jack Dempsey were a few whose endorsement in this way enhanced his own celebrity. He graced the private functions of the Astors, the Tiffanys, the Goulds and the Vanderbilts. He was especially proud to quote these words from Edison in his publicity material: 'Never have I witnessed anything as mystifying or seemingly impossible.'

One of magic's greatest showmen, Dunninger always disclaimed that he had supernatural powers. 'Any child of twelve could do what I do,' he said, 'with thirty years of practice!' That said, he would often play semantic tricks when openly asked if he could read minds. He referred to his ability as 'telaesthesia': 'You pick up a vivid impression from another mind and others follow or suggest themselves. But it isn't mind-reading; it is thought-reading.' Those who know his secrets will appreciate the difference. Perhaps more important was a simpler claim: 'I look upon myself as an entertainer.' Unlike so many psychic performers, he never abused that position. He died on 9 March 1975.

*

One reason why so many performers of mental magic have been considered authentic with regard to the effect they produce may be because of the existence of a pioneering group of stage mind-readers who threw aside the more contrived techniques of magic and deception in favour of a procedure based on sound physiological and psychological principles. These enabled them to interpret the thoughts of a second party provided they remained in hand-held contact with that person. By interpreting the slight ideomotor impulses emanating subconsciously from the brain, as the subject considered the direction he wished the performer to favour, so the latter was able to home in on a secret thought or destination without a word being spoken. Among magicians the most

Left, John Randall Brown, American pioneer of 'muscle-reading', and (*right*) Stuart Cumberland, disciple and rival of Bishop in the 'hunt-the-pin' stakes.

common names for this phenomenon are contact mind-reading and muscle-reading, although, for the latter, nerve-reading would be equally apt.

The first prominent exponent of this technique was a Chicago newspaper reporter turned showman, John Randall Brown, born on 28 October 1851. He claimed to have discovered his skills as a child playing variations of the game 'Hunt the Thimble'. In later years the *pièce de résistance* of his stage demonstration involved finding a pin hidden somewhere in the theatre he was playing. In theory there was no limit to the ingenuity of the choice of hiding-place. It could be in the spine of a book, in the stem of a pipe, in the lace of a shoe. The deed done, Brown would be escorted back on stage and, without asking any questions, would lead his subject to the exact spot where the object was hidden. In later years an assistant to Brown, fellow countryman Washington Irving Bishop, developed his own routine, history repeating itself when Bishop's assistant Charles Garner left Bishop to do the same, changing his name in the process to Stuart Cumberland. Both achieved greater celebrity than the pioneer Brown, no doubt because of the additional showmanship with which they invested the basic challenge. Bishop's special ploy was to discover the hidden object while driving a horse and carriage blindfold through the streets, a device later adapted by Dunninger to a car.

In more recent years this skill was developed to greatest sensitivity by the Hungarian showman, Franz J. Polgar. In December 1950, as part of a feature for *Look* Magazine, Polgar successfully found a small silver

Washington Irving Bishop's comprehensive demonstration was well documented in this 1883 engraving.

banknote clip which had been secreted somewhere within the 102 storeys of the Empire State Building. A further test of his skill could be gained from the description of the routine with which he finished his theatre appearances. In spite of the misgivings of his agent, the object Polgar entrusted to this eccentric game of 'Hide-and-Seek' was no less than his cheque for the engagement. If he failed to locate it, he would forgo the fee. Over the years he recovered his salary from some unlikely locations: the barrel of the gun of a Texan police chief; the hollowed-out heel of a lady's shoe; even sealed within a tennis ball. But Polgar always left the theatre more affluent than when he entered.

The theme of the hidden object test was given its most original twist by Paul Daniels in 1985 when in a latter-day 'Brain Buster' on his television show he not only waved goodbye to any prospect of contact mind-reading being used, but ingeniously turned the tables on his audience. On the day in question *he* had hidden the object and the audience was to be responsible for finding it. Neither Anneka Rice, presenter of the popular TV programme 'Treasure Hunt', who was invited to supervise the proceedings away from the studio, nor the members of the audience chosen at random for conducting the experiment were associates of Paul. All Anneka knew beforehand was that she would spend the best part of the programme in a helicopter, in the company of a surprised audience member, being directed to a point anywhere on dry land within a fifty-five-mile radius of the outskirts of London. In the studio, first a compass direction was agreed upon by the audience committee. With Anneka safely on course along this route, a distance in miles from London was selected, with the whole audience involved in deciding this figure in what Paul fairly described as 'a raffle of distance'. The map revealed the place nearest to the predetermined distance along the chosen course. When Anneka had been given instructions to land at the Cotswold village of Shipton-under-Wychwood, the committee, with a throw of a dart, chose the type of landmark for which she had to keep her eyes peeled at the destination, namely a hotel. They could as easily have chosen a windmill or a level-crossing, a church or a farm, or any other similar feature.

As the suspense built, so the mystery deepened. All the time the audience had no idea what Paul's hidden object or objects could be. Fortunately there was a hotel within a short distance of the central green where Anneka and the audience member were able to land in the helicopter. Once inside the hotel, there was nothing obvious to point towards the fact that this was the ultimate destination that would bring Paul's experiment to a successful conclusion. After a tentative search of the reception area, however, Anneka fell against the door of a private lounge. Inside stood the London Crier with a cordon of policemen and security guards in formal custody of a special locked chest. Anneka's gasp was nothing compared with her reaction to what the chest was then shown to contain – the principal Crown Jewels from the Imperial Collection within the City of London. It was the ultimate denouement to the most incredible display of what could be interpreted as either precognition or the ability to influence minds. It was perhaps appropriate that a year later Paul should buy the famous tourist attraction, Mother Shipton's Cave, at Knaresborough in Yorkshire. The prophecies of the famous witch have become part of that county's folklore. What was the name of that Cotswold village again?

5

The Magician as National Figure

In just over a decade Paul Daniels has become a celebrity of widespread fame. Not since the heyday of Maskelyne and Devant at the turn of the century has a British conjuror received such fulsome accolades. In 1982 he became the first serious magician to be nominated Show Business Personality of the Year by the Variety Club of Great Britain and, in 1986, the first to achieve a hat-trick of appearances on the 'Royal Variety Performance'. Gone were the days when he had to make excuses for himself as a magician with a billing that suggested he was not. In 1985 the BBC won the Golden Rose of Montreux (the top award in television for an entertainment programme) with 'The Paul Daniels Magic Show', against worldwide competition. He even found his way into latex on the award-winning puppet series 'Spitting Image', his natural lack of inches, toupee and high-profile ears carried to a level of caricature that must represent fame's most disconcerting reward.

In the national press cartoonists have enjoyed a field day with Paul. Franklin in the *Sun* depicted him entering the presence of a distraught Margaret Thatcher pondering the poor showing of the Tories in the latest opinion polls. The caption was entrusted to the minion opening the door on her behalf: 'She wants you to make Neil Kinnock and David Owen disappear.' Even more satisfying are those occasions when the cartoonist, unrestricted by the two dimensions of his medium, makes an imaginative leap to provide his own special form of graphic impossibility. Dredge, of *Punch*, once depicted two punks, one spraying a wall with conventional graffiti – 'City are magic!' 'Red for the Cup!' 'E.T. phone Samaritans!' – the other spraying his message in mid-air: 'Paul Daniels Rules, OK!' There the letters stayed, as happily as any physical being levitated by Paul on a conventional stage. Bill Tidy conveyed a similar comic impossibility in the same magazine when the flabbergasted expression of a fielder at a charity cricket match between the Lords Taverners XI and a showbiz team is explained by the umpire's decision: 'Paul Daniels, caught Paul Daniels, bowled Paul Daniels.'

When many years ago David Devant shaved off his moustache, his

Paul becomes the first ever subject of *two* waxworks at Madame Tussaud's in London, enabling him to appear and disappear in an uncanny display.

public accepted the cosmetic change with scarce a murmur; when Paul Daniels shed his toupee, it became front-page news. When you are then mentioned in Hansard because a member of the House of Commons considers that the Government's economic policy has as much chance of success as anyone has of winning in Paul Daniels's 'Bunco Booth', you know you have arrived. Most significantly of all, Paul has cultivated a catch-phrase on a level of recognition with that of any great comedian. Long, long ago he was heckled about his suit in a Bradford nightclub. Paul's reply was surprisingly apologetic. 'That's a shame, because I like yours, not a lot, but I like it.' The audience laughed and the line, adapted to the trick of the moment – 'You're gonna like this, not a lot, but you'll like it' – has remained a talisman ever since. When Paul lent himself to the Heineken lager advertising campaign, the usual slogan on the hoardings was subtly amended. The familiar triptych style depicted Daniels holding glass, Daniels sipping from glass, and finally glass suspended in mid-air with Daniels nowhere to be seen. Above ran the line, 'Heineken refreshes the parts that other beers can not a lot reach.'

In all history few magicians have attained such status in their own country. In the pages to come, four who undoubtedly did – Robert-Houdin in France, the partnership of Maskelyne and Devant in Britain, and Blackstone in the United States – will be examined in depth, adding to our understanding of the special gifts of Paul Daniels. Only Houdini has truly outclassed them all and he too will attract our attention in turn. But first we look to France and the magician universally acknowledged as 'The Father of Modern Magic'.

✻

In an age of Cold-War diplomacy and the sombre spectre of nuclear attack it is hard to believe that once, not so long ago, a magician's skills could have been used to avert an international incident. Such was the status in France of Robert-Houdin, however, that in 1856 he was coaxed (albeit reluctantly) out of retirement by Colonel de Neveu, Emissary for the French Government in Algeria, for this very purpose. At the time France was anxious to destroy the pernicious influence of the Marabouts, a race of false prophets whose ability to perform certain simple conjuring tricks was sufficient to make the naïve Arabs believe they were the envoys of God on earth come to deliver them from Christian oppression. The majority of revolts in Algeria at this time were excited by these fanatics, anxious as they were to sever links between the two countries. Robert-Houdin's commission was to show the Arabs that the white man was a far more influential magician than any of the Marabout intriguers.

On 28 October Robert-Houdin found himself poised to give one of his most memorable performances before an audience of tribal chiefs, interpreters, and various civilian and military dignitaries, in his own opinion the most glittering assembly to which he had ever played. He began at a leisurely pace as cannon balls, flowers, coins and sweetmeats succumbed to his manipulative skills. The magician knew only too well that it was not enough merely to mystify his spectators; he had to terrify them with a display of seemingly supernatural power. They were completely thrown off-guard by what followed.

Advancing from the back of the stage, Robert-Houdin displayed a small but solidly built chest resembling a cash-box. He then addressed the crowd as follows, 'From what you have witnessed, you will attribute a supernatural power to me, and you are right. I will give you a new proof of my marvellous authority by showing that I can deprive the most powerful man of his strength, and restore it at my will. Anyone who thinks himself strong enough to try the experiment may draw near me.'

Before long he was approached by a muscular, well-built Arab of medium height. Measuring him from head to foot, Robert-Houdin inquired about his strength. The Arab was scornful in his reply. 'And are you sure that you will always remain strong?' asked the magician. Again the reply was affirmative, whereupon Robert-Houdin delivered the *coup de grâce*.

'You are mistaken, for in an instant I shall rob you of your strength, and you shall become as a little child.'

He instructed the Arab to lift up the box, which he did with ease. A

Robert-Houdin, 'The Father of Modern Magic'.

small boy could have done the same. It was as light as a feather. After a pause, he then asked him to lift the chest once more. 'Behold! You are weaker than a woman; now try to lift the box.' The brawny assistant bent down again but this time, struggle and pull as he might, the box would not budge. Now it was as heavy as an elephant. Within seconds he was exhausted and flushed with rage. On the point of surrender, he realised that he must make one final effort to save his honour. Acknowledging the encouragement of his friends, he grasped the handle again, his legs apart so that he could brace himself more fully. To the consternation of the crowd, those legs suddenly gave way and his arms underwent a violent muscular contraction as a shriek of agony went through the auditorium. Wrapping his head quickly in the folds of his burnous to hide his shame, he catapulted himself out of the theatre.

The onlookers became grave and solemn. Robert-Houdin remembered the moment vividly. 'I heard the words "Shaitan!" "Djenoum!" passing in a murmur around the circle of credulous men, who, while gazing on me, seemed astonished that I possessed none of the physical qualities attributed to the angel of darkness.'

This illusion demonstrates perfectly the magician's flair for exploiting scientific discovery before the discovery itself has become commonplace. In the base of the chest was concealed an iron plate. Beneath the cloth that acted as carpet for the stage was a powerful electromagnet connected to a battery under the control of an off-stage assistant. At a signal, the power would be switched on. The electromagnet was so powerful that a whole tribe of the most muscular Arabs could not have shifted the box. The climax of the effect came when an electric shock from an induction coil was passed on a further signal into the box handle. In those days very few people knew anything about electricity, and so the secret required genius rather than intelligence if the innocent spectator was going to fathom it out.

Robert-Houdin had not finished with his supernatural powers yet. It was important for the magician to discredit the Marabouts' claim to invulnerability by himself proving a similar immunity while employing a far superior stratagem. One Marabout swore no bullets could harm him, and then cunningly blocked up the barrel of the gun before it was fired. Robert-Houdin informed his audience that he possessed a special talisman that rendered him bullet-proof and defied the best marksman in Algeria to fire straight at his heart. He handed a cavalry pistol to the bloodthirsty volunteer who had leapt to the stage. Having examined the weapon, the native was instructed to load a double charge of powder followed by the bullet which he had already marked with a knife. As the pistol exploded, Robert-Houdin interposed an apple on the point of a dagger. The bullet lodged in the centre of the fruit mid-flight. When the apple was cut open, the mark upon the bullet identified that which had been loaded seconds before. Nearly thirty years earlier Robert-Houdin had heard from his mentor, the magician Torrini, how his son Giovanni had been killed performing this very trick. Robert-Houdin had vowed then that he would never risk its performance himself. Now national duty had demanded that he change his mind.

He then called for a third volunteer. A young Moor about twenty years of age consented to come on stage. He was invited to stand upon a slender table that appeared isolated with a large open space beneath. The magician lowered an enormous cloth cone over the volunteer. The cone and its contents were then shifted on to a plank, the ends of which were held by the magician and his servant as they walked towards the front of the stage.

Opposite, note the 'Light and Heavy Chest' on the bottom right.

Robert-Houdin upset the cone. Its contents had gone. Panic now gripped the audience who could not leave the building fast enough, each terrified that he would be the next victim of the conjuror's devilish powers. As they scrambled through the doors some of them found themselves face to face with the Moor himself. Before they had finished cross-questioning him, he had turned on his heels, as perplexed as the crowd was petrified.

It goes without saying that with this performance Robert-Houdin succeeded in converting open hostility towards the French on the part of the Arabs into awed respect, and the threat of further rebellion disappeared. A few days later the magician was summoned to the Governor's palace where the Arab chiefs presented him with a testimonial scroll. It read in part:

> Generous-handed destiny has sent down from above, in the midst of lightning and thunder, like a powerful and fertilising rain, the marvel of the moment and the age, him who cultures the surprising arts and marvellous sciences – The *Sid* – Robert-Houdin.

Those who revere him today refer to him more concisely as 'The Father of Modern Magic'. Certainly he was to have a greater and more lasting influence on the art of conjuring, both at a secret technical level and in presentation, than anyone else up to that time.

He was born Jean Eugène Robert, the son of a watchmaker, at Blois in France on 7 December 1805, a day after the date given in his memoirs. The name by which he became famous was not acquired until his marriage to his first wife, Josèphe Cécile Houdin in 1830, when by way of celebration he became officially Jean Eugène Robert-Houdin. He was originally intended for the legal profession, but the mechanical instinct which ran through his family held sway and he soon found work in his father's profession, where in those days both mechanical skill and delicacy of touch were of equal importance. He became so adroit with his fingers that he could borrow a pocketwatch and, using only one hand, secretly open the back of the timepiece, insert a miniature playing card, and close the watch without detection before handing it back to the owner. His interest in magic as such was first aroused when a busy bookseller gave him by mistake a volume devoted to 'Scientific Amusements' and not the learned treatise on horology he had expected. The young apprentice did not notice the mistake until he arrived home, where he was soon gripped by page after page of conjuring secrets. He later recalled, 'How often since have I blessed this providential error, without which I should have probably vegetated as a country watchmaker.'

It was a foregone conclusion that his mechanical ability and his flair for deception should enhance each other. He devised a magical clock that created a sensation wherever it was displayed. This comprised a glass dial, supported upright on a glass column. The hands of the clock kept perfect time even though it was transparently clear that no motivating force was attached to them. He devised many ingenious automata, for which he received a silver medal at the Paris exhibition of 1844. One figure, which was able to write words and draw pictures of its own accord, was bought by the famous American showman P. T. Barnum, who exhibited it in London later that same year.

By now he had his own premises in Paris, a dark little shop in an unpretentious street of the Marais quarter, over the door of which was displayed the modest sign: *M. Robert-Houdin, Pendules de Précision*. One of his magic crystal clocks caught the eye of the Comte de l'Escalopier, a lover of curios of all kinds, who went in to purchase it. So began a devoted friendship between the two men. As Robert-Houdin beguiled his new patron with feats of sleight-of-hand, he admitted his desire to become a public performer, an ambition thwarted only by the lack of money. But when the nobleman offered 10,000 francs towards the theatrical venture which the magician had in mind, Robert-Houdin would not accept. After a fit of pique the Count returned some while later with a definite proposition. He explained how for the last year considerable sums of money had been disappearing from his desk. In spite of all the safeguards and precautions he had taken, nothing had deterred the thief. Fearing for the safety of his family if one of them should catch the criminal red-handed, he wanted Robert-Houdin to invent a secret device that would catch the culprit. The magician put his mind to the problem and the following day visited the Count's mansion on the Place des Vosges to install his trap. In the demonstration that followed the magician wore a thickly padded glove on his right hand. With that hand he unlocked the desk and slowly raised the lid. Suddenly a pistol shot was heard and a spring-loaded thin metal rod with a needle attachment came down on the back of the glove, only to disappear again inside the desk just as quickly when the lid fell. Proudly Robert-Houdin raised his gloved hand before the Count. There to his total amazement was imprinted in ink the word *voleur*, meaning thief. The Count asked that the device be modified to inflict just a superficial scratch. Should the wrong person open the desk, the tattoo needles which his friend had used to brand the word could prove needlessly dangerous. Robert-Houdin obliged.

Two weeks passed before the Count heard the shot he had been expecting. He raced to the bedroom, only to find his valet pointing in the direction the thief had taken. But the door was locked. At once suspicion fell on the servant. Grabbing his hand, the Count detected the tell-tale scratch. The valet signed a full confession and returned 15,000 francs to his master, a sum which the latter immediately insisted Robert-Houdin should accept on loan in order to implement his dream. This time the magician could hardly refuse. He acquired a suite of rooms on the first floor of No. 164 in the Galerie de Valois in the Palais Royal, originally the residence of Cardinal Richelieu. He converted them into a small, elegant

In time Robert-Houdin's Paris salon was taken over by magician Georges Méliès, later to become more famous as the inventor of cinematic special effects.

theatre of magic and on 3 July 1845 presented the first of his *Soirées Fantastiques*, evenings of ingenuity and wonder that would entrance Parisian audiences in the years ahead.

Ironically, the performances were not an immediate success. The first night coincided with the gala première at the new Paris Hippodrome, with the result that not a single theatrical critic covered the more intimate opening. In some ways this was just as well, for Robert-Houdin has himself confessed that his debut was a disaster. 'In my life I never passed so frightful a night as the one following my first performance. I had a fever, I am quite certain, but that was as nothing in comparison with my moral sufferings. I had no desire left or courage to appear on the stage.'

Events happily proved otherwise. By the spring of the following year crowds started to fill the 200-seat theatre to capacity. Robert-Houdin had captured the public imagination with an exhibition of 'Second Sight' that featured his 14-year-old son, Emile. While the boy sat blindfolded on stage, his father walked among the audience and invited spectators to hand him unusual objects which the son would describe in uncanny detail. The demonstration was not entirely original. Sixty years previously, the blindfolded wife of the Italian magician Pinetti had identified objects in a similar fashion. During the early 1830s an 8-year-old Scottish boy, Louis Gordon M'Kean, known as the Highland Youth, had exhibited a similar talent in London before King William IV.

Audiences today are unimpressed when such phenomena are achieved by the most blatant of oral codes, but Robert-Houdin, like the great two-person telepathy acts to follow him – the Zancigs, the Zomahs and the Trees – was more subtle in his methods. If his conversation was crucial to his son's success, how could audiences account for the times he varied the routine by simply ringing a handbell or staying silent altogether? More and more people converged on the little theatre to make up their own minds. Sceptics came with books written in foreign languages, complicated coats-of-arms, strange tools, mystery objects in sealed packages, all in an attempt to overburden or throw completely any spoken system. When this failed to happen and Emile still described the objects with microscopic accuracy, they would be all the more determined to come back for a repeat performance.

It would be wrong to imply, however, that this was the only attraction of any merit in the Palais Royal entertainment. Few magical wonders have had a more delicate appeal to members of the fair sex than that of Robert-Houdin's mysterious 'Orange Tree'. Borrowing a lady's handkerchief, the magician appeared to pass successively the handkerchief into the centre of an egg, the egg into a lemon, and the lemon into an orange. Squeezing the orange between his hands, he converted it into powder which he placed in a small spirit phial. The vapour from this when lit caused blossoms to appear magically upon the tree. In turn a wave of the wand caused the blossoms to change into oranges, all but one of which were thrown to the audience. Robert-Houdin commanded the last orange to fall apart in four sections, at which two butterflies suddenly appeared over the fruit and fluttered down to extract the borrowed handkerchief, unfolding it as they hovered above the tree.

Less romantic, but even more dumbfounding was his 'Enchanted Portfolio'. This was an artist's folder, no more than one-and-a-quarter inches thick and three feet long by two feet wide, obviously too slender to hold anything but the pictures for which it was intended. It was placed upon a pair of thin trestle legs, its spine towards the audience. The production that followed was one of the most incredible in magic's history. Having produced a two-dimensional drawing of a hatless woman, Robert-Houdin brought out two large ladies' bonnets, one for winter and one for summer. The drawing of a bird preceded the production of four live doves. A sketch of two cooks engaged in a battle of kitchen utensils led to the appearance of three enormous copper casseroles, the first containing haricot beans, the second flames of fire, and the third boiling water. After each production the portfolio was closed, its thinness verified. A large cage of canaries was brought out almost as an afterthought. And that, as far as Robert-Houdin was concerned, was that. 'Nothing here now – neither anything, nor anybody.' But then his son peered out over the edge of the portfolio: 'Yes, there *is* somebody, and I should like to come out and get a little air, for it's terribly close in here' – at which the father affectionately lifted the child free of his narrow prison.

The same son, Auguste-Adolphe, played the central role in Robert-Houdin's 'Ethereal Suspension'. In recent years this trick has become common currency, with broomsticks used in place of the poles employed by the French magician. Seldom, except when it was performed by the startling Peruvian-born illusionist Richiardi, has it really convinced. In Robert-Houdin's version, however, presentation was everything, a presentation that has to be seen within the context of its time in order to be fully appreciated now. All Paris was then excited by the recent discovery of the anaesthetic powers of ether. Controversy raged over its possible side-effects. Lending scientific credibility to his patter, Robert-Houdin would claim for ether even more powerful effects than the medical profession would admit. 'When this liquid is at its highest degree of concentration, if a living being breathes it, the body of the patient becomes in a few moments as light as a balloon.'

To demonstrate he stood his son on a small stool, then placed a pole under his extended right arm near the elbow, and another under his left arm. He uncorked a small bottle of yellowish fluid for the child to inhale. As he passed into sleep there was no mistaking the smell of ether as it wafted into the auditorium. To show the depth of his son's slumber, the magician carefully removed the stool, leaving the boy supported entirely on his arms. Then he took away the pole beneath his left arm. The boy stayed motionless. Taking hold of the boy's legs, he lifted him from the

The complete stage setting of France's greatest magician. Note the orange tree and butterflies on the left.

vertical to the horizontal, in which position he stayed suspended. To add further to the impossibility of the tableau, one of the trestles on which the bench – on which the suspension took place – rested was also taken away.

It is no secret among magicians that ether had nothing to do with it, but Parisian audiences were totally convinced, to the extent that letters of protest were written insisting that the boy's health was in danger from constant exposure to the fumes. Only Robert-Houdin knew that the trick had really been inspired by reading stories about the alleged levitation skills of Hindu fakirs.

The most ingenious mechanical figure of Robert-Houdin's creation made its first public appearance in over seventy years in 1986 on the same 'Paul Daniels Magic Show' on which Paul himself re-created in a Dickensian setting the 'Ethereal Suspension'. Painstakingly restored over a seven-year period by the prominent American illusion designer and automata expert John Gaughan (with assistance from creative genius Jim Steinmeyer), Antonio Diavolo, as he was called, was affectionately set upon his trapeze in a sitting position. First he answered questions from Paul by nodding his head from side to side. Then to the tempo of Chopin's Nocturne in E flat the gallant little acrobat, not quite three feet tall, swung himself backwards and forwards and embarked upon a series of incredible gymnastic exercises, including a somersault to a handstand position and a knee-hold that enabled him for one mesmeric moment actually to let go of the trapeze bar with 'look, no hands' defiance. At the end of the sequence he released himself from the trapeze to drop into the loving hands of John Gaughan as gracefully as he had dropped into Robert-Houdin's arms all those years ago. The mechanism and method used were exactly those crafted by Robert-Houdin for its debut on 1 October 1849. Although the French magician was himself a pioneer of electricity, that was not employed here. So ingenious was its construction, one could understand why people thought a midget might be contained inside. At the height of his fame Robert-Houdin wrote these words on behalf of his beguiling creation:

> Avec ardeur, lorsque je me balance,
> A vos bravos, Messieurs, c'est pour donner l'élan;
> C'est pour atteindre à votre bienveillance
> Dont je serai toujours le zélé partisan.
>
> Plaire, amuser, c'est ma devise
> Et mon désir est, chaque soir,
> En me quittant, que chacun dise
> – Au revoir! Au revoir!*

For all his special powers even the French magician could have had no idea how distantly prophetic that last line would be.

As we have seen from his experiences in Algeria, Robert-Houdin was skilled in adapting the one-off performance of a trick to a special occasion. On 6 June 1846, he was given his first great opportunity to display this talent when summoned to the Palace of St Cloud to entertain King Louis Philippe and his court. Here he advanced the basic premise of transporting a borrowed object from one place to another into a dimension unrivalled until, more than 100 years later, Paul Daniels, under the quizzical gaze of the Marquess of Bath in the grounds of his stately home at Longleat, caused a priceless eighteenth-century Dutch tankard from the Longleat silver cellars to be spirited into a box strapped to the body of a parachutist visible in the sky only seconds after the disappearance of the object on the ground.

---

*With eagerness, gentlemen, give me your cheers,
  As I balance myself before you;
  Your friendliness always throughout the years
  I will ardently seek to renew.

  To please, to amuse, that is my aim,
  And every evening 'tis my desire,
  That when taking your leave, each will exclaim
  – Au revoir! Au revoir!

Robert-Houdin is the only stage magician to have been honoured by a postage stamp.

Robert-Houdin's own special performance was staged in a salon attached to the Palace Orangery. For his culminating effect he borrowed several handkerchiefs which were folded into a parcel and covered with an opaque glass dome. He then distributed blank cards among the distinguished gathering, asking people to write the names of destinations to which they would like the handkerchiefs to be sent. The King was invited to choose one card from the several. He was content with the destination that read 'in the box of the last orange tree on the right of the avenue'. He sent his attendant to guard the spot in question, just visible through the door of the salon. With the King satisfied, Robert-Houdin lifted the glass cover from the handkerchiefs. Out flew a white turtle-dove with a key tied to its neck. The handkerchiefs were no longer there. Immediately the King ordered the attendant to inspect the box or tub in which the orange tree was planted. Thrusting his hand in among the roots of the tree, he found a small iron casket corroded by rust. After the earth and mould had been removed, the King was invited to apply the key attached to the bird's neck to the casket. Inside was a piece of parchment bearing the statement:

This day, the 6th of June, 1786, this iron box, containing six handkerchiefs, was placed among the roots of an orange-tree by me, Balsamo, Count of Cagliostro, to serve in performing an act of magic, which will be executed on the same day sixty years hence before Louis Philippe of Orléans and his family.

LA VOLTIGE DU TRAPEZE

Robert-Houdin with Antonio Diavolo – little did he realise that the trapeze artist would still be performing in 1987.

The parchment was not the only thing to bear the seal and signature of Cagliostro, the notorious sorcerer and charlatan; there was also a sealed packet. The King hurriedly tore this open, only to find the very handkerchiefs that had been borrowed a short time before. As Louis Philippe explained in his amazement, 'Décidément, cela tient du sortilège!'*

The Revolution of February 1848 led Robert-Houdin to close his theatre temporarily and to venture to England where he scored a major success, first at London's St James's Theatre and then in the provinces. During this visit he was honoured to appear before Queen Victoria at a charity garden party on 19 July 1848, in the company of Madame Grisi, Madame Alboni, Mario, and Lablache, the most eminent operatic performers of the day: such was the stature in which the magician was held and in which he himself had placed magic. It could not be long before he was invited to Buckingham Palace. When the moment came, Robert-Houdin, unsurprisingly to those who knew him well, produced the fitting miracle for the occasion. In 'Le Bouquet à la Reine', or the Garland of Flowers', he borrowed a glove from Her Majesty from which he immediately produced a bouquet. This proceeded to grow so large he could hardly hold it in his hands. It was placed in a vase and sprinkled with water. Thus refreshed it changed into a garland, the flowers of which were arranged to spell the name 'Victoria'.

In time Robert-Houdin returned to France and, entrusting the

---

* 'There is no doubt, it must be witchcraft!'

management of his theatre to his brother-in-law Pierre Chocat, who adopted the unlikely stage name of Hamilton, went to live in retirement in a house which he had built at St Gervais, near Blois. This retreat, known as 'The Priory', was itself one of his most ingenious achievements, a practical focal point for his fascination with mechanics, electricity, time, and deception, and full of surprises for those guests visiting for the first time. When they rapped the heavy brass knocker on the gate to the grounds, a bell rang in the house a quarter of a mile away. To acknowledge the summons, the wording on the brass name-plate attached to the gate changed from 'Robert-Houdin' to 'Entrez-Vous'. A switch pressed in the hall of the house made such entry possible. Inside the grounds the magician's inventiveness extended to an automatic feeding system for his horse and an electric thermostat that regulated the temperature of his greenhouse or rang bells in the event of fire or theft. All his clocks were synchronised electrically. The house was many years ahead of its time and it comes as no surprise that the simple peasants of the neighbouring district regarded its master with an awe that suggested he might reasonably be in league with the powers of darkness. Or of light: he produced illumination from electricity several years before Edison produced the commercial light bulb.

Robert-Houdin, saddened by the death of his son Eugène in the Franco-Prussian War, died of pneumonia at home in St Gervais on 13 June 1871. His achievements transformed the face of magic, causing other magicians to throw away their pointed hats, capacious robes, cumbersome tables, and contrived apparatus. Although earlier performers, most notably the German sleight-of-hand expert, Wiljalba Frikell, had helped to pave the way in this direction, he was the most successful thus far at directing the attention of the media of the day towards his guise of an ordinary mortal who just happens to perform miracles. His stage set, a reproduction in miniature of a salon of the Louis-Quinze period in white and gold, was as simple and elegant as the man. By conditioning the audience in this way, the few appliances he did use seemed to be devoid of the deception so obvious in days gone by.

Professor Hoffmann, the author of the revolutionary magical textbook *Modern Magic*, published in 1876, paid a fitting compliment to the man:

> The father of modern magic, as we know it, was undoubtedly Robert-Houdin. Up to his time the art of conjuring had practically stood still for generations. He wore the evening dress of ordinary life, surrendering apparently all the advantages which his immediate predecessors had derived from flowing drapery, and yet, under these more difficult conditions, he produced far more surprising effects than anyone previously attempted.

The Frenchman also wrote textbooks himself which predated Hoffmann and would in time be translated by the English author. They are still studied today – pioneering treatises in which he stressed the equal importance of applied psychology and digital dexterity in the performance of magic and laid down the axiom, paradoxical but true, that it is easier to deceive an intelligent person than an ignorant one. Others before him had described how tricks were done; Robert-Houdin was the first to describe how to do them.

Ironically his performing career spanned just eleven years. However, his theatre, which in 1853 had moved from the Palais Royal to a new address at 8, Boulevard des Italiens, continued until the early 1920s under various directors, the last of whom was Georges Méliès, the magician and film pioneer. Today a Robert-Houdin museum stands as a monument in his home town; streets have been named after him in Paris, Bourges, and Caen, as well as in Blois; on the centenary of his death the French Government saw fit to honour his image on a postage stamp: all in fitting tribute to the magician about whom the critic in the *Illustrated London News* wrote after witnessing one of his London performances:

> We feel our breath taken away; he entirely beats us. He is the sole Monarch of the world of wonders; all other conjurors and wizards, from whatever point of the compass they arrive, sink into insignificant imitators before him.

In other words, he set the standard for the rest to follow.

6

The House of Cards

' "Do you like card tricks?" he asked. I said "No". He did five.' Thus in thirteen terse words W. Somerset Maugham escorted his reader into that nadir of tedium experienced every time a hackneyed amateur proffers the pack. The ubiquitous pasteboards have arguably done more to cause audiences to fight shy of magic than any other prop or motif. However, it is their very accessibility that enhances those memorable moments when they fall into the hands of an accomplished master. Because everyone *has* fumbled his or her way through a card trick at some point in life, because everyone is mindful of the rewards which the combination of cardboard and dexterity could produce in the gaming houses and casinos of their dreams, they are prepared to give the edge in the applause stakes to the cardman *par excellence* at the expense of equally skilled practitioners with billiard balls, dice, or coins.

One of the earliest detailed records of a conjuring performance with playing cards is to be found in the writings of the gambler, mathematician and astrologer, Girolamo Cardano. Francesco Soma, the magician who came under the scrutiny of his pen, could be said to have been one of the first to make card tricks respectable in that he brought card magic into the salons of high society from the al-fresco booths of the itinerant jongleurs. According to Cardano's 'De Subtilitate Rerum', Soma was a young aristocrat from Naples who had scarcely reached his twenty-second year. He would start by spreading a pack of cards face-down on the table and then, according to the eye-witness account which derives from circa 1550:

He asked us to take one card and conceal it. Then he took the pack, shuffled it, and guessed what card it was. This might perhaps have been attributed to quickness of hand, but that is by no means the case with what he did next. For when the card was put back in the pack and it was laid on the table, he asked several of us to draw a card, and we realised that the man who had drawn the card on the earlier occasion always drew the same card now, as though Soma were compelling us to draw the same card, or else were changing the face of the card . . . The act was too wonderful to be understood by human cogitation. And if he had not asked us at various times to draw different cards, I would have suspected that he had substituted a pack consisting of cards of a simple kind, namely, the 'Two of Flowers'. For with that device it would happen that whoever drew a card would always seem to chance upon the same card. But, as I have said, the diversity of the remaining cards precluded that explanation.

As a result of the inexhaustible permutations possible between the fifty-two assistants and the two jokers in their casual attendance, this field of magic reveals a diversity of effect and method shared by no other. It has been estimated that at least half of the new material currently published privately for magicians relates to playing cards. If the flow were to stop tomorrow, there would be card tricks and sleights enough to meet an infinite demand. And yet catch Paul Daniels relaxed in a social situation with a pack of cards in his hands and the likelihood is that he will launch into a routine with more than a passing resemblance to that of Soma. The most telling effects are not necessarily those employing the most advanced modern techniques. Everything rests on the presentation, and that is inseparable from the personality of the presenter.

One litmus test of a magician's showmanship has been his ability to present card tricks, as distinct from card manipulation, on the largest of stages. Anyone who has seen his presentation of the classic comedy item known as 'The Six Card Repeat' will know that Paul Daniels passes with ease. The effect was invented in the early years of this century by the British magician Ellis Stanyon, but remained virtually unknown until reinvented and popularised in 1933 by the American entertainer Tommy Tucker, who would achieve fame later as half of one of the world's leading two-person telepathy acts. Paul recounts the tale of the first magician he ever saw. He counted six cards, threw away three, and still had six left. Paul's narrative takes him on a quest to purchase the illusion. Each time he describes the trick, his hands act out the effect using the same single source of cards. At no time is anything added or taken away, apart from the cards which Paul throws down with snappy relish at the opportune moments of the story. The climax comes when the magician behind the counter explains that he doesn't sell the trick: if you take away three cards, you can have only three cards left. And so, this time, has Paul, until he turns the tables on the salesman and demonstrates that it is still possible to take away three and 'get one, two, three, four, five, six cards back again'.

The history of stage magic this century contains some towering personalities whose principal act has been built around little more than a pack of cards. Paramount among these is Nate Leipzig. Born in Stockholm on 31 May 1873, he became a prominent attraction in American vaudeville. Before a small committee invited on stage, the four aces inserted into different parts of the pack each rose mysteriously to become the face-card

If the trick has
worked for Leipzig,
the two chosen cards
will be either side of
the blade.

in turn. With his card chosen, returned, and shuffled into the pack, one
spectator was asked to deal the cards face-down and to stop at any point
with a card in his hand. When he did so, he was invariably holding his own
card. For his feature trick Leipzig had two cards chosen, replaced and
shuffled in the pack. All the cards were wrapped in newspaper. With a
table knife in one hand and the package in the other, Leipzig stabbed
through the paper. When the paper was torn away the knife was shown to
be between the two chosen cards. The American magician Judson Cole
summed up Leipzig's manner on stage, 'Very few acts have real authority.
Nate had it, plus that intangible glamour which has been called everything
from stage presence to personal magnetism; but call it what you will, he
literally electrified an audience when he walked out on stage.' In later years
Paul Rosini and Paul Le Paul in America, and Lionel King and Billy
O'Connor in Britain, would all present similar acts with their differing
personalities, acts in which cards played a part bigger than their size could
ever suggest.

Howard Thurston (1869–1936), long before he became the leading
American illusionist of the early part of this century with a show that took
ten railroad baggage cars to transport, had also specialised in an act with
playing cards. The highlight was the card trick which over the years has

probably had the greatest appeal not only to audiences but also to magicians, if the number of different methods they have contrived to achieve it is anything to go by. Ordinary conjurors before and since have caused selected cards to rise unaided half-way out of the pack. In Thurston's version the chosen cards would float one at a time to his waiting hand from the pack held in the other. He would even allow spectators to call out the names of the cards. Once summoned, each card would still glide up and away from the others, rising and falling at the spectator's command and sometimes soaring way above the magician's head. No one made the 'Rising Card' trick a more spectacular or more perplexing item. All the time Thurston's hand would demonstrate the non-existence of threads above and below the pack. And there were memorable moments of humour. Involving a small boy in the audience who wished his card to rise, Thurston would tell him to take a firm grasp on his father's hair and say 'Rise'. The spotlight fell on the boy and his father, who almost invariably turned out to be bald. Inevitably the chosen cards were scaled into the audience followed by an endless succession of 'Good Luck' souvenir cards, the music getting louder and louder as the pasteboards were thrown higher and higher.

It was in order to perform a card trick that Paul Daniels found himself in possibly the most unlikely location for demonstrating his magical skills. And yet the Cabinet War Rooms, situated beneath the sedate but sturdy stone and concrete of London's Whitehall, where Winston Churchill conducted the affairs of the Allies during the darkest moments of the Second World War, were the obvious place for Paul, with the assistance

Thurston's skill enabled him to throw lucky cards, depicting himself and his daughter, to the furthermost reaches of the theatre.

Paul Daniels in 'Mississippi Magic' – 'Never Play Cards with Strangers'.

of Dame Vera Lynn and noted war correspondent Wynford Vaughan Thomas, to re-create the card trick that could have changed the course of history. Such a claim might appear a rash assertion until qualified by the statement that it was arguably responsible for holding up the course of the Second World War for several hours.

At the height of hostilities Churchill was entertained to dinner by a select group of friends who were anxious to relieve his mind of the pressures that being a wartime Prime Minister entails. The meal over, Churchill would have made a dash straight back to Parliament had not his hosts prevailed upon him to watch a cabaret they had arranged featuring the magician Harry Green. The latter had first become famous on the American vaudeville stage, not as a wizard, but as George Washington Cohen in the comedy sketch 'The Cherry Tree'. An enthusiastic amateur conjuror, he had developed the right social connections upon arriving in England and now found himself in the position of being able to present to the Prime Minister what many still consider to be the most baffling card trick of all time.

Taking a new pack, he extracted a red card and a black card and placed them on the table face-up about six inches apart in front of Churchill. Having explained that these were to be known as the leader cards, he handed the rest of the pack face-down to Sir Winston, with instructions that he should proceed to deal cards one at a time face-down on top of the leader cards. If he had a hunch that a card was red, he was to deal it on to the red leader. If he felt instinctively that a card was black, he should likewise place it on the black leader. At no point was he to look at the faces of the cards. The ritual was continued until all fifty cards were exhausted. At this point Green pointed out the unlikelihood of the Prime Minister being 100 per cent correct. In fact the odds were in excess of 200 trillion to one against such an occurrence. And yet, unbelievable as it may sound, when Green showed Churchill the results of his efforts the reds and the blacks were totally separate.

Someone as tenacious as Churchill could not resist the challenge the trick presented. The War could wait while Green presented the impossibility again. Maybe this time Churchill dealt the cards more slowly, maybe his concentration bit deeper, yet still he divided the cards as before. Four more times the miracle was staged at his insistence until, none the wiser, Churchill left for the House. It was 2 a.m. when he at last arrived for his appointment in a condition best described by *The Times*, which wrote up the occasion, as 'befogged'.

The trick Churchill witnessed that night is now known to magicians as 'Out of this World'. In the late 1940s, when the distinguished New York magic magazine *Hugard's Magic Monthly* ran a poll among its readers to nominate their favourite card trick, it was a runaway winner. Green was only one of many professional magicians to turn it to his advantage. However, if any one individual should have received the Churchillian accolade that evening it was its inventor, Paul Curry, doyen until his death in 1986 of the backroom boys in magic whose ingenuity acts as life-blood to those who perform it as a profession. Curry's own profession was that of executive for a large medical insurance company. He also invented that incredible close-up illusion performed by Paul Daniels on television where in a flash the name of a freely selected card appeared scorched on a piece of paper held between two coins, in addition to the sequence in which Paul influenced a member of the audience to pick up nine visiting cards, numbered haphazardly on the reverse side from one to nine, in correct numerical sequence.

During the War the German Ministry of Propaganda printed thousands of coloured postcards depicting Sir Winston smoking one of his giant cigars. The caption read 'The Great Illusionist', subtitled 'In the Dense Smoke of His Cigar'. The words were not meant to be complimentary, but Churchill is unlikely to have been ruffled by them. Impressed as he had been by Green's performance, he is unlikely to have looked upon the title with anything less than humour and the boyish pride of wish fulfilment. Such was the impact of a card trick at such a crucial time.

7

Come a Little Closer

Paul Daniels's success on television has tended to obscure the fact that television and magic, like most branches of the variety arts, have long tended to enjoy a love–hate relationship. The presence of a small coterie of magicians kept magic alive on television during the 1950s and 1960s, but their entirely personal success bore no true relationship to the status of magic in the big world of show business outside, where the music halls and variety theatres, long the principal arena for the magician to display his talents, closed as the new medium took hold.

In the early days of televised magic in Britain a monochrome Robert Harbin brought a quirky inventiveness to his new illusions and a few of the old ones; in America first Milbourne Christopher and later Mark Wilson pioneered the big spectacular coast-to-coast magic specials. In both countries, Chan Canasta with his brilliant psychological magic kept audiences on the edge of their seats at the turn of a playing card: here was one performer who, working in the more uncertain world of mentalism, was able shrewdly never to guarantee his success. Al Koran successfully combined a more positive approach to mind-reading with classic sleight-of-hand, a combination taken to even more adventurous extremes in recent years by David Berglas.

The quintessentially British David Nixon, with a bashful showmanship unrivalled since, succeeded more through personal charm than through any high degree of technical ability and, until the arrival of the inventive Ali Bongo late in his career, was far more limited than Paul – who is helped by a far larger team of which Bongo is a crucial part – in finding the new material essential for a weekly series. Maybe it was this latter shortcoming that made him more reliant than others on the use of camera trickery or 'switchcraft', as it was wittily dubbed. It must have been impossible to resist the new toy, a medium more magical than the magic it presented. In fairness, David always admitted when he was using it, but by doing so he caused doubt to be cast on performers – including himself – who did not need such a prop. The audience could not now accept authentic television magic at face value, and in the estimation of many the art of hocus-pocus

Chan Canasta and Al Koran, favourites on British television screens in the 1950s and 1960s, with their contrasting styles of psychological magic.

sank into the doldrums. The subsequent success in the mid-1970s of Paul Daniels in Britain and Doug Henning in the United States, a success which on so vast a scale could not have been achieved without television, was rooted firmly in the public's restored confidence that no such technical chicanery was taking place. Everything Paul has ever presented on the screen could as readily be performed on the stage of an authentic theatre, with the exception of those occasions when outside broadcast cameras allow the honest use of a special location in an original or spectacular way.

Whereas technology once worked as a lazy magician's aid, it can now act as the touchstone of a fine magician's skill. The introduction of home video recording, with its freeze-frame and replay facilities, has been much publicised in recent years as the key which could unlock a magician's secrets. In defiance, Paul Daniels and his colleagues have thrown out a 'catch-me-if-you-can' challenge to technology, as a result of which their visual magic can appear only more impressive when viewed in slow-motion. In any case, no matter how scrupulously you inspect the taped performance of a fine magician, you will be unable to detect any flaws in his technique if they are not already visible to the naked eye.

Sadly, in more recent years the credibility which is so crucial for a magician to succeed on television, and which Daniels and Henning have gone to such great lengths to achieve in their respective countries, has been undermined by the emergence as television star of the stylish young American illusionist David Copperfield. No one can fault the showmanship of the ideas featured on his programmes. On separate, equally talked-

Left, David Berglas, enduring British magic star, and (*right*) David Copperfield, current American magic success.

about shows he caused a seven-ton Lear jet to disappear, the Statue of Liberty to succumb to a similar fate, and himself to be levitated across the Grand Canyon. Ironically, the least credible of the three, the Statue if Liberty sequence, was the one that was staged before a 100-per-cent bona-fide audience. It is too much to suppose that Copperfield actually made the statue disappear, but he assuredly created the illusion that it vanished. If only the presentation and advance publicity had chosen their words more carefully, conceding to David the ability to render the statue invisible and not the utter impossibility of dematerialising an object so massive and immovable. Then the cynicism and accusations of camera trickery that greeted the illusion in many quarters might have been avoided. In the case of the levitation, however, there is no way this could have been viewed by an audience at the Grand Canyon without those present realising part, if not all, of the secret. The illusion did not involve trick photography as such, in that the actual pictures shot on tape were viewed untampered-with by the home audience, but it certainly relied upon the special use of editing procedures to bring about the overall effect. While there were no spectators present at the Grand Canyon, the aeroplane illusion did, in fact, have a large committee circling the jet prior to its disappearance, but even this was not all the vox-pop interviews shown after the illusion implied it to be.

Dishonest as his profession may openly proclaim to be, the television magician has always to remember that without credibility his role is little more than that of a cypher. Give the public the merest iota of an opportunity to interpret magic as the result of camera technology, whether it has been used or not, and the whole foundations of the art are shaken. In conjuring, from the point of view of the audience, there are no such things as wrong solutions. Once it thinks it knows how a trick is done, whether right or not, the illusion is destroyed. There are signs that Copperfield now recognises the dangers. On a more recent television special he magically dematerialised his body through the Great Wall of China in full view of an audience at the scene. There is no reason to surmise that their amazed reaction was not genuine. The inclusion of a similar feat in his stage show suggests that he has come to reckon with the disappointment of live audiences who discovered that in the flesh their hero was less miraculous than on screen. That said, Copperfield as a box office attraction is for the time being one of the biggest in America, his concert income rivalling that of Bruce Springsteen, Joan Rivers, and Diana Ross in their respective fields.

On one occasion Paul did cock a snook at principle by performing a camera trick. More accurately it was 'a trick with a camera' and represented the most sensational vanish he had achieved at that point in his career. It is, in fairness, about the only trick recorded indoors that he could not present on a conventional stage, unless he were every night to install five cameras and monitors for the theatre audience. Then they would see exactly what the studio audience saw on the occasion in question, which is exactly what the audience at home saw as well. A bona-fide representative

David Nixon, genial master of quiet showmanship and television superstar.

of the audience was first invited to inspect a wooden crate, about the size of two telephone kiosks standing side by side. In the wall at one end was a porthole that would play a crucial part as the illusion developed. Paul then drew attention to the five cameras. Numbered from one to five, all were seen to be working as they each took a shot of the next in sequence, daisy-chain fashion. The spectator was asked to nominate one. He chose camera four. The camera was driven up a ramp into the crate by its technician, who entered as well. Quickly the ramp was removed, the doors closed, and the crate raised on a fork-lift truck. At all points the camera cable dangled out of the front of the crate, while the camera, still live, continued to transmit (in the corner of the screen) a picture of the studio through the porthole. The talking presence of both Paul and the spectator in this shot proved that it was not a pre-recording. The truck now turned 180 degrees in the centre of the solid concrete studio floor. In this way everybody in the studio was allowed to see all around the crate. Paul took a gun and on the count of 'three' fired. Instantly the view of the studio in the bottom corner of the screen changed to the disturbance pattern known as 'noise'. From its raised position the crate disintegrated into planks. A bewildered cameraman could be discerned surveying the empty end of the cable in his hand. The camera had gone. The illusion represented one of the most spectacular effects of Paul Daniels's entire career. More important, the conditions under which the trick had been performed and recorded left Paul's own integrity intact in the process.

*

While the platform which television has provided for large-scale illusions may at times have transgressed the reasonable bounds of credibility, nevertheless it has given the presentation of close-up magic increased importance. When a visiting American magician watched a tape of the hands of Paul Daniels in close-up producing a mouse from an empty matchbox, he was heard to comment, 'Well, who needs lions and tigers?' In so doing he was making an astute comment on the way television not only magnifies the total audience able to watch an intimate close-quarter performance, but also magnifies the image, seen to a size greater in the drawing-room than the most grandiose effect may appear from the back of the largest Las Vegas showroom.

As I have already revealed, the very roots of magic as we accept it today were in the close-quarter performances given at markets and fairs since the beginning of time. Television has helped to bestow upon the direct descendants of those pioneers a status and following unheard of in a less technological age. Not that it is roses all the way. It would be unfair not to point out that in one respect the close-quarter wizard faces a far greater challenge the moment he steps before the all-searching eye of the television camera. Misdirection has always been his greatest weapon, in simple language the ability to look you – his special audience of one – directly in the eye while just out of your vision his hand deviously performs the sleight that achieves the effect. What about other people present? Well, they're not going to miss anything, so they'll be looking where you're looking. Such a procedure will not work on television. If the camera comes away from the performer's hand, it will be obvious that some chicanery is taking place out of frame; if the camera moves back to take in the full picture, the distance of distraction as measured between his hand and his eye becomes minimal and ineffectual. One of the greatest myths in magic is that 'the hand is quicker than the eye'. In circumstances where that might appear applicable, getting the audience to focus its attention on the wrong place at the right time is almost certainly the true key to the mystery.

Recent years have seen an upsurge of interest in close-up magic among magicians, amateur and professional alike. Among the *cognoscenti* its skills and techniques have been taken to technically intricate lengths which their fairground forebears could never have envisaged. Almost certainly the turning point for this revival took place at the Magic Castle. Here in the Hollywood headquarters of the Academy of Magical Arts members and their guests can be entertained every evening in the most intimate surroundings by some of the world's leading sleight-of-hand performers. The building was the brainchild and life's ambition of American magician William Larsen Senior, and brought into reality in 1963 by the sheer will-power, graft, and dedication of his sons, Bill Junior and Milt. Arguably they have done more to advance the cause of magic behind the scenes than any other two individuals in the world. The influence of the club extends beyond the immediate entertainment and refreshment of its lay clientele. The profile the Larsens have achieved for their enterprise in the world's entertainment capital has led more than a few producers and stars to think of and subsequently use magic to their professional advantage where they would not have done so before. If one building represents the unofficial headquarters of the magicians of the world, this is it. The time and hospitality given to visiting magicians by the Larsens, together with Bill's captivating wife Irene, is legendary. Less well publicised are the stunning acts of generosity extended by them away from the limelight to deserving older members of the magic profession.

The Magic Castle, a mass of turrets and spires in true storybook fashion, is quite simply a wonderful piece of theatre in its own right, the most recent in that select architectural line which includes Robert-Houdin's salon and Maskelyne's Egyptian Hall. It is impossible to enter from the book-lined reception area until you whisper 'Open sesame' to the stuffed owl that eyes you suspiciously from the corner. Then the wall melts away before your eyes and a special atmosphere envelops you. Among the unique attractions within is the Houdini Seance Room, a private dining-room for twelve people with thirteen places, the last not taken until midnight when a magician enters to prove without any shadow of doubt that things do go bump in the night. Further dining-rooms are devoted to

Above, these two playing cards depicting Dai Vernon remind one that he turned his hand to silhouette-cutting before concentrating on magic as a profession. *Below*, the Magic Castle, magic's unofficial headquarters, tucked away in the Hollywood hills.

the names and memorabilia of the two greatest illusionists of this century's middle years, Blackstone and Dante. In another room, all to herself, you will find Irma. Irma is a piano, special in that she has no pianist at her keyboard. Nevertheless, name her a tune, however obscure, and her keys will mysteriously play it for you. The keys go up and down by themselves. Irma has never failed to respond with the tune of the moment.

Remarkable as Irma is, it is unlikely that she will excite the visiting magician as much as the presence in some other corner of this rambling edifice of a distinguished, silver-haired Canadian, eternally youthful in his ninety-second year at the time of writing. His name is Dai Vernon, but he is better known to magicians as 'The Professor'. The elder statesman of American magic, he has in recent years found at the Magic Castle an Indian summer of recognition, the just reward of a career as performer, writer, innovator, teacher, sage, and catalyst. The books by the author Lewis Ganson, in which Vernon's methods for performing essentially close-quarter magic were explained, have been the most influential of recent years, leading more magicians away from pocket-trick gadgetry to the studious application of sleight-of-hand than any other single influence. His technique for both the 'Cups and Balls' and the 'Chinese Linking Rings' has influenced virtually every serious newcomer to those classic tricks in the last thirty years, not least Paul Daniels. The man himself represents a paradox worthy of his impish sense of humour: on the one hand he is shy of performing, yet on the other he represents the touchstone of artistry in close-quarter magic to a generation that has never seen him perform. The knowledge he holds and the sheer respect in which he is held demands for him a very special mention in these pages. If we were greeted on our arrival at the Magic Castle by that mystic owl, we now make our departure in the presence of Merlin himself.

The position approaching that of guru held by Dai Vernon on the West Coast of America is matched at the opposite end of the country in New York by the equally legendary Tony Slydini. Slydini's real name is Quintino Marucci. Born at the turn of the century in the tiny Italian village of Foggia, he emigrated in early childhood to live with an uncle in Buenos Aires. There his Italian background intertwined with the predominantly Spanish culture to shape the discreetly flamboyant, but always dignified style associated with his name. More than any magician he has developed the basic principles of misdirection to a precise science, but there is nothing academic about the mischievous way he coaxes a spectator to sit at his table to behold the next miracle. 'I'm-a gonna show you something you not-a gonna believe.' What follows will be as close as possible to seeing real magic, as Slydini causes coins to pass through the table top, cigarettes to multiply, and securely knotted handkerchiefs to untie themselves under your rigid gaze. In possibly his most visual deception he tears a lighted cigarette in two. The separate pieces are held in a V-shape at the very tips of his left thumb and forefinger. A few loose shreds of tobacco are sprinkled in the angle between them. Slowly and delicately his right forefinger rubs against the gap. Visibly the cigarette becomes whole. There would appear to be no room for deception. In his hands objects vanish while you are looking at them, but his magic does not merely play tricks on your eyes. In another effect he pours salt from a salt-shaker into his hand. You know it is salt because he allows you to taste it. He makes a fist, then opens it. The salt has dematerialised without trace. His other hand now makes a grab in the air and instantly pours the salt back into his palm. He asks you to taste it once more. It is still salt. He asks you again. Now the salt has changed to sugar, but you know it couldn't possibly have changed. 'That's-a good, eh?'

When Slydini sits at a table top to perform his miracles you know instinctively you are in the presence of a far more significant event than anything achieved by the casual throwaway style of the average magician anxious to impress at close quarters. This approach has been taken to even greater lengths by another American, Albert Goshman, to the extent that the table at which he performs becomes a miniature stage of its own. The effect is reinforced by the background music he carries with him on a cassette recorder. Every detail of Goshman's act is planned as meticulously as if he were a manipulator on stage. The fact that he is sitting in your

Irving Desfor catches Slydini as the knots in the handerkerchiefs dissolve.

Left, 'Magic – by Gosh' – apt billing for Albert Goshman. *Right*, Bill, Milt (*foreground*) and Irene Larsen, the first family of magic.

drawing-room is incidental. Before becoming a professional performer Goshman was a baker in Brooklyn, New York. There is still something about his homely eyes and crumpled lived-in appearance that suggests his earlier profession; still something in his approach that suggests the friendly tradesman dealing with cherished individuals rather than anonymous members of the crowd. But from the moment he announces, 'I'm going to magish for you,' you know you are in the hands of an intuitive performer. Marvellous as his individual tricks with coins and cards and sponge balls are, it is the incidental asides surrounding them that fix him in your mind. At the end of each sequence he will ask you to lift up his magic salt-cellar. If you say 'please', there will be a coin underneath. Lift it up without saying 'please' and it will not be there. Then you put it down, say 'please', and when you lift it up, it *is* there. The device becomes a challenge, but you will never see him load the coin beneath the salt-cellar, not even the enormous Japanese coin with which he concludes the sequence, so big that it extends around the edges of the shaker. And with each appearance, of course, the laughs build. Seldom do audiences leave a Goshman show without tears in their eyes.

The scope for humour in the close-quarter relationship between mystifier and mystified has been explored most skilfully of all by the justifiably proclaimed 'Amusing and Confusing Johnny Paul'. A genial bear of a magician with the largest heart you will find, Johnny has pioneered not one, but two important movements in the area of close-up sorcery. Born on 15 January 1912, he was one of the first, if not *the* first, magical bar-tenders to operate out of Chicago in the late 1930s. At a

The young Johnny Paul (*centre*) working in his favourite milieu.

succession of locations culminating in his own Magic Lounge on Cermak Road in Cicero, one-time headquarters of the Al Capone gang, Johnny would juggle ice cubes and glasses, perform appropriate magic, and tease the customers between serving drinks. One line from those days still re-surfaces. 'Don't applaud. Keep drinking. The more you drink, the better I get.' The style caught on. Today there are many such performers in the United States. In the late 1950s Johnny headed West, eventually settling in Las Vegas to become host and entertainments director of the Showboat Hotel. Today there are possibly more professional close-up magicians performing in the lounges, casinos and bars of the gambling city than anywhere else in America. Once again, Johnny Paul set the trend.

No magician is held in greater esteem by Paul Daniels himself, and in fact Johnny Paul is no stranger to regular viewers of 'The Paul Daniels Magic Show', although you need to see him 'live' to appreciate fully the sheer wonder, hilarity, and *joie de vivre* this life-enhancing entertainer creates around him. Hand him a dollar bill and he will do with it practically everything it is possible to do with a dollar bill. He will tear it up, restore it, cause it to grow to ten times its size, then to shrink to the size of a visiting card. He places it in a glass and it jumps through the air into his hand. About the only thing that doesn't happen is for President Washington's picture to blink back at you in amazement.

He was the first performer in magic to feature the skilful technique of dice-stacking. Taking an empty upturned dice cup, he sweeps four

Johnny Paul, the Clown Prince of Magic, as few will now remember him.

conventional dice off the table one after the other in four clean moves. When he lifts the cup they are stacked in a tower of four. Even more bewildering is his ability to control the numbers on those dice. Call out any number from one to six and that will be the number at the top of the stack. The climax, when he asks someone merely to think of a number, is incomprehensible. There is no way he can manipulate the dice once the number has been called. You lift the cup yourself. Snap! All the while the miracles are peppered with jokes and one-liners accumulated over a lifetime's experience of performing. 'Years of practice and self-denial – you don't get it? – I didn't either!' He could be referring to his most famous routine. For this he needs two pretty ladies, the more buxom the better. 'Can I call you Susie? How about tomorrow morning?' He asks each in turn to count out ten cards and to place them inside their blouse. 'Not too far down, I have to reach for them. I have never lost a card yet.' Delicately he mimes transferring three invisible cards from one girl to the other. In the end courtesy dictates that they take them out, but when they count them, one has only seven cards, the other thirteen. His billing describes him as 'The Clown Prince of Magic'. It is a modest claim for the comedy king of legerdemain.

In the wake of Vernon, Slydini, Goshman, and Johnny Paul a whole new wave of close-quarter magicians has emerged. None has impressed quite so much as the refreshing young Israeli-born magician, now resident in New York, Meir Yedid. He could be said to have given a totally new

Left, Johnny Paul as he is today. *Right*, Meir Yedid brings a new meaning to digital dexterity.

interpretation to the phrase 'sleight-of-hand'. He demonstrated how when he came to London to appear on 'The Paul Daniels Magic Show'. Meir disregards the conventional accessories of the close-up magician, the coins and cards, sponge balls and cigarettes. His hands offered a self-contained magic show of their own, his right fingers and thumb proving as versatile as Johnny Paul's dollar bill. His little finger telescoped backwards and forwards; each finger disappeared in turn; his thumb travelled up his arm. At one stage he actually cut off his little finger and replaced it with a spare. Cold print cannot convey the sheer impossibility of what the eye saw. We have all attempted simple finger tricks in childhood. Using these as no more than a basis, Meir added advanced digital skills and misdirection to convey a sequence of genuine illusions as original as anything in magic. Tragically, since that recording Meir has been involved in an automobile accident in which his car overturned four times. He was lucky to escape. When he arrived at the hospital doctors miraculously discovered no limbs broken, no concussion sustained, but the little and ring finger of his right hand severed. A medical helicopter crew flew instantly to the scene of the crash to find the two digits in the tangle of twisted metal. They were rushed back to the hospital under refrigeration in the hope that micro-surgery might restore them to the hand. At the time of writing seven operations have been performed and it is possible that one finger will be restored, if only cosmetically. While other magicians pray, Meir himself rehearses his old routine with his left hand and thinks about ways in which he might incorporate the unique advantage of a genuinely missing finger on the other. The irony of his misfortune is beyond belief, like the talent and the courage.

8

England's Home of Mystery

On 22 December 1839, the sedate and unlikely English town of Cheltenham, long a bastion of all that is discreet and above board, saw the birth of the British magician whose subtle showmanship and Machiavellian mechanical skills were to have a devastating effect throughout the world of magic.

Even more auspicious was 7 March 1865, for it was then that the adult John Nevil Maskelyne, now a watchmaker by profession like Robert-Houdin before him, attended a performance by the famous spiritualist team, the Davenport Brothers, and caught a glimpse of Ira Davenport's hand, released from the ropes supposedly restraining it, as it threw musical

Ira and William Davenport, restrained in their spirit cabinet, with bewildered spectators in 1864.

John Nevil Maskelyne, founding father of a magical dynasty.

instruments out of the wardrobe-style cabinet in which they sat. At a crucial moment mid-seance a curtain, draped at a window to black out light from the Town Hall, had fallen, producing a beam of light that allowed Maskelyne this privileged view.

John Nevil was already known to the townspeople as an amateur conjuror of some merit: this had led to his being chosen as one of the committee whose task was to ensure that throughout the seance no trickery took place. The Davenports' presentation was always claimed to be authentic and due to genuine spirit aid. Maskelyne now knew otherwise and, equipped with the secret of the trick (whereby the pseudo-spiritualists appear restrained by ropes one moment, secretly free the next, and then retied again in an instant), announced his plan to duplicate such dexterity in an exact replica of the performance in the same hall.

Two months later Maskelyne, with the aid of his friend George Alfred Cooke, a cabinet-maker and fellow cornet player in the local Volunteer Rifles Band, fulfilled his promise. The performance was an immediate success and the partners were now firmly set upon a professional career as magicians. On 19 June 1865, Maskelyne and Cooke made their first professional appearance at Jessop's Aviary Gardens, Cheltenham. The bill proclaimed:

The Egyptian Hall, Piccadilly, during its magical heyday.

The latter was to become a signature trick in the Maskelyne repertoire. John Nevil, all five feet eight inches of him, was locked in a deal box three feet long by two feet wide by eighteen inches in depth. A few small holes at each end allowed the passage of air, but thorough scrutiny could reveal nothing in the way of sliding panels or other means of exit. The chest was securely roped by a committee from the audience, placed upended in the cabinet, bells set upon it, and the doors closed. Immediately the bells began to ring and were then thrown through the opening in the cabinet. When the curtains were pulled back, Maskelyne was sitting triumphant on the receptacle, the locks and cords still intact. In time he got the escape down to seven seconds *after* the box had been laced inside a canvas cover! Maskelyne had proved beyond doubt that within the arena of magic, spirits themselves were not necessary to produce supposedly spiritual phenomena.

Together the new partnership toured the provinces for eight years, until on 1 April 1873 they began a short season with 'their entertainment of pure trickery' at the St James's Hall, Piccadilly, their first in London's West End. They took a short lease, intending to stay in the capital for only a few months. Their success, however, was beyond expectation, and before May was out they found themselves taking out a longer lease on the Small Hall within the Egyptian Hall on the opposite side of Piccadilly. They opened there on 26 May 1873, and were to stay in the same building, for most of the time in the Large Hall upstairs, until the end of 1904.

The Egyptian Hall at 171, Piccadilly had been built in 1812 by William Bullock of Liverpool to house his collection of '16,000 natural wonders', a vast assortment of stuffed reptiles, birds, mammals, geological specimens, armoury, and other artefacts. Over the years there had been exhibited in this curious mixture of entertainment and educational establishment Chang, the Chinese Giant; Michel Boai, who tapped out tunes upon his chin; Christine and Millie, Siamese twins known as 'the Two-Headed Nightingale'; the legendary General Tom Thumb; Artemus Ward cracking his jokes; and Albert Smith discoursing on Mont Blanc. For most Londoners, however, the building now became synonymous with Maskelyne and Cooke. Never before, not even at Robert-Houdin's salon in Paris, had one place become more vividly associated with the performance of magic pure and simple. England's 'Home of Mystery', as it became known, was always billed under the joint names of the two men, but it is now known that they were not partners in the accepted business sense. The Maskelyne and Cooke company was the sole property of John Nevil Maskelyne. The partnership was essentially that between magician and confidential assistant, Cooke never holding the limelight as an individual performer, playing only subsidiary parts in sketches. But Maskelyne's debt to his friend, fourteen years his senior, was committed: Cooke's technical skill as a cabinet-maker was an integral part of the younger man's success.

One of Maskelyne's principal contributions to magic was the skilful embodiment of tricks and illusions in dramatic sketches, a form revived today by the top American performer David Copperfield. In a decapitation illusion, for instance, the severed head of a besmocked Gloucestershire farmer (played by Cooke) was placed on a table where it continued to converse with the surgeon (played by Maskelyne). After a short time the corpse rose from its chair, picked up its head, and walked around the stage, literally 'with its head tucked underneath its arm!' This sketch was called 'Elixir Vitae'. More sedate was 'The Temptations of Good St Anthony', incorporating a topical deception known as 'Cleopatra's Needle', in which three people were produced from a small model of the famous monument, the obelisk standing on a raised platform throughout. Nor was spiritualism forgotten: in 'A Spirit Case or Mrs Daffodil Downy's Light and Dark Seance', a violin played while suspended in the air and the Piccadilly ghost was produced in a cloud of white light.

The 'Box Escape' was also worked up into a magical playlet, 'Will, the Witch and the Watch', probably the most famous and successful of the genre. The original trunk now had its canvas cover. The cabinet became the village lock-up. Everything was examined by the audience before the sketch began. The leading lady, Dolly (played by John Nevil's wife) was in love with Will (played by Cooke) who also doubled as a gorilla. Maskelyne on occasion would play three parts, Daddy Gnarl the Watchman, Joe Killbull the butcher, and the Witch. J. B. Hansard, a comedy actor and regular member of the Maskelyne company, completed the cast. The plot itself had as many twists and turns as Hampton Court Maze. Will was locked in the cabinet. Killbull then cut off part of the gorilla's tail (sic) which danced around the stage with a life of its own, while the gorilla was put into the original box, which in turn was secured within the canvas cover and laced tight. There followed a succession of appearances, disappearances and changes so rapid that audiences dissolved into laughter in their confusion as to who was which and where. Never has the public been given a test of identity and of geography so tantalising and so skilfully executed. The sequence became so popular that it was performed more than 10,000 times over a period of four decades.

In the final assessment, the illusion which will be considered Maskelyne's greatest creation is probably his 'Levitation', made all the more remarkable

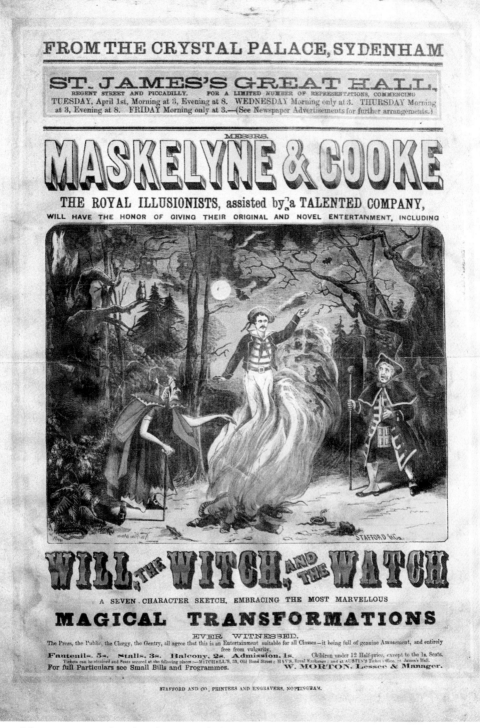

The most popular sketch in Maskelyne's repertoire dated back to pre-Egyptian Hall days.

by the seeming absence of any apparatus. Until Maskelyne applied his mind to the problem, magicians had been suspending, but not levitating, their assistants in mid-air. In 1867 at the Crystal Palace, London, Maskelyne caused his wife to rise from the stage in a standing position and return. When this trick was later presented at the St James's Hall in 1873, *The Times* described the breakthrough with effective simplicity. 'The lady simply rises directly off the floor, where there is no trap, and remains suspended, full in the light, with nothing under her feet, over her head, or in any way visibly connected with her.' Over the years the illusion became streamlined with constant performance and technical modification until, in May 1898, Maskelyne's son Nevil added the most convincing touch of all. In a magical sketch entitled 'Trapped by Magic', it was proved beyond all doubt that there were no extraneous supports or attachments, however invisible, when a large solid hoop of flexible steel was passed completely over the assistant not once, but twice.

So impressive was the levitation by now that the great American illusionist, Kellar, after failing to work out the exact method by watching it countless times from the front stalls, finally bribed Paul Valadon, a magician in Maskelyne's employ, to join his company in America in order to obtain the full working knowledge. But Maskelyne had not been content to restrict himself to one solution to the levitation problem. Inspired by the publicity obtained by the great Scottish medium Daniel Dunglas Home (who was supposedly able to soar up to the ceilings of private houses and on one occasion in 1868 had allegedly floated out of an upper-storey window and in at another at Ashley House, Westminster), the magician had also set about levitating himself. In 1876 he unveiled his 'Levitation Extraordinary'. Having been securely tied in a cabinet, he would emerge eerily from its doors, his hands folded across his chest, and then in an upright position slowly rise to the domed roof of the hall above the heads of the audience; there he would turn to a horizontal position before drifting all the way back into the cabinet. Throughout the experience two lanterns were beamed directly upon him. When the doors of the cabinet were opened at the conclusion, Maskelyne was seen to be tied as securely as at the beginning of the performance.

It is arguable, however, that the most baffling creation of his career was not an illusion in the strictest sense, but an automaton which set the whole country talking when introduced on 13 January 1875. Two years previously he had become acquainted with a Lincolnshire farmer, John Algernon Clarke, who had been toying with the idea of a machine that played cards. Maskelyne was able to supply the technical knowledge that made the dream a reality. The result was 'Psycho', a turbanned Hindu figure, about twenty-two inches high, who sat cross-legged on a box supported by a clear glass cylinder. All three components could be examined by members of the audience to reveal nothing but machinery within the doll and the box, and nothing extraneous attached to the glass.

When reassembled, 'Psycho' would perform under the closest possible scrutiny. He would solve arithmetical problems set by the audience by opening a little door beneath his left hand and sliding out numerals to give the correct answer. He would identify playing cards by striking a bell to denote their appropriate suit and value. In time he learnt to smoke. His greatest talent, however, was for playing whist. Three spectators sat at a card table on the stage and one of them dealt the cards in the customary way. Maskelyne took the fourth hand and set the cards upright individually in a rack in front of the automaton, their backs facing the other players. *Macmillan's Magazine* for January 1876 contained a detailed description by a certain Dr Pole, FRS:

> When it is Psycho's turn to play, his right hand passes with a horizontal circular motion over the frame till it arrives at the right card; he then takes this card between his thumb and fingers, and by a new vertical movement of his hand and arm, he extracts it from its place, lifts it high in the air, and exposes it to the view of the audience, after which, the arm descending again, the card is taken away from the fingers by Mr Maskelyne and thrown on the table to be gathered into the trick.

The even more amazing thing is that Psycho not infrequently won.

To this day the exact details of how he performed his incredible feats remain a closely guarded secret. One thing, however, is certain: there was no way a child or midget (the most often volunteered solution) could possibly have been concealed within the torso. He became the most popular of all Maskelyne's originations and made well over 4,000 consecutive appearances before being withdrawn for rest and repair, the proud patriarch of a family of automata that embraced 'Zoe', a mechanical lady who sketched the portrait of any celebrity selected by the audience; 'Labial', a mechanical trombone-player with perfect lip and finger movements; and 'Fanfare', who performed a similar service on cornet. Psycho himself became the subject of countless articles, cartoons, and poems in the national press, achieving prominence as a national figure on a level with John Nevil himself.

Maskelyne's inventive ability also found a successful outlet in the wider commercial field, where the reward of patents superseded that of an audience's applause. In 1869 a cash register of his design won a major award at the Paris exhibition. Between the years 1875 and 1913 he acquired more than forty patents, embracing, among other things, railway signalling, wireless telegraphy, and devices for issuing tickets and checking money. Probably the most financially successful was his patent in 1892 for the coin-operated lock that became widely used on the doors of public lavatories throughout the United Kingdom until well into the 1950s. The most famous, however, was almost certainly his typewriter of 1889, acknowledged now as the most complete exponent of differential spacing

No name is more associated than Maskelyne's with the development of the levitation illusion.

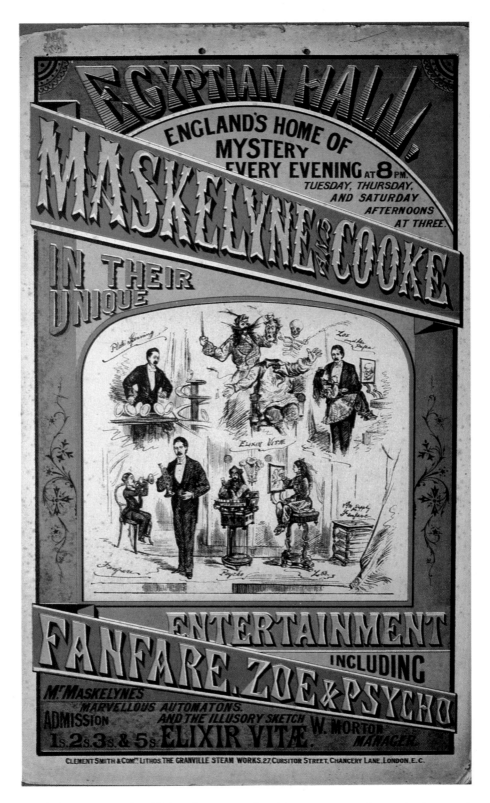

Maskelyne received additional renown for his automata, plate-spinning, and decapitation mystery.

ever produced, ahead of its time by some fifty years. Today a Maskelyne typewriter can be viewed at the Science Museum in South Kensington. One has to travel to the London Museum within the Barbican, however, to view, by special request, 'Psycho' himself. But do not expect to uncover his secret. He remains as inscrutable in retirement as ever in performance.

Maskelyne's scientific aptitude is in keeping with his forebear, the Reverend Nevil Maskelyne, who won distinction as Astronomer Royal by having a crater on the moon named after him. It has also tended to overshadow any talent he may have had for more conventional sleight-of-hand. He was, in fact, one of the great exponents of the 'Japanese Butterfly' trick, a classic effect in which pieces of tissue paper are twisted to represent butterflies and, by deft and graceful manipulation of a fan, subjected to the illusion of flight. The easy, natural manner of his presentation and the skill with which he made the creatures hover and fall around a bouquet, before catching them in a hat, aroused a special sense of wonder in those lucky enough to have seen it.

This elegance was carried over into his presentation of 'Dancing Delf'. As a boy he had seen a performance by Antonio Blitz – not only a magician, but also a pioneer of the art of spinning plates. Maskelyne is on record as crediting his first desire to become a conjuror to this event. His own prodigious skill in Blitz's speciality was not just a matter of setting eight or nine plates spinning simultaneously on a table; he used plates, bowls and basins of indiscriminate size. Beneath his cunning fingers the plates did not merely spin, they waltzed, galloped, danced the hornpipe, performed quadrilles, descended an incline only four inches wide, ascended a helter skelter, and even played at see-saw.

As a publicist and entrepreneur Maskelyne had few equals. He is often wrongly credited with the invention of the theatrical matinée, but it is virtually certain that he was one of the first, if not the very first, theatrical producer of modern times to feature daily afternoon performances, allowing him the frequent luxury of being able to advertise 'The Only Entertainment in London This Afternoon'. He was less successful, however, when he transferred his impresario's role outside the theatrical sphere. On the occasion of Queen Victoria's Diamond Jubilee he undertook to build a grandstand as a luxurious vantage point on top of a building in St Paul's Churchyard. When the building was declared unsafe, he demolished it and created the grandstand on the site with a promise to renew the building after the parade. Maskelyne had difficulty in finding the labour required, with the result that the grandstand was only partially finished by the big day, and there was little public interest in the expensive seats.

If Maskelyne was loath to accept the loss incurred, there were nevertheless other projects which he recognised as sound investment in the cause of publicity. No magician became involved more often in famous law suits. When he lost, he was always reconciled by the advertising they

MR. MASKELYNE'S SCHEME IN ST. PAUL'S CHURCHYARD.

MR. MASKELYNE, TO HER MAJESTY:—"I AM A CONJURER BY PROFESSION, AND IF I SUCCEED IN MAKING THOUSANDS OF SOVEREIGNS OUT OF ONE, I AM SURE YOUR GRACIOUS MAJESTY WILL APPLAUD THE FEAT."

Maskelyne attempts to make capital out of Queen Victoria's Diamond Jubilee, 15 May 1897.

brought him. He appeared to have an insatiable appetite for issuing challenges which usually led to litigation. Riled not least by the imposture of a rival performer, Dr H. S. Lynn, who attempted to claim a version of Maskelyne's 'Box Trick' as his own invention, he made a standing offer of

£500 to anyone who could discover and reproduce the secret as used by him. In December 1897, Stollery and Evans, two young clerks who worked in an engineering office, accepted the challenge. Maskelyne soon found himself in an untenable position. In order to prove beyond all doubt to the lay public that they were not duplicating his method, the master magician would have to reveal the secret of his own version. All Maskelyne could do was dispute the claim. Action at law became inevitable. At the first trial the jury could not reach a verdict; at the second it found in favour of the claimants. The Court of Appeal held no light for John Nevil, who determinedly took the case to the House of Lords, where a decision of three to two was made in favour of Stollery and Evans. Maskelyne paid over £500 and the court costs and then issued a new challenge, more subtly worded, whereby he would pay £1,000 to anyone who could prove they knew the secret of his box. That challenge outlived its author.

His crusade against bogus mediums took him inside the court room several times. In 1876, he gave evidence for the Crown at Bow Street Police Station against the American medium Henry Slade, by demonstrating in the witness box how messages could be produced convincingly on a slate through trickery without the need of spirit aid. Slade was sentenced to three months imprisonment, but managed to escape on a technicality.

Another controversy centred around a clergyman and avowed spiritualist, Archdeacon Thomas Colley, who offered Maskelyne £1,000 if he could reproduce any one of the manifestations Colley had witnessed twenty-nine years previously under the mediumship of the notorious Dr Monck, who ironically had already been exposed by the magical profession. The most significant of these phenomena was described by Colley as 'the extension of a materialised spirit from Dr Monck's side in a cloud of vapour'. In response to the challenge Maskelyne produced on stage in October 1906 an illusion entitled 'The Side Issue'. As he stood with his right side to the audience in full view beneath the glare of an electric chandelier, a vapour appeared to emanate from his left side. A hand appeared and then the full spirit form, head first and horizontally out of the magician's body amid clouds of smoke. The form then walked to the footlights to demand of the audience, 'Where am I?' The critic for *The Times* was so convinced that his review ended, 'We conclude that Mr Maskelyne has won £1,000'. Colley, however, refused to hand over the money on the grounds that the spirit had not returned to Maskelyne's body. The magician explained that had he reversed the illusion, he would have ruined the trick through anti-climax. It was enough to send Maskelyne scurrying once again to the law courts. While the magician sued Colley for the award, Colley countersued for libel. The jury came out in favour of the Archdeacon and ordered John Nevil to pay damages of £75 plus costs. Before Maskelyne had time to implement the missing part of the illusion, the Archdeacon withdrew his offer. Nevertheless 'The Side Issue' was incorporated into an extended sketch, 'Spectre of the Inner

Sanctum', and the newspaper coverage achieved by the controversy kept Maskelyne's theatre full for many months.

By now Maskelyne had moved from the Egyptian Hall to a new location, St George's Hall in Langham Place, literally next door to the present BBC's Broadcasting House. Two years previously, in 1904, the Crown Estate Commissioners had issued a demolition order on the Piccadilly building. To lesser men the event would have signalled the end of an era. In one respect it was, but in another Maskelyne drew renewed zeal from the set-back. He completely rebuilt both stage and auditorium of his new purchase with the special technical demands of magical entertainment in mind, and after the initial false start of a full-length play incorporating magic in place of the distinctive mélange of acts, sketches and illusions, he played his trump card in offering a partnership to the great magician David Devant, long a box-office stalwart at the Egyptian Hall. Cooke had died in February 1905 within weeks of the opening of the new theatre; two months later the era of 'Maskelyne and Devant's Mysteries' had begun. Maskelyne himself died on 18 May 1917, two years after the partnership with Devant was dissolved, although his family, principally under his son Nevil and then his grandsons Clive, Noel and Jasper, would keep the tradition of magic alive in Langham Place until

Left, John Nevil in his workshop. This picture is dedicated to Gil Leaney.
Right, George Alfred Cooke, Maskelyne's first partner.

1933. The longest-running magic show in the world then came to a close.

During John Nevil's lifetime the name of Maskelyne became synonymous with magic in Britain. To play on a Maskelyne bill set the seal of distinction on the careers of many magical performers. Indeed, one of John Nevil's greatest contributions to the twin worlds of mystery and show business was his astute patronage of special talent. Apart from David Devant whose own career we shall now explore in greater detail, Buatier de Kolta, Charles Bertram, Karl Germain, Owen Clark, P. T. Selbit, Charles Morritt, Martin Chapender are just some of the names, now legendary to other magicians, who secured important engagements at 'England's Home of Mystery'. And yet there was one occasion when he did let slip a rising star. Disenchanted with America and determined somehow to break into the prestigious London theatre scene, this performer wrote to John Nevil asking for an engagement. On 24 March 1898, the master sent his reply:

> Dear Sir,
> I have no room for any addition to my company.
> I seldom change my artists.
> Yours very truly,
> J. N. Maskelyne

That letter can be seen today in the prestigious John Mulholland Collection in Los Angeles. What makes it especially noteworthy is that it is addressed to none other than Houdini, who within two years would be presenting a strong threat to Maskelyne as a starring attraction in London's West End.

Today on the site of Maskelyne's St George's Hall there stands an architecturally impersonal, even if eponymous, hotel; on the site of the Egyptian Hall in Piccadilly a more discreet office block, happily known as Egyptian House, remains another essential place of pilgrimage for the serious student of magical history. It was in the minuscule, wood-panelled entrance hall of the latter that, on 23 September 1985, Paul Daniels (on behalf of the members of the Magic Circle, Britain's most prestigious magical organisation) unveiled a special plaque in honour of Maskelyne's achievement, in the company of Mrs Althea Kelsey, a great-granddaughter of the master, and Mrs Joan Maskelyne, the widow of his grandson Noel. That it took so long to acknowledge the man universally regarded as the pioneer of modern magic in the English-speaking world is its own mystery. However, the delay was appropriate. No British magician over the years has come closer to rivalling the public acclaim and technical virtuosity possessed by Maskelyne and his partner David Devant (also honoured by the plaque) than Paul Daniels himself.

On more than one occasion Daniels has had cause to be grateful in specific terms to the ingenuity of his predecessor. When Paul in an appropriate story-book scene caused the sleeping body of Snow White to levitate in a recent Christmas show, it was the groundwork of Maskelyne and his son Nevil that allowed the illusion to appear so convincing, even if the final touch of showmanship, where Snow White is awakened from her magical slumber by the kiss of a small boy from the audience, owed more to Devant than John Nevil. When on another show Paul escaped from the innermost of a nest of three wooden chests scrupulously examined ahead of time by members of the audience, as well as under the more critical scrutiny of furniture expert Bernard Price from the 'Antiques Roadshow', he gave credit on screen to George Grimmond, a prominent magician in seaside concert party and society circles during the middle part of this century. Certainly the triple box presentation had been the distinctive feature of Grimmond's act at the height of his career, but it is hard to imagine that he would have got to use even one box without the pioneering work by Maskelyne in this field.

The whole world of magic has so much to be grateful to Maskelyne for, but away from the legacy of individual tricks and methods there is a wider debt. Perhaps his greatest contribution came out of his work as an impresario. By booking guest magicians on to his programmes, he showed them the advantage of working together on a friendly and co-operative basis. There is no doubt that this encouraged them to form their own organisations in a way unknown in those early days among acts of other kinds. For almost half a century the theatre of the Maskelyne family was one of the indispensable sights of London, on a level with the Tower, Madame Tussaud's and the Zoo as part of the established order of things as far as family outings were concerned. As such it held its own through innumerable changes of taste and social habit. The definitive showman, Maskelyne always had some new wonder, some new controversy up his sleeve with which to intrigue or provoke the great British public. No one knew better how to turn an apparently adverse situation to his gain in the cause of publicity. Above all, he was a true British gentleman of enormous integrity to whom David Devant, who far surpassed him as a performer, never failed to refer as 'The Chief'.

9

'All Done by Kindness'

David Devant is universally revered as the greatest magician Britain produced at the time when magic was at the height of its popularity with the theatre-going public. When John Nevil Maskelyne went into partnership with Devant the combination of their names quickly became as much a by-line for both quality and popular demand as 'Gilbert and Sullivan'.

The younger magician was born David Wighton, the son of James Wighton, a Scottish landscape painter, at Highgate on 22 February 1868. According to Francis White, the President of the Magic Circle, the artistic connection had some influence on his subsequent change of name. As a boy, David was attracted on a visit to an art gallery by a biblical painting with a descriptive caption beneath it in French: 'David Devant Goliath'. The young Wighton mistook the preposition for the subject's name and, inspired by the painting, filed it away mentally for professional purposes in later life.

By 1890 his early boyhood enthusiasm for conjuring had already matured sufficiently for him to hold an acknowledged position as a minor attraction on the leading London music halls. It was at one such venue, the Trocadero, that he was seen by Maskelyne. The illusion that impressed was called 'Vice Versa' and had been inspired by F. Anstey's popular novel of the same name. Whereas in Anstey's book, however, a man changed into a boy, Devant himself changed a man into a woman under seemingly impossible conditions. Throughout the presentation members of the audience held the ends of a ribbon which were tied securely around the waist of the man in question. When the curtains of the cabinet containing him were drawn back, however, the ribbon was now inextricably tied around the waist of a lady. The whole trick took not much more than thirty seconds.

In August 1893, Devant made his debut at the Egyptian Hall, beginning an association with Maskelyne that would run intermittently for more than two decades. Ironically the stage of the theatre in Piccadilly was too small to present 'Vice Versa'; but John Nevil had faith not only in the technical prowess of the young illusionist – who quickly adapted the

Opposite, an early poster depicting Devant's skill as a shadow artist as well as magician.

principle behind the illusion to produce a new effect known as 'The Artist's Dream' in which the picture of a young woman on an easel came to life – but also in the special quality of his presentation. This embodied a rare blend of faultless appearance and perfect taste, leisurely ease and charming humour, and the widest popular appeal. If people were to accuse Maskelyne himself of not keeping pace with the times – not that they did – he would have only to point to his new recruit. Others before had performed entertaining magic, but Devant, like Paul Daniels, would have been an entertainer whatever the performing skill to which he addressed himself.

Early in his career he resolutely broke with tradition by casting aside the magic wand which had been the *sine qua non* among all aspiring conjurors. He favoured technical subtlety to sleight-of-hand if the illusion became more impressive as a result, albeit less clever from a manipulative point of view. He was an illusionist in the sense that he performed large-scale magic with human beings, but wherever possible he abjured the use of any apparatus which had obviously been made specially for magical purposes, tailoring what few cabinets and trunks he did need to be wholly natural in appearance. As the elaborate and cumbersome Victorian age drew to a close, so Devant was to lead magic out of the nineteenth and into the simpler, more streamlined twentieth century.

This desire to keep abreast of the times technically also involved Devant in the early workings of the British cinema. Impressed by the new moving pictures presented by the Lumière Brothers in London in 1896, he tried out the novelty at the Egyptian Hall. Soon three road companies of 'Mr David Devant's Animated Pictures, direct from Maskelyne and Cooke's Egyptian Hall, Piccadilly' were playing the provinces. It is possible that the first film of any magician actually performing was taken of Devant by the cinematographer R. W. Paul, on the roof of London's Alhambra Theatre. Producing a rabbit from an opera hat, Devant suddenly split the animal into twins. Subsequent movies showed his egg manipulation, hand shadows, and paper-folding. The hundreds of pictures that went to make the films were transferred to the pages of small flick-books which re-created the effect of movement. They sold in their thousands, making Devant even better known than before. In time he had to make the choice between magic and specialising in the new entertainment. Fortunately magic won the day. Maybe Devant himself did not fully appreciate the potential of the new craze he had helped to launch.

Between seasons in Piccadilly Devant took the Maskelyne and Cooke show on tour. Then, when Maskelyne moved his London-based operation from the Egyptian Hall to St George's Hall in Langham Place, and instead of the usual magical-based variety bill offered an elaborate magical science-fiction fantasy, 'The Coming Race' (based on Bulwer-Lytton's satirical novel), the public stayed away and Devant was rushed back to London from his tour to prove once again the box-office value he had already

David Devant showed warmth and extreme charm in everything he did.

displayed. With the death of George Cooke the path was clear for John Nevil to bring in Devant as a full-time partner. The great performer's presence revitalised both the show and public interest, with the result that for ten more years, until the partnership dissolved in 1915, 'Maskelyne and Devant's Mysteries' became a household phrase throughout the English-speaking world.

The audiences who attended Devant's shows saw a redefinition of what magic could make possible. In 'The Magic Mirror' they looked on as Devant and a volunteer from the audience put on black cloaks and goggles. The magician walked the spectator around to examine a full-length mirror or cheval glass, which stood isolated in the centre of the stage. He then asked the assistant to gaze intently at the reflection. As the lights dimmed, a small red glow appeared in the glass. It grew and grew until it materialised into the scarlet-clad figure of Mephistopheles. All the time Devant and the spectator could see their own faces reflected in the mirror

Few magical appearances were more enchanting than that of the girl created by Devant's excursion into horticulture.

through the figure. The devil faded away and in turn apparitions of a bride in her wedding-gown and an alarmed Devant himself in evening-dress materialised. As the silvered image of the magician threw up his arm in anguish, the supposed real-life Devant on stage threw off his cloak. It was not Devant, but Mephistopheles.

Equally spectacular, and recently revived by Paul Daniels himself, was the strangely titled 'Biff'. In conversation with an amateur conjuror in Scotland, Devant had offered to pay ten pounds for a new idea, however impossible that idea might sound. The hobbyist suggested that the magician should make a motorcycle and its rider disappear in mid-air with the engine still running. Devant rose to the challenge and in a short while audiences saw a motorcyclist, after several laps of the stage, drive his spluttering machine up a ramp into a large white deal packing-case which stood in the centre of the stage on eighteen-inch-high legs. The case was closed and winched into the air. There was no doubt that the motorcycle was still within: the sides of the crate shook from the reverberation of the engine. Devant then beamed an 'Invisible Ray' of pale green light at the case. Suddenly the crate disintegrated into planks and the noise of the motorcycle ceased, leaving not a trace of rider or machine.

Of all his larger miracles, the one for which Devant still receives most acclaim is the one which he himself considered to be his masterpiece. It has to be the most wonderful vanish of a human being ever devised and yet, so complicated is its mechanism, so delicate its handling, that it has rarely been attempted since. The inspiration came to Devant one night as he stared at a flickering candle. He imagined the devil tempting a moth with its flame. As the moth came close, it disappeared. Eventually that is exactly what the audience saw. A girl assistant in a flowing silk dress, painted to represent a moth with wings attached, fluttered across the stage. Devant approached with a lighted candle. As he came near, she stood still, folding her wings across her body to shield herself from the flame. Then, just as the magician stepped in front of her, she was no more. With no covering of any kind, she literally dissolved into thin air. It is a measure of Devant's status in general and not merely of the brilliance of this illusion in particular, that no less than E. Nesbit, the prominent children's author of that time, was inspired to write a play for Devant around this most incredible of disappearing tricks. Like her better known *The Railway Children*, *The Magician's Heart* in story form remains well-loved today, a minor children's classic in its own right.

Devant's reputation would have been secure based entirely on the ingenuity of his original conceptions in magic, but there was something more. His success as a public figure was due in no small part to something about the man. From the moment he made his entrance on stage, audiences responded to the quiet command and the impish twinkle in the eye of this lovable uncle. Even when presenting his larger illusions, he was able to project the intimacy of the drawing-room in the largest of theatres. He

In 'The Mascot Moth' the bewinged creature disappeared in full view of the audience.

allowed nothing unnecessarily gaudy or shoddy on his stage. The result was that no magician ever exerted a greater sense of wonder, transporting young and old alike down a yellow brick road of whimsy and delight, where cynicism and disillusion have no name.

The overall pace of his performance would not be acceptable today, a criticism not of the man, but of the age in which he worked. Between tricks the band would play 'The Narcissus Waltz' as he explained, 'I leave the stage for a few moments after each experiment in order to give you an opportunity to tell each other how it is done.' But as this comment reveals, humour was never far away from his performance. While Maskelyne's presentation tended towards the straightforward and matter-of-fact, with Devant, even in something as essentially serious as 'The Magic Mirror', there was still scope for laughter. When the first figure of Mephistopheles had appeared, he would explain to the young audience volunteer, 'You have seen your awful past, now I will give you a glimpse of the future.' As the vision of the bride materialised, Devant would secretly cue the man to reach towards her, only to check him seconds later, 'No, that is for the future.' Many of his lines appear pedestrian today, but only because they have been appropriated by each successive generation of aspiring magician. His sense of humour was totally off-beat for its day, friendly and informal, in keeping with the man. Whether addressing the young boy about to come up on stage, 'That's right, bring the other foot with you', or advising the audience as jury, 'Now I want everyone to keep one eye on this ball, the other eye on this hat, and another eye on this rabbit', or searching for feminine assistance, 'I'm looking for a lady . . . a lady I can trust . . . with an envelope, that is', he pioneered a style. It was a mark of their effectiveness that after Devant's time many of his lines became ossified as cliché. Thankfully there were those which only Devant could successfully use: 'May I close the bag? I do this myself because I do these things so gracefully, don't I? Like an elephant getting off a bicycle on a muddy day!'

Devant was never seen to better advantage than in his handling of children. If it was possible to use them in preference to adults he would. His secret was to enter a conspiracy with them; he never made fun of them. Their shyness cast aside as a result, they became equal partners with the magician. A favourite routine was entitled 'The Lesson in Magic'. 'I want to teach a boy a trick. I will teach any boy how to turn a handkerchief into a lemon if I can get the loan of a handkerchief and a boy. Any handkerchief will do. It can be either scented or clean. We have got a clean boy, anyhow. Whose handkerchief is this? Yours, sir? Will you please notice that I do not move it from your sight. The only reason why I borrow the handkerchief is because I find that when you borrow anything it adds interest to what you are doing.'

The boy with the handkerchief has to copy all the actions which the magician makes with his own red silk square. First he must knead it between his hands, but he presses too hard and produces a heap of disintegrated scraps. Further kneading turns these scraps into one very narrow strip several feet long. Devant takes the strip and transforms it into the fruit, but as he explains, 'You can't expect the gentleman to go home rubbing his nose with a lemon . . . ' The fruit is cut open. There is the

Devant surrounded by some of his greatest creations, including Diogenes produced from an empty barrel.

Devant's name was not necessary. He had made the trick his own.

handkerchief impeccably restored, but the catalogue of errors has really only just begun. The boy is shown how to cut a piece out of the centre of the handkerchief and then how to mend it in the heat of a candle flame. Both red and white handkerchiefs get burnt in the process, but when their flames are extinguished it is seen that they have both been restored. Alas, the borrowed one now has a red centre, and the red one a white centre! The owner of the handkerchief is offered a glass of claret by way of compensation. That claret mysteriously appears in place of the handkerchiefs in an empty glass held by the boy, while the handkerchiefs themselves find their way into the bottle that was full a moment ago. It has to be broken open with a hammer. At last both handkerchiefs are completely restored.

That Devant was so much at ease in this type of situation is proved by the decision to feature a similar routine in the most important performance of his career. He was the only magician among the twenty-two featured acts invited to participate in the first Royal Command Variety Performance, held at the Palace Theatre, London in the presence of King George V and Queen Mary on 1 July 1912. In the company of such great stars as Harry Lauder and Paul Cinquevalli, Little Tich and Anna Pavlova, Devant had hoped to feature both an illusion and an audience participation item. Pressure of time meant that one had to go. The props for 'The Artist's Dream' were conveyed back to St George's Hall and Devant made his leisurely entrance on to a bare stage. This time he invited both a boy and a girl to participate in the surprises to come. For this special occasion he knew them ahead of time – his daughter Vida, and Jasper Maskelyne, the grandson of John Nevil, himself to be a considerable performer in later years. Once they had been ushered on stage to the tune of Mendelssohn's Wedding March, Devant was on course for another performance of his funniest trick, the production of an apparently unlimited supply of eggs.

With an empty bowler taken from an audience member in one hand, the magician pointed into the air with the other. 'Can you see those little white atoms floating about? I don't suppose you can. They are quite invisible except to a magician. All you have to do is to catch one of them, develop it, and it becomes an egg.' Using the cover of the hat as a 'developing chamber', he produced an egg and passed it to the girl, to pass in turn to the boy. Gradually the production of eggs quickened, the mystery of where they could be coming from competing with the sheer slapstick hilarity of the situation as the poor boy at the end of the line wrestled with the overflow of eggs he was expected to hold safely. That they were genuine was proved by the uncooked omelette that accumulated at his feet. As you watched you could roll with laughter, sit back amazed, or, if you were a father or mother, quite simply feel the warmth in your heart at the way the magnificent Devant handled the boy and the girl.

There was not another Royal Command Performance until 1919, but little more than a year after the first, on 7 July 1913, Devant found himself entertaining the King and Queen again at a special private gala at Knowsley Hall in Cheshire, the home of the Earl of Derby. He was the only performer from the previous year to be invited back. On this occasion the highlight of his presentation was the illusion known as 'The Chocolate Soldier', its supposed intention being to show the possible side-effects of exposure to electric light. An assistant in coloured make-up wearing the full costume of a British guardsman – scarlet coat, white trousers, and busby – was hoisted to the top of a completely isolated platform where he (sometimes she!) marched stiffly to the topical music. Surrounding him were three separate lighting battens, one red, one white, and one blue. Union Jacks on staffs were now secured to the top of the battens forming a triangular enclosure. When Devant gave the signal, the flags fell. The soldier was still marching, but he had shrunk to the size of a doll. To prove that it was a chocolate soldier, Devant would break off a finger and give it to a lucky child in the audience.

The only performer to have come near to matching Devant's success in his own country is Paul Daniels himself. Their styles, separated by three-quarters of a century, are totally different, courtly on the one hand, cocky on the other. But just as there was always a layer of irreverence lurking beneath the surface of Devant's dignity, so there resides a level of charm, warmth and repose beneath Paul's more obvious cheekiness. One is tempted to ask whether, had each been born at the time of the other, the roles would have been reversed. All popular entertainers are moulded by the social conditions in which they exist and the resultant audience demand. If nothing else, both Devant and Daniels stand as men of the people, easy-going personalities capable of evoking laughter, mystery, and respect in their own time, sharing the keenest appreciation of every single degree of fun that can be drawn from any situation.

It is appropriate that of all the past masters of magic, Paul himself has drawn as much inspiration from Devant's material as from anyone's. When Daniels caused an audience member magically to turn upside-down when strapped into an upright cabinet just large enough to hold him, he was repeating an earlier success of Devant's known as 'The New Page', a title derived from a newspaper competition that awarded fifty pounds to the lucky winner and massive publicity to Devant himself. When the Yorkshire cricketer Freddie Trueman found himself bowling a pack of playing cards at a Paul resplendent in cricketing whites, it was Devant whom Paul acknowledged when he caught all three previously selected cards on the bat in his hands.

The most visual motif in Paul's stage act is that of 'The Electric Chairs', in which for no reason at all ordinary unsuspecting members of the general public find themselves leaping off their seats only to discover that the chairs on which they sit are totally innocent and unprepared. Paul uses the device as a hilarious catalyst in a comedy of errors with borrowed money.

Devant, all those years ago, used the same device to add hilarity to a similar chain of events with a borrowed watch.

In recent years technical advancement in magic has made it possible to take the impossible one step further than in Devant's day. When Paul made a live television camera disappear mid-transmission, his presentation resembled not a little Devant's earlier 'Biff', but Devant himself would have been the first to acknowledge the impressiveness of the effect achieved in the openness of a fully lit television studio, with visual proof that the object to be vanished was there right until the last moment.

'The Eternal Triangle' was a full-stage presentation of a card trick in which Devant caused two cards, merely thought of by members of the audience, in one half of the pack to travel along the sides of a triangle marked by ribbon into the other half securely held by a third member of the audience. Once again Paul catapulted the effect into the television era, inviting viewers at home in their living-rooms also to think of a card. Still the trick worked, in spite of the geographical separation made necessary by the new medium and the even stranger time-shift occasioned by the fact that the show was pre-recorded!

Paul's greatest technical leap was in his presentation of 'The Magic Kettle'. Although it was founded on ancient principles, Devant had made this trick his very own. Using a simple tin kettle he poured any drink called for by members of the audience, whether wine, spirits, liqueurs, soft drinks, or milk. Paul himself has presented the item twice now on television and on each occasion has been able to enhance the mystery beyond the already puzzling level established by Devant. Some people suspect the glasses, but on the first occasion Paul asked a member of the audience to wipe out a glass, hold it herself, and only then name her drink – 'cherry brandy' – which he poured for her to taste. It was genuine. Other people suspect the kettle, but in what may possibly be the most baffling sequence Paul has ever performed, he must have allayed even those doubts. Having dispensed drinks in the normal way to members of the studio audience, he invited a small group of spectators to join him on camera. One was given the kettle, was told to name a drink and to pour, then to hand the kettle to one of the others. This person in turn was to do the same, again handing it to either of the other two. The penultimate person was to repeat the process, passing the kettle to the last person who had merely to think of a drink, then pour just the same. When all four drinks were tasted at the end, everyone confirmed that they had the real thing. At no point had Paul touched the kettle! After the programme the magical press, as stunned by the miracle as the general public, criticised Paul for using paid confederates. This underestimated the power of the magician. No one was more baffled by the sequence than the four volunteers. It is appropriate here to acknowledge the genius of magician Robert Swadling, who devised the secret foundation upon which Paul's routine was based.

Devant pours 'any drink called for' from his Magic Kettle, and Paul follows suit.

Sadly, the latter years of Devant's career were beset by ill-health, causing his eventual retirement from the stage. The story is told that during his Christmas season in Manchester in 1919 he asked the small child helping in 'The Lesson in Magic' to hold the handkerchief exactly as he did. Devant could not understand why the child insisted on waving it from side to side, until he looked down in anguish at his own hand shaking in the early stages of nervous palsy. No worse end could come to a magician than the inability to control his hands. After 1920 he could no longer perform on stage and was eventually forced to end his days in the Royal Hospital for Incurables at Putney. Ironically, modern medication could easily have treated his disease today.

When he died at the age of seventy-three on 13 October 1941, *The Times* called him quite simply 'the greatest magician of all times'. Certainly no one since has combined the performing flair and inventive acumen of Devant. He was at the height of his powers when magic was at its peak. In 1912 the other leading magicians of the day deputed a spokesman to convey a message along the following lines to him: 'We are of the unanimous opinion that none of us can ever hope to equal your standard. We ask you to do us the honour of being our guest at a special private function, when we can acknowledge your supremacy.' On 3 February 1913, the great magician was presented with a testimonial signed by, among others, Houdini, Horace Goldin, Howard Thurston, and John Nevil Maskelyne himself, in which he was acclaimed as the embodiment of perfection in all things magical. It is significant that in his vast repertoire

there are no effects involving any kind of human mutilation, so conscious was he of his public persona. Devant, to underline the point, even had a catch-phrase that featured on one of his most memorable publicity posters. It said simply, 'All done by kindness'. To the vast majority of his public, there could have been no other way.

An original poster design for Britain's greatest magician by John Hassall, one of the most popular British poster designers of all time. Another example of his talent is shown on the dedication page. Both capture the essential wit and humour of Devant.

10

Some Great Illusionists

The Selbit Mysteries

If an audience for sensationalism in magic existed during the early years of this century, no one went to greater lengths to accommodate it than the British magician P. T. Selbit. If he lacked the warmth and charm of David Devant, he nevertheless came close to rivalling him for inventive prowess. He was born Percy Thomas Tibbles on 17 November 1881, eventually dropping one 'b' and reversing his actual name to obtain his *nom de théâtre*. Prior to the First World War he had presented a magical act with an Egyptian theme under the name of Joad Heteb, 'The Wizard of the Sphinx', but he did not really come into his own until he brought his impeccable manners and academic, even clinical style to a ghoulish succession of torture effects. More than anyone Selbit established the identity of the magician's assistant as hapless victim, but fortunately no blood flowed, no complaints were voiced by the girls themselves, and the feminists of the day were more concerned with the suffragette cause than the harmless make-believe of a fiendishly clever wizard.

A list of some of his inventions tells its own sadistic tale. In 'The Human Pin-cushion' the victim was impaled on eighty-four sharp spikes projecting from a metal panel which slowly penetrated her flesh as a wheel was turned. 'The Elastic Lady' involved ankles and wrists being tied and fastened; when the ends of the ropes were fed through a screen and pulled, so her limbs became elongated with all the facility of an animated cartoon, her neck distended for good measure. 'Avoiding the Crush' had nothing to do with traffic conditions: the crush in question was the descending weight of two girls in an oblong box just large enough to fit snugly into a larger box containing a third. There could be no room for the last girl unless she were crushed flat. She *was* crushed flat, but like all the other girls quickly restored to healthy, three-dimensional normality.

In recent years one of Selbit's magical tortures, 'Through the Eye of a Needle', has become a standard part of Paul Daniels's repertoire. Selbit himself used barrels and a steel plate the size and shape of a manhole cover;

Opposite, Selbit's versatility as an inventor was promoted in this advertisement.

P. T. SELBIT'S
MYSTERIES.

"Mr. P. T. Selbit has achieved a world-wide reputation as a producer of sensational novelties; in fact, the name Selbit is the hall-mark of perfection in mystery and of excellent showmanship."

PERFECT
Demonstrations of
Spiritualistic
Wonders.

—

A Triumph of
Unique
Artistic Novelty.

—

Effects that
REALLY
baffle Scientific
explanation.

IN ACTIVE

PREPARATION—

"THE TALKING

TEAPOT,"

"THE LIQUEFIED

LADY."

The Latest Sensation:—
'THE WRESTLING CHEESE.'
THE STRONGEST CHEESE ON EARTH.

Which defies six men to put it down; **GOTCH** and **HACK.** specially invited. Presented in conjunction with

"MY SPIRIT STENOGRAPHER," "THE GOBLINS' CUBICLE," "CAGLIOSTRO'S SKULL," "GRANDMOTHER'S SUNSHADE."

The World-Famous Mystery :—
"SPIRIT PAINTINGS."

"THE
SELBIT MYSTERY"

Sole Agent—

Julian Wylie.

Paul now uses tea-chests and a giant examinable Chinese coin, but the basic effect is the same. The 'eye' in question is a two-inch hole in the metal disc. A long rope is fastened around the waist of the girl assistant. One end is threaded through a hole in the base of one chest, which the girl then enters. The other end of the rope is then threaded through the coin and through a similar hole in the other chest. The two chests on their sides on platforms are pushed tight against the coin, thus enclosing the girl. The only way from one to the other is through the 'eye', but metal rods are slotted down to remove any further possibility of access of any kind. On cue the girl waves her hand through the flap in the top of one chest; a split second later the same hand emerges from the corresponding flap in the other. The chests are separated, the rope is still intact. The girl has literally passed 'through the eye of a needle'.

It would be unfair on Selbit to project him as a performer concerned exclusively with inflicting mock pain and discomfort on showgirls. That he was capable of his lighter moments is proved by his invention of the 'Mighty' or 'Wrestling' Cheese, one of the most unusual items in the history of magic, in which six strong volunteers from the audience were invited to turn a full-size circular Edam cheese on to its side. Those who tried found themselves struggling violently with the object, sometimes being thrown to the floor in the process. Only the magician could actually accomplish the task. There have been more intriguing mysteries, not least on Selbit's own stage, but few producing greater laughter.

Selbit died on 19 November 1938. In addition to the dazzling arcana of his displays, his inventive talent produced a device for tilting beer barrels without disturbing their sediment and first floated the idea of 'Football Pools'. Tried out on a local basis in Berkshire, the latter idea quickly faded into obscurity; by the time it was revived to become a national habit, Selbit had lost out commercially. However, there is still one magical invention of Selbit's that demands mention in these pages. It was the most commercial illusion in the history of conjuring. Quite simply, Selbit was the first to saw through a woman.

As magic fell into quickstep with the Roaring Twenties, no illusion captured the imagination of the public faster, Selbit pushing the plight of the ever-suffering magician's assistant to the limit of both taste and possibility. He always insisted that his presentation should be regarded as 'a problem, not an illusion', but since he first performed the item at Finsbury Park Empire in London on 17 January 1921 few tricks have been pirated more ruthlessly, changed more dramatically.

Everyone carries around a mental image of this illusion which they have seen in one form or another at some time in their life, but it is unlikely that it corresponds to Selbit's original version, even though Paul Daniels himself opted to present a modification of the original when the time came to saw through a woman on his television series. In Selbit's presentation five long ropes were tied securely around the neck, wrists and ankles of the victim, spectators marking the knots for identification with small luggage labels. The girl then stood in a tall crate, the ropes being threaded through holes in the side. The spectators were told to hold the free ends taut throughout the trick, enabling them to feel the movement of the girl if she attempted to change her position. The lid was snapped in place with padlocks and the crate placed horizontally on a wooden scaffold. Selbit then took three sheets of plate glass about four feet long and nine inches wide and plunged them dramatically through slots in the lid and base of the crate without meeting any resistance. Two steel blades were similarly inserted from side to side. Selbit pointed out with relish that the criss-cross pattern achieved in this way divided the crate into eight equal sections not much larger in area than a cigar box. How could the woman survive? The saw, a two-handed affair with vicious teeth, was now brought forward and Selbit, with the help of an assistant, proceeded to saw the box dramatically into two parts. The sawing necessarily took time. The glass and steel blades were then quickly withdrawn and the two halves of the crate drawn apart showing the complete woman inside. The knots were found to be intact and cut off with the luggage tags to be left with the spectators as souvenirs.

Shrewd publicity on Selbit's part led to huge press coverage with the magician advertising for victims at five pounds a night and offering a salary of twenty pounds a week to Christabel Pankhurst, daughter of the famous suffragette. After each performance assistants carried buckets of ersatz

Selbit with the most famous of all his inventions.

blood to pour into the gutter in front of the theatre. Standing-room-only notices became the order of the day for the illusion, while George Johnson, editor of a popular magical journal *The Magic Wand*, advised Selbit to put the first plagiarist of the idea into a crate, saw through it, and leave him in pieces. He did not realise how quickly prophetic his remark would be.

As Selbit reached his finest hour, the career of the Polish/American illusionist Horace Goldin had fallen on thin times, the magician having lost both his props and the profits from a long overseas tour in a shipwreck at Hawaii in 1918. By July 1921, however, he was back at the Palace Theatre in New York scoring the biggest success of his own career with a sawing illusion. In fairness it was not an exact copy. In Goldin's version you could see the head, hands and feet of the victim extending from the box. Whereas Selbit's version had been totally puzzling, Goldin's method was obvious to any person of average intelligence. The box was so large it was hardly any secret that two girls were employed. But there was a subtle difference in the effect. After sawing through the box, Goldin inserted two metal plates to seal off the two box halves and then pulled the two halves apart. If Selbit was the first to saw through a woman, Goldin, to be semantically correct, was the first to saw a woman in two.

If Goldin produced the weaker trick, nevertheless he was more than a match for Selbit when it came to publicity. Doctors and nurses with stretchers ready were posted in attendance at all theatres. Ambulances drove through the towns he played announcing, 'We are going to Keith's [the name of the theatre circuit] in case the saw slips.' His own use of press advertising was even more provocative than Selbit's: 'Girls wanted to be sawn in half at B. F. Keith's next week. Guarantee $10,000 in case of fatality.' When a local girl did volunteer there was one qualification – she had to wear a mask 'to hide her identity'. It goes without saying that Goldin ensured a supply of 'local' girls.

Within a short time Goldin had five units franchised to perform the act in his name. Selbit had gone to similar lengths in England, but by the time he reached New York to play the rival Shubert circuit in person he found himself outflanked. Once Selbit's itinerary was published, Keith's arranged for Goldin or one of his deputies to play the week ahead of Selbit in every town he was due to visit. Notwithstanding, Selbit's better product enabled him in time to launch seven units of his own. A wealthier if not happier man, he returned to England where he was honoured to become only the second magician to perform an act on the 'Royal Variety Performance', at the London Hippodrome on 12 December 1922. Naturally it was 'Sawing through a Woman' which the King wanted to see.

In fairness to Goldin he, before anyone, saw the shortcomings of his own method and worked relentlessly to improve the mystery. By 1931 he was advertising an entirely new version. He called it 'A Living Miracle' and its striking visual impact more than compensated for the amateurism

Goldin added even greater danger to the illusion with a circular saw.

of what had gone before. Boxes were now obsolete. The girl in Oriental costume lay in full view on a slender table top. A huge circular saw, the sharpness of which was demonstrated by cutting a log of wood, was made to revolve at speed and the table slowly moved beneath its teeth. Audiences saw the steel slice through her body with macabre ease. The saw was stopped, and saw and table turned sideways so that everyone could see that the thirty-six-inch circular blade really did go right through her midriff. Within seconds the saw was withdrawn, the girl 'de-hypnotised', and Goldin stood there taking the loudest applause of his career. Audiences now found an easy solution less forthcoming, but this did not stop them advancing every possible theory from the use of mirrors to mass-hypnotism. They were as far removed from the truth as Selbit and Goldin were from a handshake.

A Whirlwind of Wizardry

It would be an injustice to Horace Goldin to reduce his role in magic's history to his part in the 'Sawing' controversy. He has two other important claims on the attention of any student of that history. As 'The Whirlwind Wizard' he pioneered the high-speed style of presentation which had a considerable effect upon the tempo of most subsequent magic acts. Again with his finger on the pulse of the times, he possessed a magnificent flair for linking his illusions to the most topical stories of the day.

He was born Hyman Goldstein in Poland on 17 December 1873,

emigrating to Nashville in the United States at the age of sixteen. His first words of English were learnt as he assisted in his uncle's grocery store, but the language, not helped by the trace of a stammer surviving from childhood, did not come easily to him. When he broke into vaudeville in the late 1890s, the critic of *New York American* praised his conjuring skills, but advised those who intended to see the show to put cotton wool in their ears. Goldin, however, was resilient and instantly set out to prove that his act could survive without speech. Fast music was scored and two assistants hired. Goldin had decided to cram in more magic where otherwise he would have been talking. The criticism proved the turning point of his career.

In the years to come few illusionists, when presenting a full evening magic show, would fail to open their performance with a rapid-fire sequence of as many miracles in as short a time as possible. 'Blink and you miss a trick' became a tradition, but Goldin was its pioneer. The tactic pushed his salary in dollars into four figures and proved the vast money-making potential for magicians on the vaudeville stage at that time. One reviewer described him as 'lightning in a dress suit'; another wrote, 'It is a treat to meet with a conjuror who gets through his performance as if he had a train to catch, and not as if he meant that you should not catch yours.' Goldin himself boasted that at one stage in his career his rate of performance was no less than 'forty-five tricks in seventeen minutes'. He still had his detractors. One described him as a 'pull-the-string magician', another as 'a salesman demonstrating as many mechanical toys as possible', but his speed was such that audiences never really had time to rationalise one secret before he went on to the next. Flags, flowers, handkerchiefs, goldfish, canaries, rabbits, bowls of fire, bowls of water, not to mention his assistants themselves, were produced, vanished, transposed, transformed in a wild harlequinade of mystery. As he matured, so his performances became more subtly varied in pace, but they never lost their urgency.

It was inevitable that at some stage the historical precedent set by these fast and furious sequences would be reflected in an item on 'The Paul Daniels Magic Show'. However, television is more subtle. It was not enough for Paul, just for the sake of it, to present at hell-bent speed a succession of the quickest tricks (individually not often the most baffling ones, particularly those of the 'pull-the-string' variety). There had to be a *raison d'être*. It came from the *Guinness Book of Records*. In 1953 Dr Roger Bannister had broken the 'Four-Minute Mile'. Paul, with the gracious consent of editor and publisher Norris McWhirter, would attempt to inaugurate a record for 'Four-Minute *Magic*'. In November 1983, under the statistical scrutiny of McWhirter himself and the schoolmasterly gaze of Francis White, the President of the Magic Circle, watching carefully to see that the magician did not perform the same trick twice in a different guise, Paul raced along with a dash and a hustle that would have left Goldin breathless. From the moment he changed his

Opposite, Goldin's flair for keeping pace with the news was typified by this illusion.

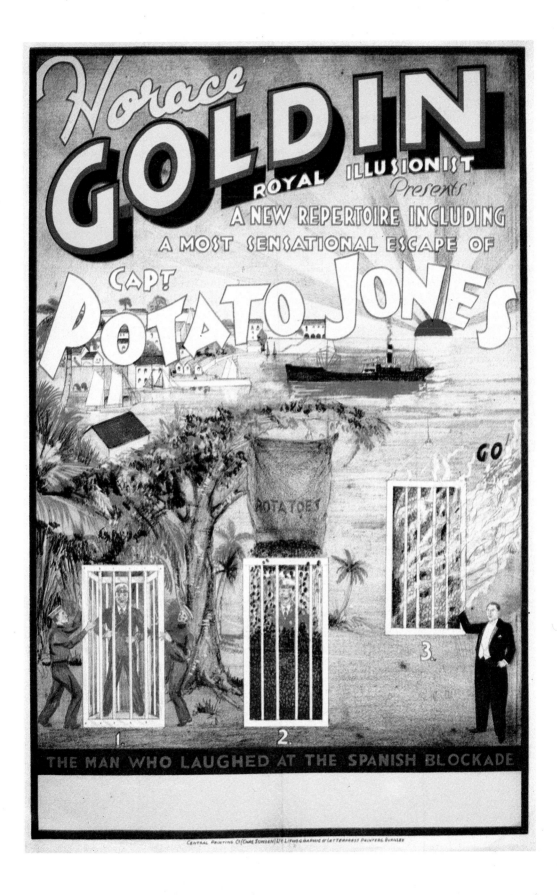

handkerchief into a boutonnière, through a succession of tricks most magicians would have long forgotten about, to magically filling the stage with a profusion of confetti, ribbons, silk, ducks, a pig, a pony and its rider, he came in at an official count of forty-seven tricks with not a second to spare! In the subsequent issue of the *Guinness Book of Records* Paul was listed as 'the most versatile' magician. The categorisation, while complimentary, proved a little puzzling. 'Fastest' would have been more apt. He had surely already proven his claim to versatility over the several years he had been presenting magic on television.

Goldin would have loved the challenge of the new medium with its topical urgency and insatiable demand for new material: appropriately, he had been one of the few magicians to be featured by the BBC on its pre-war service. Paul has found to his advantage that the one-off nature of a television performance makes possible the participation of topical celebrities in specific illusions in a way which would be out of the question for the duration of a theatre season or while touring in vaudeville. Nevertheless Goldin's mind was for ever active in capitalising on the latest headline. Within hours of the Ascot Gold Cup being stolen in 1907, he was ready to present his own Gold Cup Vanish, in facsimile of the theft, at London's Palace Theatre.

During the Spanish Civil War Captain 'Potato' Jones was a member of the British Merchant Marine, who captured headlines by running his tramp steamer loaded with potatoes through the blockade, thus saving thousands of the Spanish civilian population from starvation. Goldin was quick to see the value of this popular hero. One of his assistants, disguised as Jones, entered a large wooden cage covered with wire netting. As soon as he was secured inside, other assistants began tipping sack after sack of potatoes in from the top. When 'Jones' could no longer be seen, the whole unit was hoisted high above the stage. Goldin blew a whistle, the cue for an assistant to release the bottom of the cage. Potatoes cascaded everywhere but 'Jones' was no longer to be seen, until the spotlight shifted purposefully to the back of the audience to discover him waving wildly. If Jones could beat the Spanish blockade, his *alter ego* could well survive the most fiendish plight a magician might devise for him.

At the beginning of Goldin's career, one of the greatest spy trials of all time inspired an illusion which he called 'Dreyfus Escapes from Devil's Island'. In this he himself portrayed Captain Alfred Dreyfus who had been brought before a military tribunal in Paris and found guilty of betraying secrets to a foreign power. An assistant played the probable culprit, Esterhazy, dressed as the devil, overlord of 'Devil's Island', the dread penal settlement off the coast of French Guiana. The audience saw the red-robed officer tear the buttons and epaulettes from Goldin's uniform and break his sword across his knee before forcing the captive into an apparently escape-proof cage. The cage was covered, soldiers fired, the cover fell and there in his place was Madame Dreyfus, who moments

A characteristic puzzle-portrait of Horace Goldin on a Swedish publicity brochure.

before had been pleading for his safety. Esterhazy dismissed the soldiers, took off his devil's mask and cloak, and there was Goldin.

Goldin died suddenly on 22 August 1939, ironically after an appearance at the Wood Green Empire, the theatre where Chung Ling Soo had been fatally shot twenty-one years before. His career had known many extremes. Once when he received a command to appear before the King of Siam, there was no room in the palace to house his full spectacle and a theatre was specially built in the grounds. During the dark days of the Depression, rather than give himself a very necessary holiday Goldin would transport his whole show to a town like Tonypandy as a treat for the miners, losing money in the process, but no doubt becoming recharged by the additional enthusiasm he felt towards him across the footlights. For all the controversy that surrounded the 'Sawing' illusion, it is hard to believe that at heart Horace Goldin was not a nice man.

'Sim Sala Bim!'

No illusionist succeeded better in portraying the public impression of a storybook wizard than Dante. Indeed 'Sim Sala Bim', the title of his spectacular stage show and the cry with which he would impishly demand audiences to accord him their applause, were nonsense words derived from an early book of nursery rhymes in his native Danish. Fortunately, however, Dante's portrayal was more thorough than his make-up and publicity techniques would suggest. Beneath the veneer presented by his silver hair and Van Dyke beard was a true showman whose immense personal charisma shone like a beacon from his roguish blue eyes. His ability to look the part of a magician was effortless both on and off stage. However, if Dante possessed the authority and bravura that made you believe he really did perform the miracles you saw, he was also able, like Devant before him and Daniels since, to project across the footlights a cosy informality that enabled him to secure a fingertip control over the reactions of his audience. He never failed to meet the expectations raised by his imposing appearance, but only on his own terms as, tongue-in-cheek, he played a cat-and-mouse game with the traditional procedures of magical entertainment. Illusions – however grand – were dismissed as mere 'swindles' and the twinkle in his eye revealed that his glamorous assistants meant more to him than all the magic put together.

The tone was set the moment he ambled on stage. He made it clear right from the start that he was too old to keep running backwards and forwards from the wings to acknowledge applause. Besides, constant bowing was liable to 'bring on rheumatism'! He explained that when the audience responded, he would instead show his appreciation by placing the tips of his fingers together and parting them to express a hundred thanks: 'Sim'. If the applause continued, he would raise his hands to signify a thousand thanks: 'Sala'. If there was still more, he would raise his hands still higher to denote a million thanks: 'Bim'. By the end of the performance the 'Sim Sala Bim' ritual was etched for life on the memory of those fortunate enough to have seen the great man.

The lazy Californian drawl in which he conducted his show belied his actual beginnings. He was born in Copenhagen on 3 October 1883, his real name August Harry Jansen. He was six years old when his parents moved to St Paul, Minnesota and was scarcely out of his teens when he began to tour America with a small magic act. The name Dante was acquired in 1923 at the suggestion of the prominent American illusionist Howard Thurston, who had confidence enough in the younger performer to place him in charge of one of his road companies. He toured with the Thurston unit in the United States for four years, continually frustrated by the need to restrict himself to the lesser towns where his sponsor did not himself appear, until he managed to persuade the older performer that it would be to their mutual financial advantage for Dante to take the show overseas.

No one played the part of the story-book wizard more affectionately than Dante.

This proved the turning point for the international recognition Dante had craved. He was no longer fettered to another man's reputation and gradually the streamlined style for which he became famous began to evolve. If Goldin had injected speed for speed's sake into his presentation, Dante's premise was to capture the pace and appeal of a musical comedy revue, making his own more leisurely presence the hub around which it revolved. Many of his illusions and much of his smaller magic were given production values that would be impossible today outside the major Las Vegas-style entertainment centres, spectacular settings and showgirls galore enhancing the magical effect.

Nowhere was his showmanship seen to better advantage than in his version of one of the oldest tricks in magic, 'The Cords of Phantasia' (sometimes known as 'The Grandmother's Necklace') in which objects tied to and threaded on a pair of ropes fall free when the magician's wand, itself tied to their centre, is withdrawn. The item is one of the oldest and simplest in the conjuring manuals, favoured by aspiring young magicians since the beginning of time. And yet when Dante used it to illustrate his impression of a lazy magician, it became elevated to the status of a masterpiece. Throughout he sat with one leg crossed over the other, his top hat tilted at a rakish angle, every inch the elderly roué. To the lilting strains of Dubin and Herbert's 'Indian Summer', he beckoned on stage two dancers to hold the ropes outstretched between them, then signalled a third, his principal assistant, Moi-yo Miller, to light his cigar. As he tied first his cane and then four handkerchiefs to the cords, one at a time on alternate sides, so the girls were choreographed to glide back and forth, causing the magician the minimum of movement and inconvenience. The handkerchiefs were slid to the centre of the ropes against his fingers. Taking his hat, he bunched them inside, pulling out the cane. The girls tightened the cords and the handkerchiefs fell free in the hat, their knots still intact. Dante, however, had eyes only for Miss Miller, his cigar smoke wafting in her face. Then, gathering the handkerchiefs together, he held them to Moi-yo's waist, pushing his cane against them and presumably right through her, never to be seen again. In this one item magic and music, humour and choreography, with Dante's winsome personality the chief catalyst, all came together to create a magical whole greater than the sum of its parts.

Most of the illusions that have stayed associated with Dante's name embodied a twist that suggested as sure a grasp of comedy as of magic. One of his favourite items took place in a barber's shop. Dante (playing the barber) put on a large grotesque carnival head. One of his assistants (playing the customer) did the same. When, after much by-play involving lather and a giant razor, the heads were removed, the customer had become the barber, while Dante was sitting in the chair. The transposition of people was a favourite motif with Dante. In a starker presentation he would raise all the scenery to reveal a totally bare stage and, in hat and overcoat, though still smoking his big cigar, present the effect as a magician's rehearsal. Now a girl being interviewed for a position as assistant would change places with an established member of his team. In a simpler version still, a coloured boy holding a pole with a black lollipop disc on top and a blonde girl carrying another pole with a similar white disc were wrapped in black and white sheets respectively, with the discs always visible. When the cloths were unrolled, the boy and the girl had changed places.

Dante's wittiest and probably most original presentation was entitled 'Backstage with a Magician'. If its description sounds familiar, that will be because Paul Daniels, endorsing its sheer entertainment value, has seen fit to revive it several times, not least on the occasion of the Royal Gala Performance in aid of the Falklands Appeal in 1982, when Debbie McGee became transformed into Twiggy. No one was more surprised than Roger Moore, specially recruited to receive a lesson in magic on-stage from Paul for the event.

Dante, having produced his own assistant from a simple double-box arrangement, would explain that he was going to take the audience into his confidence and allow them backstage to see how the trick was done. The magician turned his back on the audience in readiness for the repeat performance, running a comb through his hair and twirling the ends of his moustache as an assistant held a mirror in front of him. When the back curtains opened, the actual theatre audience found themselves staring at a

Dante about to make
horse and rider
disappear in mid-air.

backdrop on which was painted a sea of faces, another audience entirely.
Also on the stage were the two boxes, isolated from the floor on a
platform. Behind one secretly crouched a girl. Dante addressed the make-
believe crowd as both boxes were in turn shown to be empty and then one
was placed inside the other. Meanwhile the actual audience could follow
what really happened as the girl crawled from behind one box to the other
and then into the nested boxes through a secret panel in the back. When
she jumped out of the box, however, the tables had been turned. She was
now Dante's Chinese boy assistant. As the magician bowed to his
imaginary audience, a real pair of hands emerged through the backdrop to
join in the applause. So adroit was his presentation that right until the very
last moment audiences were convinced they knew precisely what was
happening.

The Dante show reached its spectacular finale with the maestro's
presentation, often in full mandarin costume, of a traditional Chinese
effect, the 'Water Fountains'. This commenced in low-key fashion, Dante
pouring rice from one bowl to another only for the rice to appear to
double in quantity and then change to water. He poured the water into a
coconut shell from which it gushed forth in a magical stream. When Dante
touched this with his wand, the latter then spurted a mysterious jet of its
own. Whatever he touched with the wand sprang its own spray at the
point of contact. In turn all his assistants received this bizarre baptism,
water spurting from their fans, swords, and shoes, heads, shoulders and

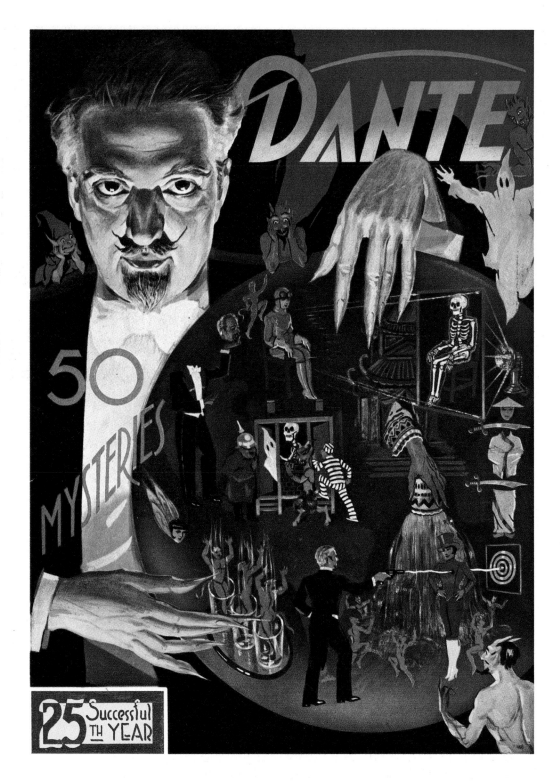

The Silver Jubilee of 'Sim Sala Bim!'

Dante's most spectacular effect – the audience could feel the spray.

fingers. As spouting finger impregnated finger, spraying sword sword, so the water continued on its mysterious, self-propagating course. At the conclusion of the performance the whole stage was a dazzling cascade of fountains with coloured lights playing off the dancing waters.

Dante's full evening magic revue was one of the most travelled theatrical ventures in the world, enjoying long runs in London, Paris, Buenos Aires, New York, Madrid, Tokyo and countless other prestige locations throughout the 1930s and 1940s. The show was the first all-American production to appear in the USSR, Dante taking fifteen curtain calls on his opening night in Moscow, with the audience still shouting for more. His only conceivable competition as an American resident came from Blackstone, but Dante was more than happy with an arrangement that acknowledged the father of today's great American performer as the leading magician in North America. With some justification Dante could look upon himself as the top box-office attraction in magic throughout the world.

As the 1940s came to a close, the great showman slowed down into semi-retirement, spending more and more time at his ranch in Northridge in the San Fernando Valley, where he died of a heart attack on 16 June 1955. A combination of Mephistopheles and Buffalo Bill, with just a dash of Santa Claus, he had, as the *New York Times* proclaimed, provided an echo of a time 'when the world was young and kind'. What better excuse could there be for becoming a magician?

Some Suave Deceivers

It will come as a surprise to his countless followers to realise that one of the earliest acts performed by Paul Daniels, talkative as he is today, was a manipulative magic act done to music without speaking. Featuring both Paul and his former wife Jackie, the act pioneered the use of pop music – in this case the early 1960s style of prominent British group, 'The Shadows' – as accompaniment. Billed with an anagrammatic twist as 'The Eldanis', they jived their way through a succession of magical effects both in unison and individually, sharing the spotlight as magician and magicienne rather than further exploiting the stereotyped image of the magician and his assistant. As they both demonstrated card fanning it became a challenge to audiences to spot the slightest detail out of step between them – from the identical colour patterns on the backs of the cards in their hands to the corresponding body movements danced to the rhythms that gave the act its drive. Individually, Paul would manipulate billiard balls and levitate the traditional silver sphere beneath a cloth; Jackie would conjure with fans and silk handkerchiefs in a magical version of the Cinderella story. Both played an equal part in the climax, which saw a seemingly endless flow of ribbon cascade from a tube considerably too small for the ribbon in the first place. The technicolour fountain continued to gush forth on to the stage as the couple took individual curtain calls. And still it flowed.

Acknowledged enthusiastically by the magical profession at the time, The Eldanis were the latest in a long line of performers combining pantomime, prestidigitation and music within the limited confines of a short act. The vogue began in music hall and vaudeville where managements were often better disposed to offer work to the magician with a concise, original novelty than to the performer with a bulkier, and invariably lengthier illusion show. In this way Birmingham-born Gus Fowler (1888–1960) became the acknowledged 'King of Watches and Clocks' with an act devoted exclusively to time, a motif kept prominent with immense style today by the cheerful Dutch magician Richard Ross. Fowler, who later adopted the billing 'Always Doing Time', produced, vanished and

Gus Fowler,

The Watch King,

"Always doing Time."

Telegrams: "WATCHFUL."

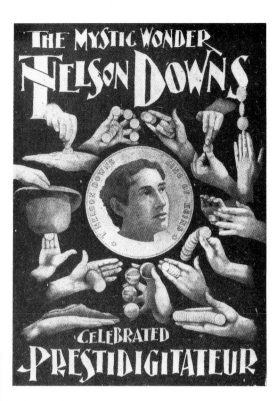

Left, Gus Fowler's visiting cards depicted his speciality. *Above*, T. Nelson Downs made pure sleight-of-hand theatrically acceptable.

transposed both mechanically and by manipulation watches and clocks of every conceivable kind, his act culminating in the production from an empty hat of over thirty alarm clocks, each one ringing and differently tuned.

T. Nelson Downs (1867–1938) brought a similar approach to an act devoted solely to the manipulation of coins. The witty American, also known as 'The King of Koins (sic)', popularised the title 'The Miser's Dream' now used by magicians to describe the continual production of coins from the air, but originally Tommy Downs's description for his whole act of which this sequence was only a part. Many consider Downs to have been the greatest pure sleight-of-hand artist of all time. To make his technique register on the largest of stages, however, required superb pantomime ability and immense showmanship. So accomplished was he with regard to the former that when one night at the Folies Marigny in Paris he forgot to palm a stack of coins prior to producing them individually at his fingertips, he pantomimed the production and received no less applause. As for showmanship, before he did anything on stage he would assume a stance, roll up his sleeves, and tense his fingers before undertaking a single feat of magic. Audiences knew they were about to witness something important.

Today the format is superbly tailored to the demands of the international cabaret circuit. In America Marvyn Roy as 'Mr Electric', following in the footsteps of 'Voltaire', has tailored an exciting act in which light bulbs predominate, while Jeff McBride has taken classical magic themes and blended them dramatically with Kabuki-style masks of every possible expression. This Japanese motif has also been exploited by that country's leading magician Shimada, whose stylised act culminates in the appearance of a long, sinuous fire-breathing dragon. The Hungarian Paul Potassy, with the urbanity of a diplomat, can hold a stage with just six silk handkerchiefs and the knots that invisibly travel back and forth between them. The walking definition of 'suave' on today's nightclub circuit, Potassy, unlike the others, actually talks – fluently in eight languages, on occasion displaying them all for the same cosmopolitan audience.

The leading exponent of the specialist manipulative act today is the Wisconsin-born magician Norm Nielsen, whose exquisite talent has been given a very special welcome on 'The Paul Daniels Magic Show'. Taking as his theme 'Musical Magic', this warm, engaging performer weaves a very special spell of wonder as first a flute disintegrates into silver dust the moment it touches his lips. Coins appear mysteriously at his fingertips, to be dropped melodically upon what resembles a vertical xylophone, down which they tinkle with a distinctive melody of their own, faster and faster until his hands are overflowing. The whole sequence has that Cartier stamp of dazzle and class. Nielsen's speciality, however, is his floating violin, rightly considered to be one of the most beautiful illusions in magic. The instrument takes on a bewitching life of its own as it soars, spins, and plays hide-and-seek behind a silk scarf in Nielsen's hands. Balanced precariously across the strings, the bow moves tantalisingly to and fro to produce its own special music. When the bow is taken away, the strings play hauntingly of their own accord. In a last attempt to tame the instrument, the magician throws the scarf high into the air. In less than a second, the violin literally melts away. Nielsen walks forward to acknowledge his applause; from the wings the violin enters at ground level and makes its way to his side. As Nielsen takes his bow, the violin dips the head of its fingerboard as its own cheeky mark of respect. Seldom has a magician endowed a supposedly inanimate object with such telling personality.

Nielsen's casual approach is in perfect contrast to the more formal attitude of his predecessor as the acknowledged master of this kind of speciality magic act. Channing Pollock, who made his impact in the 1950s, has now retired as a full-time performer of magic, although his interest in the art is unabated, as shown by his continual presence at magicians'

Norm Nielsen and co-star – a violin with a life of its own.

conventions where he is more than content to sit back and allow his colleagues to entertain him. To gauge the impact he made on the theatrical scene, one has to acknowledge that other magicians *had* produced doves ahead of him, most notably the Mexican Cantu in the 1940s. However, from the moment you saw Pollock perform this classic feat of magic it was as if no one had gone before. He made the motif of the dove his own and suffered more imitators than any other magician. Not that it is fair or accurate to talk of Pollock simply producing doves. He did more than that. He sculpted the air between his sinuous fingers and they appeared. His artistry was enhanced by a film-star arrogance redeemed by the merest shadow of a smile that clung subtly to his lips. No performer invested the birds, or even the playing cards and vivid red silk handkerchiefs which also featured in his manipulation, with a greater sense of mysticism. Like Paul Daniels, but in a totally different way, he made audiences care, engaging them emotionally at a level beyond mere puzzledom. Today his spiritual heir, the young American card and dove manipulator, Lance Burton, does the same and manages brilliantly to redefine Pollock's aristocratic aloofness within the context of contemporary rock culture.

Although Pollock is himself an American, his most memorable platform came to be the stage of the London Palladium, where twenty years previously the third in a special trinity of manipulative showmen achieved one of the greatest triumphs of his own career. Both Pollock and Nielsen would today acknowledge that the example set by the legendary Cardini, in technique, in suavity and in career achievement, shone the light for them. It is probable that Cardini has still not been surpassed as both an entertaining and an artistic exponent of pure sleight-of-hand within the limitations of a short vaudeville act.

There could be no greater contrast between the level of sophistication which Cardini's act came to epitomise and his early background. He was born Richard Valentine Pitchford on 24 December, probably in 1895, in Mumbles, a small fishing village close to Swansea in South Wales. The exact year is difficult to determine since Cardini, no doubt prompted by vanity, claimed several during his lifetime. His one link with show business was a father who played fiddle in the local variety theatre, but by the time he was five his ever-bickering parents had separated. His mother opened theatrical lodgings in Treharris, but before long the young Richard, now nine years old and desperate for the attention he could not find at home, ran away on a picaresque adventure that embraced spells as a butcher's apprentice, a page boy in a Cardiff hotel, and an exhibition billiards or pool player. His contact with the card-sharpers who also frequented the billiards hall reawakened an interest in magic and manipulation dormant since the days when, while very young, he had watched the impromptu tricks of the magicians who stayed at his mother's boarding house.

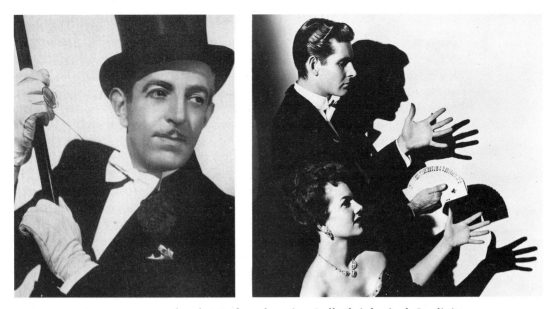

Left, Cardini, the epitome of style. *Right*, Channing Pollock inherited Cardini's crown.

On the outbreak of the First World War he joined the King's Shropshire Light Infantry under Lord Kitchener. Soldiers were allowed to carry a pack of cards on their person and the challenge they presented kept Cardini this side of sanity. In the trenches the weather was so excruciatingly cold it was impossible to manipulate the cards at all without gloves. So he practised with them on and laid the groundwork for the exquisite skill and sensitivity that would come to inform his act in later years. Indeed, in 1916, having recovered consciousness after being invalided during the second battle of the Somme, he found that he could not perform his sleight-of-hand without the gloves. In later years they would become as much a part of his total image as his top hat, cape and monocle. Another quirk of wartime fate led to one other development in card technique. In the extreme conditions of the trenches his cards inevitably became sticky and dog-eared, and it proved impossible for Cardini to emulate a feat attributed by some to Houdini – the ability to produce one at a time a whole pack of cards skilfully concealed behind the fingers, a technique known among magicians as the back palm. Cardini could manage to produce the cards only in bunches or small fans. Today, when magicians do the same intentionally, we should not forget the straitened circumstances in which Cardini, by default, pioneered the technique.

If Paul Daniels's participation in the act of 'The Eldanis' now seems an unusual step along the path to success, Cardini's own progress in that direction contains its surprises too. Turning to magic as a career on the cessation of hostilities, Pitchford changed his name several times before finding the label that became synonymous with his style. His first experience on a stage, in an army concert party, was as Madame Juliet, the transvestite receiving-end of a second-sight act! Once demobbed he became variously Val Raymond, Professor Thomas and Valentine, until around 1923 an Australian booker suggested, 'Get a name like Houdini.' 'Why not Cardini?' asked Pitchford. It was as simple as that, although the act that would become immortalised with the name in years to come still had to find itself. Touring Australia he found it was the custom for a management to hold over an act for as many weeks as the performer could vary his presentation. So for the first week he performed with cards and billiard balls; the second, cigarettes and silk scarves; the third, rabbits and flags; the fourth, liquids; the fifth, thimbles and fire. The digital dexterity was present throughout, but he still persisted in being a talking magician upon whose lips jokey asides like 'there is nothing in my hand except my fingers' clung uneasily.

In 1926 he arrived in the United States and by March of the following year was playing New York's prestigious Palace Theatre. Cardini was a success, but he wasn't satisfied. He placed himself under the guidance of a professional director, and when he was re-booked at the Palace the following December the results showed, as the reviewer of *Billboard* made clear: 'In two seasons Cardini has improved his act many times over. From a fumbling, faltering lad using a fair line of chatter he emerges on this ace-house date as a finished product of the magician's art.' Billed as 'The Suave Deceiver', Cardini had now put his patter days behind him. In October 1930 he was reviewed at the Palace once again: 'Cardini is grace and suavity personified . . . when he took the bows one might have thought by the clamour that Al Jolson had paid the house another visit.'

The characterisation that Cardini developed for his act was as memorable and as important as the manipulative skill. Teetering on stage in full formal attire to the tentative, lazy strains of 'Three O'Clock in the Morning', every inch of his body contributed to the portrayal of an ever so slightly tipsy English reveller plagued by hallucinations on his way home from a night on the town. Audiences first saw him trying to focus his attention on a newspaper. From the opposite side of the stage came a page boy – played unobtrusively throughout his career by his wife Swan – shouting the only words spoken during the entire act, 'Paging Mr Cardini! Paging Mr Cardini!' Tipsy as he is, he is glad for the boy to take the paper from him, only to find a moment later that a fan of cards has appeared at his gloved fingertips in its place. Exasperated, he throws them away into the newspaper now held by the boy as a tray, only for another fan to appear, and another. He is as bewildered as the audience by the seemingly wayward independence of the objects around him. Unsteadily he attempts to insert a cigarette into the holder clenched between his teeth. After considerable effort he succeeds, only for the cigarette to vanish and then reappear back in the holder. The holder is too much trouble and is discarded. Then a lighted match appears in his hand. He lights the cigarette, puffs it, throws it away. The lit cigarette comes back to his fingertips or between his lips, and again, and again, and again. By now the monocle has dropped from his eye in amazement, only for a lighted cigar to present itself. As he walks towards the wings the cigarettes still persist, until a large, smoking meerschaum pipe cues his final curtain. Along the way his buttonhole has spun around in his lapel, a knotted handkerchief has untied itself, billiard balls have appeared and changed colour. But the most important thing of all is that everything that has occurrred has been part of an invisible conspiracy against the performer.

A priceless moment of comedy occurred when Cardini went to adjust his monocle. Blowing smoke at it in the process, he could not fathom how the smoke went through the lens. At moments like this, no eyebrow had ever been raised to more telling effect. He was such a master of pantomime that he could register the slightest movement of this kind in the largest of theatres. He played Radio City Music Hall, one of the largest theatres in the world with 6,000 seats, on at least six separate occasions. Happily he would boast that to do so he needed only a pack of cards, a few cigarettes and a billiard ball or two. In point of fact his props must have been invisible to at least half the people there, but the aura surrounding him compensated.

Audiences became won over by the 'Sorcerer's Apprentice'-style whimsy of his scenario, the wit and sophistication of his characterisation, and the technical originality of Cardini's manipulative skill. To purists he was not, in fact, the first performer to manipulate cards with gloves on: an ambidextrous British magician called Paul Freeman had established that claim as early as 1913 when producing five cards singly using the back and front palm. Likewise Cardini was not the first magician to perform with lighted cigarettes: the continuous production of such objects had been introduced to vaudeville by the Spaniard José Florences Gili around 1915, as well as made into a feature by his descendant, the Spanish magician Frakson, billed as 'The Man with 1,000 Cigarettes' and a contemporary of Cardini. Cardini's achievement, however, transcended that of his rivals. By placing his rare skills in a dramatic context, he was able to raise them above the basic level of the showing-off process. Few would dispute that by so doing he made them his own. The point to remember is that with Cardini there was never any suggestion of *manipulation*. Objects just materialised or dissolved to his total dismay. He died on 11 November 1973, at his home on Long Island, New York. In his lifetime he had received virtually every accolade a magician could have achieved, performing for presidents and kings, and being generally acknowledged among his peers as the standard by which perfection in his kind of magic should be set. He was quite simply the Fred Astaire of sleight-of-hand.

12

The Menagerie of Magic

Animals and birds have played a popular part in the activities of the magician from the earliest of times. The first known recorded detail of a professional magic performance is contained in the Westcar Papyrus kept in the State Museum of East Berlin. The document itself, the work of an Egyptian antiquarian, is over 3,500 years old; the events it records go back to about 4000 BC. At that time in Memphis at the court of King Cheops, the builder of the Great Pyramid, a wonder-worker by the name of Dedi was challenged to restore a severed head. The monarch was anxious to supply the magician with a prisoner condemned to execution, but Dedi diplomatically declined, insisting that the performance could take place as effectively and less sinfully with a bird. A goose was brought. Dedi cut off its head. He placed the body on one side of the court and the head on the other. Even then magicians uttered magic words, upon which 'the goose began to hop forward, the head moved on to it, and when both were united the goose began to cackle'. So great was the applause that Dedi was persuaded to repeat the miracle, first with a pelican, and then again with an ox, on both occasions with equally telling results! He returned home laden with royal favours.

The first British magician of whom any precise record has been handed down is Brandon, the principal 'juggler' at the court of Henry VIII. The Shrewsbury Corporation Accounts for the years 1521 and 1535 show payments to him, as do the accounts of Thetford Priory for unspecified years. To learn about his performing skills one must turn to Reginald Scot's *The Discoverie of Witchcraft*, published in 1584 to combat the witch-hunting craze and the first book in the English language to give a detailed explanation of how to perform conjuring tricks. The trick with which Brandon would impress at a later court, possibly Hampton Court no less, again featured a bird, but in a less direct, almost surreal fashion. In the King's presence, Brandon drew the crude outline of a bird on a wall. He then pointed to a pigeon sitting on a rooftop in the distance. Taking a dagger, he uttered the words, 'Lo now your grace shall see what a juggler can doo, if he be craftes maister', and stabbed repeatedly at the effigy.

A 1595 engraving of Banks and his wonderful horse, Morocco.

After a while the three-dimensional bird fell down 'starke dead'. Brandon's reward was less material than that accorded Dedi – survival at the hands of a paranoid King on the understanding that he never perform the feat again, 'lest he should emploie it in anie other kind of murther'.

The most famous animal in the history of magic is probably the learned horse, Morocco, or Maroccus, celebrated enough to be referred to by both Shakespeare in *Love's Labour's Lost* and Sir Walter Raleigh in his *History of the World*. Exhibited by a showman named Banks, Morocco was a white steed which could, by stamping its hoof, announce the total number of spots on a pair of dice, the amount of change in a spectator's pocket, or the age of anyone who whispered it to the master. For good measure the horse could also dance to music, tell fortunes, return a glove to its owner, and discover a chosen card. The act left England to tour Europe in 1608. When they performed in France, Morocco, confronted with foreign currency for the first time, had no difficulty in denoting the correct rate of exchange. In Orléans, however, Banks was summoned before the local church council on the charge of possessing an animal in league with the devil: when the horse was brought forward, it sought out a crucifix in the crowd and went down on its knees in front of the cross. Both man and beast were acquitted on the grounds that no devil would come near the cross in this way. It is possible that they were less fortunate in Rome, where one account says they were burned alive by decree of the Pope on similar charges, although there are references to a Banks who 'taught his horse to dance and shooed him with silver' in England in 1637.

Fortunately nothing so drastic befell Paul Daniels when more than three centuries later he re-created Morocco's act with Goldy, the magnificent steed belonging to Joan Rosaire of the famous circus family. A modern audience was still intrigued as the horse performed simple feats of mental arithmetic, discovered a chosen card, and even conducted the band. Indeed only half a century ago, Dr Joseph Banks Rhine, the prominent American investigator into psychic matters, had conducted an inquiry into a three-year-old filly, Lady Wonder, with similar powers. He came to the conclusion that Lady had to have telepathic powers of some kind. Neither Goldy nor Morocco (nor Lady Wonder for that matter) was telepathic at all, but Banks, like Paul Daniels, was an exceptionally adept deceiver.

No animals have appeared more successfully with Paul than chimpanzees. In a hilarious sequence on the television show that was awarded the prestigious Golden Rose of Montreux Award in 1985, Paul discovered the true meaning of the advice which says that actors should not share the stage with animals. The participation of chimpanzees was inspired by the memory of another television show in which the great American comedian Jack Benny featured the act of Gene Detroy and the Marquis chimps, a top animal act in Las Vegas during the 1950s and 1960s. Benny, as self-

The most magical moment of Paul's television career.

OWEN CLARK'S
LATEST INVENTIONS.

Left, Owen Clark, the first to involve a chimpanzee in a magic act. *Right*, John Henry Anderson, the Wizard of the North, Scotland's greatest magician.

effacing as ever in T-shirt and diapers, actually played the part of a chimp himself, needless to say the one ignored by the others. Conjuring, however, could obviously present a different challenge altogether to such intelligent creatures. The idea of Paul giving a lesson in magic to William and Jambo, two untrained baby chimpanzees from Twycross Zoo, was instantly appealing. As one wrestled mentally with the riddle presented by a mirror concealed in the base of an empty box – could he really have a twin he had not met before? – the other, shocked by the sudden appearance of a whole family of spring snakes, found in Paul's arms a comforting if surprised welcome that conceivably produced the most appealing television moment of the year. Research for this book, however, has proved that nothing is new in magic. At the height of the Houdini craze, Owen Clark (d. 1929), a stalwart of many bills presented by the Maskelyne organisation, conceived the novel idea of an act in which a chimpanzee escaped from a box. The act had a short life, no doubt due to the refusal on one occasion of 'Betty', the animal in question, to escape, until its lady trainer, obviously undressed for the stage, rushed on in full view of the audience to coax the creature out. Successful as the idea of chimpanzees with magic proved, it was not new at all.

The animal most readily associated with the performance of conjuring is, of course, the rabbit. So common today is the image of a magician pulling this small, furry creature out of a top hat that one overlooks the anachronism of an item of apparel which a hundred years ago could easily

FAWKES,
(Slight of Hand-man.)

MARY TOFTS,
(The Pretended Rabbit Breeder.)

be borrowed from a gentleman in the audience. The trick is the most famous in magic, but the precise moment when a live bunny first made its theatrical entry in this way is clouded in obscurity and controversy. There has long been imagined a link with the bizarre case of Mary Tofts, a housewife from Godalming in Surrey who towards the end of 1726 claimed that whil̶e̶ ̶w̶a̶lking home through the woods she had been assaulted by a h̶a̶r̶e̶ ̶a̶n̶d̶ ̶a̶ ̶rabbit. Her husband Joshua initially dismissed her tale as a h̶a̶l̶l̶u̶c̶i̶n̶ation, but had to revise his opinion when over the next few weeks M̶a̶ry was delivered of a succession of small white rabbits. The news spread like wildfire. So intrigued was the country at large that George I himself sent medical representatives to investigate. After consultation with Tofts's local physician, John Howard, confirmation was sent to court that the births had indeed taken place. Others remained sceptical, however, and when Tofts announced her next pregnancy she was removed for stricter supervision to a London bagnio where, when threatened with a dangerous operation, she was ultimately unveiled as a common fraud. Numerous poems and prints were published depicting the affair, and it has been suggested that a magician then performing in London jumped on this early satirical bandwagon by billboarding a new illusion, 'The Birth of a Rabbit', the trick under discussion.

The noted magical historian Professor Edwin A. Dawes, however, has recently pointed out that the customary headgear in London in 1726 was the tricorne hat, a most inconvenient shape when compared with the capacious topper. No record has come down to us of the name of the

Even Paul could not resist producing a rabbit i̇

magician in question if the trick was actually performed. At that time the most prominent magical celebrity in London was Isaac Fawkes (d. 1731), possibly the greatest of the fairground showmen who popularised the egg and bag trick and received considerable media attention. Had he produced the rabbit, records – if only newspaper advertisements – would exist to prove that fact. Certainly, as Dawes states, if an unknown had beaten him to it Fawkes would have latched on to the sensation somehow. Ironically there is no actual documentation of a rabbit being produced from a hat until well into the nineteenth century, over 100 years later, when the iconography with which we are now so familiar first began to materialise. At around this time posters of John Henry Anderson (1814–74), the 'Wizard of the North', once described by Houdini as 'the greatest advertiser in the history of magic', depict the illusion. Since Anderson never had qualms about duplicating the best feats of his rivals, we shall never know whether he was the first to perform what has become magic's trademark trick.

Apart from the obvious appeal of the cuddly bunny, why the trick should have become such a pervasive trademark is itself a mystery. It would not appear to have been so popular with magicians themselves, fraught with inconvenience and requiring great skill to accomplish properly. The moment the audience sees the empty top hat in the conjuror's hands, something says that the end result will be a rabbit. If the assumption is correct, the difficulty facing the magician in secretly loading the creature is increased; if incorrect, the likelihood of disappointment is almost certain. Paul Daniels has skilfully skirted around these problems by teasing his audience with the presence of an obviously unreal, but still cheeky, puppet rabbit. When, apparently unbeknown to Paul, the front of his tablecloth falls down, it is no secret that his hand must go through a hole in both hat and tabletop to secure the creature. When Paul slides the hat across the table, the rabbit darts across of its own accord in the opposite direction. It is never where Paul requires it to be. A game of magical hide-and-seek ensues in which the rabbit finally makes its getaway in a toy car. When Paul next surveys the top hat in his arms, a real live bunny has appeared. Whatever its origins, there can be no doubt that Paul Daniels has brought the trick up to date for modern audiences, while still retaining all its original wonder and charm.

The Magical Farmyard

One of the most spectacular of all magical sequences involving the use of animals did not feature a single wild zoological specimen. The clue to its appeal is instantly apparent from its title, 'The Magical Farmyard'. It was the brainchild of one of magic's most ingenious performers and inventors, Jean Henri Servais Le Roy, the son of a Belgian hotelier and a British mother, who was born in Spa, Belgium on 2 May 1865. As a boy he ran away to England, where a friend of the family which adopted him so impressed him with a display of sleight-of-hand that the young Le Roy soon became an accomplished exponent of the 'Cups and Balls'. His greatest impact as a performer would not register, however, until in partnership with two colleagues he formed the act of Le Roy, Talma and Bosco, known throughout show business at the turn of the century variously as 'The Monarchs of Magic' and 'The Comedians of Mephisto'.

Le Roy first met Talma during an engagement at London's Royal Aquarium where she played the part of assistant in the act of a lady mind-reader and snake-charmer. Her real name was Mary Ann Ford, but in 1890 she became Mrs Servais Le Roy. Her husband soon spotted her natural aptitude for magic and began to coach her in coin manipulation. A lady of startling beauty, she lost no time in becoming a successful solo act, answering to the full billing of 'Mercedes Talma, the Queen of Coins'. There was no mistaking her presence on stage where, sheathed in a stunning black gown against a plush crimson backdrop with a single red rose in her hair, she made coin after coin materialise at her pretty fingertips. In their combination act the sleight-of-hand contribution devolved upon her, leaving Le Roy free to devote more time to the invention and presentation of large-scale stage illusions.

If Le Roy was happy for his wife to take the accolades for manipulative skill, he was equally content that the laughter, which he saw as an integral part of any total entertainment package, should be directed at Bosco. The full name of the original Bosco was Leon Bosco, a knockabout comedy performer discovered by Le Roy on the British music halls, whose lumbering, fumbling style was particularly appropriate to the presentation of burlesque magic. Over the years, however, Leon would be replaced by a succession of other performers, while the name of Bosco and his basic comedic appearance would remain constant: such was the investment Le Roy had in full-colour illustrated publicity posters! The most distinguished of all the Boscos was Dr James William Elliott, a pioneer of much that is now standard practice in card manipulation. To emulate the total effect of his predecessors this relatively slender former physician had not only to pad his stomach, but also to grow a full beard and shave the top of his head.

As an inventor Le Roy was a pioneer in both effect and technique. His earliest significant contribution to large-scale sorcery was an illusion known as 'The Three Graces' in which, standing within an obviously

'The Comedians of Mephisto.'

The act the stagehands dreaded.

empty open-fronted cabinet of wardrobe size, he held up one after the other three large cloths. Each time a mysterious form materialised beneath the cloth and hopped forward in a crouching position to the front of the stage. When he shouted 'Appear', the shapes cast their cloths aside and stood revealed as 'The Three Graces' of Greek mythology. In time Le Roy devised an even more effective presentation of the same illusion. At its conclusion only the two outer forms stood up to reveal themselves as beautiful young girls; when the centre shape rose, it turned out to be none other than Le Roy himself.

In 'The Flying Visit' Le Roy conjured with his own body at even greater speed, using for the first time a principle which has been much abused by many lesser performers. On the stage were set two small cabinets with curtained fronts, one on short legs at floor level, the other raised to such a height on veritable stilts that it would be impossible to reach it secretly without the aid of a ladder. Both cabinets were shown to be empty and their curtains drawn. Le Roy, costumed for the occasion in a scarlet skull-cap which gave him a true Mephistophelean appearance, entered the lower cabinet, disappearing from sight behind the curtain. Instantly a girl would appear in his place, calling out, 'Where are you?' 'I am here' came the reply as Le Roy appeared out of the taller box. Le Roy ducked out of sight as the girl went to pull back the top curtain, only to discover that the magician

Opposite, Servais Le Roy's flair for transposition was demonstrated not once, but twice in this illusion.

had dissolved again. 'Where are you now?' she cried. 'I am here!' shouted Le Roy as he came racing down the aisle of the theatre.

His most famous invention involved, as with Maskelyne before him, a completely new approach to the problem of levitation. Le Roy's innovation was that at the point in the illusion when there was nothing further to achieve but to cause the floating lady (in his version covered by a flimsy white silk sheet) to come back to earth again, he simply pulled on the cloth, causing her to disappear in full view of the audience. When he first presented it at the Empire Theatre, Johannesburg in 1905 he had grave misgivings regarding its ability to be a success, doubtless needing to convince himself that the eventual vanish did not negate the very floating effect that preceded it. To cover his insecurity he had Leon Bosco standing in the wings ready to dash on stage to make a funny fall with a tray of crockery in order to divert attention away from the illusion if it failed to be taken seriously by the audience. The device was not required, but Le Roy did not present the effect again until he played London's Alhambra Theatre six weeks later, when the manager of the theatre actually came on stage after the act to compliment Le Roy on what he described as the greatest illusion ever. The press endorsed this, describing the miracle as 'a new and positively electric effect'.

Over the years 'Asrah', as the levitation became known, has been adopted by many magicians with varying degrees of success. Few have added any touches of originality to it: Paul Daniels is one of those few. In his version, presented in his current theatre show within a futuristic space scene, Paul himself is levitated under the piercing gaze of a masked Darth Vader-style clone. When the sheet is pulled away he too has disintegrated. Many might expect Daniels himself to come rushing down the theatre aisle at that point, but the denouement with his subsequent reappearance is far more startling, more impossible than that. To reveal it here, however, would be to spoil the enjoyment and excitement for those still with the treat in store of seeing the spectacle for themselves.

As clever and baffling as these individual creations within the Le Roy repertoire were, it is doubtful if for sheer entertainment value they rivalled 'The Magical Farmyard' presentation, which itself was the inspiration for the hilarious, if more specific, vanish and reappearance of ducks featured by Paul Daniels on his television show. The humour of the Le Roy sequence was as basic as the general effect was rumbustious.

'Permit me,' he would begin, 'to introduce my partners, Mademoiselle Talma and Herr Bosco, *without any hair.*'

'That's not right,' chided the gruff fat man, 'this is my *hare*', upon which he reached into an empty opera hat to produce not a hare, but a rabbit. Handing the hat to Talma, he challenged her with a boisterous, 'Let's see what you can do.' Not to be outdone she produced a white pigeon, before passing the hat to Le Roy.

'What would you like?' he asked, 'black or white?' If black was chosen, so he produced a pigeon of that colour, only to follow with, 'Had you asked for white, I have a white one here too.' It was now time for Bosco to interrupt.

'Hi – look here!' he shouted. Having been quietly stroking his rabbit one moment, he now (with a rapid movement of his hand) apparently split the pet in two so that he was left with one kicking vigorously in each hand.

'And now,' announced Le Roy with calm understatement, 'we will commence to *do* something.'

Bosco's most memorable illusion within the sequence involved supposedly twisting the heads off two ducks, one black and one white. He put a body in each of two boxes, and then a head also. In due course when the ducks were shown to be restored, the white duck waddled forth with a black head and the black duck with a white head. In later times he would perform the same effect with a duck and a rooster with even more hilarious results. Le Roy was so protective of this trick that while he allowed the great American illusionist Howard Thurston the rights to perform a version of it – as he explained, more as a personal favour than as a business transaction – he stood his ground in refusing those rights to extend to the young Dante, then being groomed as Thurston's successor. So valuable was the laughter and surprise it caused in the Le Roy show.

Even more controversy would surround the incredible vanish of livestock, the centre-piece of Paul Daniels's own routine, known among magicians as 'Where Do the Ducks Go?'. This particular item is one of the most foolproof optical deceptions in all of magic. Le Roy introduced a patter story involving a thief in a poultry yard as he placed two ducks, in the company of a rooster, a rabbit and a pigeon, into a simple box affair. A flash suddenly leapt forth from within the box which was then quickly taken to pieces, each piece being placed flat one upon the other. There was nowhere a humming-bird, let alone a duck, could have been concealed. Le Roy always claimed the trick as his invention and there is no reason to doubt this, despite the rival claims of his contemporary W. J. Nixon, better known as 'Doc', who travelled with a show entitled 'Hong Kong Mysteries', and almost certainly did invent the title by which the trick became known. When Nixon claimed the effect for his own in *Billboard* magazine, Le Roy got the National Vaudeville Managers' Association to take up the matter on his behalf. They proved that Le Roy's claims could be substantiated and that Nixon was suffering from a well-known disease 'Ducksoophitis'! Le Roy's ingenuity also extended to a method whereby ducks might return. He himself considered his 'Duck Tub' one of the most perfect deceptions he ever originated. This was in effect an old-fashioned and obviously empty wash-tub which he and Bosco built up on stage between them, first the slender base, then the metal sides. The completed tub was filled with twelve buckets of water. At the shot of a pistol the surface was suddenly full of ducks swimming to and fro.

These detailed descriptions do little to convey the sheer pace of the act.

Ducks placed in newspapers disappeared. Others placed in cages vanished when flags were waved over them. Poultry flew from supposedly empty stew-pans, more than they could ever have contained had the birds stayed in their shells. A larger shallow paper-covered drum yielded an avalanche of flags and more livestock still. From the flags themselves flew ducks and chickens, pigeons and geese. Then Bosco produced another goose, but this one was plucked. The whole stage was a flurry of feathers, as the proscenium arch became transformed into a squawking, flapping, quacking barnyard of a spectacle. Much excitement also came from the odd creature escaping into the auditorium, in spite of a special wire fence raised between audience and stage. The laughter of the crowd vied for volume with the cacophony produced by the cackling and crowing. Stagehands who had to clear the stage afterwards loathed the act as much as the public loved it. At the finish, when a long line of quacking ducks waddled into the wings – only to return in line to acknowledge the audience's applause as the curtain fell on Le Roy, Talma and Bosco, each brandishing a gigantic flag on a staff at least twelve feet long – there could be no doubt that those fortunate enough to have seen this great act would never forget it. And never would they look on a hen or a duck again without a smile coming to their lips, or a wrinkle of bafflement to their brow.

Le Roy eventually settled in the United States where in 1930 his professional performing career came to an end when he was struck by a car near his home in Keansburg, New Jersey. He recovered sufficiently to make a single comeback performance in 1940 for a special audience, principally of magicians and their friends, at the Hecksher Theatre in New York. In spite of the standing ovation that greeted the great artist when he first walked out on stage, it was as if he had forgotten everything that the combined years of apprenticeship and stardom had taught him. His hands trembled, props were dropped, assistants mis-cued. The following day he set about destroying the equipment and impedimenta acquired from a lifetime in magic. Four years later Talma died, although a straitened Le Roy, dejected as he was, would endure until 2 June 1953 – a tragic end totally inconsistent with the glamour and gaiety of his achievement as a magician of distinction.

Conjuring at the House of Commons

In one of the most deceptive tricks ever involving livestock, a cage containing a canary, without cover of any kind, literally dissolves in the hands of the magician. The trick is one of the most visually impossible in the whole world of magic. When recorded in recent years for television, it has defied the searching scrutiny of the most persistent stop-frame video fanatic: in one frame it is there, in the next it has gone. Of all the tricks it is possible to perform, it sets a test for baffling durability that is hard to beat.

Le Roy used moments of low comedy to enhance his more dramatic sensations.

It was introduced in 1873 by the innovative French magician Buatier de Kolta and in time would become a prominent feature in the act of the portly, bewhiskered Charles Bertram, the most successful of London's society entertainers in the latter half of Victoria's reign and the then Prince of Wales's favourite performer. But the magician who achieved the widest impact with the effect was an American, Carl Hertz, noted as much for the overgrown schoolboyishness of his showmanship as for any great technical ability. Early in his career he played a season in Melbourne, Australia, to promote which he placed an advertisement in a local newspaper: 'Wanted 1,000 cats of all descriptions. Apply at Stage Door, Opera House, with cats, at 9 a.m. One shilling or a free seat for the evening performance will be given for each cat.' The following day children crowded round the theatre with their own pets and any strays they could find. Hertz showed no discrimination as he attached a paper collar to each feline neck. On each neckband was the message, 'See Carl Hertz at the Opera House tonight.' The cats ran all over town advertising his show and Hertz played to capacity for six whole weeks.

Born in San Francisco on 14 May 1859, his real name Louis (or Leib) Morgenstern, he would undergo the most exacting performance of his career far from home in London when he became, to one's knowledge, the only magician in history to perform a conventional conjuring trick before a Select Committee in the House of Commons. At the time attempts were being made to pass a Bill through Parliament that would restrict the appearance of animals in public performances. Inevitably propaganda was to lash out against certain performers as the Bill gained momentum, with Hertz foremost in the accusers' line of fire. Officials of the RSPCA claimed, maybe with some justification, that the canaries used in his performance of the trick were maimed and killed. Before and since, imitation birds have been used to no less effect, but Hertz's flair for sensation refused to take the additional life out of such a stunning illusion.

The Committee was formed and Hertz went on the defensive, claiming that he had used the same birds for years and, out of the sheer bravado that comes as second nature to self-publicists, defying anyone to prove injury to the birds. Nervous as he was on the day, nothing was to prevent the magician on trial once more becoming the suave showman of past renown. The cage was there and, as his hands moved outwards, was there no longer, whereupon Hertz retired briefly and came back with the canary unharmed. The *Daily Express* account of the incident on 3 August 1921 is worth quoting:

A lively canary entertained the Select Committee on Performing Animals at the House of Commons yesterday. The canary's name is 'Connie', and she disappears four times a day, explained Mr Carl Hertz, who is the canary's owner. He had brought 'Connie' (in answer to a hundred-pound challenge by an earlier witness, Mr Haverley, formerly

Left, Carl Hertz and canary. *Right*, Hertz successfully met the challenge.

a theatrical manager), to disprove before the Committee the allegation that he killed a bird each time he made it disappear together with the cage. Mr Hertz placed 'Connie' on the centre table and asked members to mark it, so that there should be no deception. 'That is not necessary,' said Mr James O'Grady, MP. 'I know something about birds. Let me examine it, and I shall recognise it again.' Mr F. O. Roberts, MP, removed the canary and placed it in the cage. 'One! Two! Three!' cried Mr Hertz, and suddenly threw up his hands. Sir John Butcher was startled and half-rose from his seat, and meanwhile both 'Connie' and her cage had vanished. Mr Hertz took off his coat, retired a moment, and reappeared two seconds later holding the bird, which chirped happily, and everybody was satisfied that it was indeed 'Connie'.

'I do not want Mr Haverley's hundred pounds,' said Mr Hertz in evidence; 'I am glad to do the trick for nothing, in order to refute one of the wild charges made by an earlier witness. The statement that I kill a canary at each performance is absurd on the face of it; I have had this bird for twelve months, and some of my earlier birds have remained with me for six years.'

Mr Carl Hertz's performance is unique, as it is the first time in the annals of history that a conjuring performance has ever been given within the Houses of Parliament.

Hertz had correctly sensed that parliamentary committees could be as gullible in matters magical as scientific ones are in the investigation of the so-called paranormal. Even so it seems incredible that no one would insist upon searching the performer immediately after the dematerialisation of the cage, and that Hertz got away with what was probably a straightforward substitution of a similar bird. At the end of the episode, however, the one indisputable fact was the publicity Hertz collected in its wake. Soon after the event his visiting cards carried the message, '£50 if Carl Hertz got the bird'. Hertz's career, flagging until that point, enjoyed an Indian summer until his death in March 1924.

Today the trick still thrives in the hands of Harry Blackstone, using a presentation inherited from his equally successful father and namesake. He in turn had been inspired by a little-known conjuror called Del Adelphia, 'The Cowboy Magician'. This 'Billy the Kid' of a wizard would vanish the cage along the lines attributed to the other performers, then pronounce to the crowd, 'I will now get another canary and another cage and do the trick again.' When he returned to the stage, he did just that. Blackstone, however, would invite members of the audience to crowd around on the stage for the second vanish, permitting the volunteers to touch the cage with their own hands. With equal speed the vanish re-occurred, those close at hand as dumbfounded as anyone else in the audience. To witness today's Blackstone perform this presentation with an on-stage committee made up exclusively of children is to witness one of the most charming moments available in contemporary popular theatre.

A Magician's Best Friend

No performing animal has ever been held in higher esteem by its master than the dog Beauty, a gift from Houdini to fellow master showman Lafayette when they were both playing Nashville, Tennessee, at a lowly stage of their respective careers. So fanatical was the owner's affection for the animal that at his London home at 55 Tavistock Square guests were greeted by a plaque that proclaimed, 'The more I see of men, the more I love my dog', and a notice to the effect, 'You may drink my wine; you may eat my food; you may command my servants; but you *must* respect my dog.' A bachelor all his life, Lafayette ensured that Beauty's own suite (complete with miniature sofa and porcelain bathtub) was set aside within the house, as well as insisting that in all hotel reservations on tour the dog must have her own accommodation. A roll-call of the more prestigious hotels at which they stayed was engraved on her special silver and leather

Lafayette arrives in style with his beloved Beauty.

collar. When guests were entertained, Beauty was served a full-course meal at table in advance of the dismayed onlookers. She even had her own compartment in the private train in which her master travelled across the United States. While the dog was of uncertain origin, Lafayette ensured that an appropriate pedigree was invented, claiming that the mongrel was a rare *gheckhund* from the island of Gheck in the Azores. No animal ever had a more eccentric iconography lavished upon it. Beauty's image extended from the radiator mascot on Lafayette's limousine to his Credit Lyonnais cheques which carried an image of her begging beside two bags of gold and the caption 'My two best friends'.

We are quite obviously in the presence of a most extraordinary man. He was born Sigmund Neuberger in Munich, most probably on 25 February 1871. At an early age he went to the USA where he changed his name to 'The Great Lafayette' by deed poll and acquired American citizenship. To forestall anyone challenging the first two words, he always signed his initials 'T.G.L.', invariably in purple ink. Purple became the overriding colour motif for his stage show, from the scenery to the costumes which he designed himself. This artistic side of his character was offset by an innate militarism. He demanded that all members of his vast company should salute him when they passed in the street. Military-style uniforms were *de rigueur* on stage. Regimented precision was the order of the working day. Alcohol was forbidden to pass their lips at any time.

In America he failed to achieve the recognition he craved, so in 1892 he came to London. Within a short time he became the highest paid theatrical performer in the United Kingdom, soon grossing a phenomenal £400 a week, rising to a colossal £1,000 by 1910. In return he provided the public with a spectacle as elaborate and magnificent as they had ever seen on the vaudeville stage. While there may have been magicians technically more capable, Lafayette won through on the sheer power of his showmanship and an unstinted commitment to give value for every penny he earned. His shows were a flamboyant kaleidoscope of sharp-shooting, impersonations, quick-change artistry, illusions, colour and razzle-dazzle. Although not an imposing man, he cut a courtly figure in his black silk knee breeches and knew exactly how to sell an effect so that it achieved the biggest possible impact. When he appeared at the London Hippodrome in August 1900, he was driven across the arena to the stage in a limousine, an amazing novelty for the day, but typical of his panache.

We will concern ourselves with two of his most famous illusions. In 'The Lion's Bride' he was the first to bring true circus flair to the conjuring arena, paving the way for today's most exciting and most glamorous performers of large-scale magic, his fellow countrymen Siegfried and Roy, whose Las Vegas wild animal spectacle is the nearest thing extant today to the Lafayette show. First, however, in an illusionary playlet entitled 'Dr Kremser – Vivisectionist', we encounter a star part for Beauty herself. The great hypnotic surgeon of the title was played by Lafayette with a gothic seriousness worthy of Edgar Allan Poe. From the beginning he is distraught. His only daughter is terminally ill with a mysterious disease. A

T. G. L. astride the steed that may have cost him his life.

revolutionary new operation might save her, but he soon realises that the only means of discovering its effectiveness is to experiment on the dog, the only animal available to him. He recoils at the thought, but paternal duty demands that the dog's life be risked. The doctor prepares the anaesthetic and summons his negro servant to get the pet ready for the operation. When the servant remonstrates, he is rapidly hypnotised by the doctor, who in his less than careful haste is overpowered by his own potions and slumps to the ground. The tortured hallucinations that go through his mind are now acted out on stage in all their grotesqueness. He is approached by a monster with the head of a dog and the body of a human being. Apparitions of his own dog, and then of his daughter pleading for the animal, arise before him. He makes towards the vision, but it dissolves. The dog-headed monster now passes in front of Kremser with his back to the audience, attacks the surgeon with a knife, and decapitates him. As the torso slumps out of view, he hurls the head into a blazing pit. At this moment the daughter rushes to her father's aid, Kremser regains his head and, as he lovingly strokes her hair, he calls the dog to their side. Kremser ponders his surgeon's knife, hurls it out of the window, and the curtain falls.

If Lafayette brought a science-fiction approach ahead of its time to the traditional decapitation mystery at its most melodramatic, he used Arabian Nights splendour in all its magnificence to transform the basic substitution illusion that was the *raison d'être* for 'The Lion's Bride'. Amid all the spectacle paraded on stage, all eyes were drawn to the large cage in the centre. Prowling angrily behind its bars was a savage lion. The plot revolved around the plight of the beautiful Christian princess Pari Banu, who survives a shipwreck in the Persian Gulf only to fall into the hands of the Pasha who gives her the option of becoming his wife or being thrown into the lion's den. Preferring death to dishonour she is bound and left to contemplate her fate. Prince Hashim Ne Bari, an officer in the Persian army and her true love, alias Lafayette resplendent with gleaming scimitar, now gallops to the rescue on his Arab steed. Gaining admission to the harem, the magician encounters a burly negro guard whom he kills in a duel, thus allowing him the opportunity to disguise himself as the princess, whom he dispatches to safety on his horse. The supposed princess is now bundled into the cage. The lion pounces on the body. The girl lets out a blood-curdling scream. The lion rears on its hind legs and a chill descends upon the enthralled audience. Then, without bathos, but with a combination of surprise, relief and stunning theatricality, the lion removes his head to reveal Lafayette, who then lifts the yashmak to reveal the princess all along!

Sadly for Lafayette, the happy endings of the playlets did not extend into real life. Tragedy first struck on 4 May 1911, when Beauty died of apoplexy at the start of a two-week season at the Empire Palace Theatre, Edinburgh. In his grief Lafayette was determined that the dog should be

Descriptive detail and pictorial simplicity both played their part in Lafayette's publicity campaign.

Opposite, Lafayette brought science fiction into the magical arena ahead of its time.

buried on consecrated ground. The authorities at the Piershill Cemetery on Edinburgh's Portobello Road eventually acceded to his request on the morbid condition, guaranteed by signature, that the great showman would himself be buried on the same plot, no matter where in the world he might die. The animal was embalmed and entrusted to an elaborate silk-lined coffin with a glass lid.

Lafayette felt emotionally betrayed. The 'Dr Kremser' sequence was withdrawn from the programme and the grief-stricken magician wrote, 'I have lost my dearest friend. Beauty was my mascot, and I feel, I know that I shall not be much longer in this world. Our lives were irrevocably bound together.' Lafayette's intuition was to prove horrifyingly correct. As he took his bow after the second performance of 'The Lion's Bride' on the following Tuesday, 9 May, an Oriental lantern burst into flames setting fire to the adjacent scenery. At first the audience assumed it was all part of the spectacular effect for which Lafayette was famous. Then the stark reality dawned. Wheelan, one of Lafayette's musicians, went on stage and played the National Anthem, an act of heroism that cost him his life. His bravery, however, prevented a stampede and the audience of some 3,000 people was able to make its way to safety. Backstage, however, an inferno raged. At first reckoning nine people were killed, including Lafayette himself, together with the lion and horse which figured so prominently in 'The Lion's Bride'. The magician's charred body, identified by the scimitar he carried, was taken to Glasgow for cremation, a facility unavailable in Edinburgh. Lafayette's lawyer, however, was intrigued by the sudden absence from the corpse of two distinctive diamond rings which the showman always wore both on- and off-stage. The day after the fire another body was discovered in the basement of the burnt-out theatre. Although unrecognisable, it was without doubt that of Lafayette – it wore the rings. It looked as if Lafayette might well be able to claim that he died twice. And in a sense he did. The corpse already cremated turned out to be that of Dick Richards, a drummer with an incredible resemblance to the magician, who off-stage posed as a bandsman, but who actually played Lafayette's secret 'double' in some of the illusions. It was ironic that the performer in magic who carried the effects of transformation and substitution to levels of impact never dreamed of before, should in death flaunt that very talent; it was tragic that in the process his most closely guarded secret was revealed.

The subsequent funeral on 14 May proved to be one of the most spectacular sights Edinburgh had seen. Thousands thronged the three-mile route to the Piershill Cemetery. Out of respect public transport was stopped. Four Belgian horses drew the hearse containing Lafayette's ashes. No less than sixty vehicles followed, transporting floral tributes, mourners and, in the magician's own motor car, Mabel, his Dalmatian dog, second only to Beauty in his affections. At the burial ground the casket containing his ashes was placed between the paws of the embalmed dog, and poignantly they were interred together in a vault marked by two memorial stones that may be seen to this day. Close at hand was Houdini's tribute, a floral effigy of Beauty's head inscribed, 'To the memory of my friend from the friend who gave him his best friend'.

People still debate whether Lafayette needed to die. Certainly the fire backstage was worse than it should have been, as a result of his general rule that all but one of the exits from the stage had to be locked or barricaded by scenery in order to preserve his secrets. It is generally accepted that Lafayette did have every chance to escape, but turned back in a noble attempt to save his horse. One report states that when the skull of the latter was examined, a bullet wound was found. Having saved the steed from a more lingering death, he found his own survival impossible. It is not inconceivable that if a tragedy had to occur, he would not have wished for his own part in it to end in any other way. Many years later Mr Nelson, the publicity manager for the Edinburgh Empire Palace at the time of the fire, wrote about the tragedy in the *Edinburgh Evening Dispatch*. In the issue of 18 May 1961, he stated that Lalla Selbini, Lafayette's lover and principal assistant to whom he bequeathed his show, had attempted to persuade the magician to follow her to safety in the heat of the disaster. The true facts will never be known. It is hard to accept that this master showman was only forty when he died.

The Master Phantasist

The undisputed immediate successor to Lafayette as magic's most extravagant showman was 'The Great Carmo'. This resourceful and courageous performer was born to staid Scottish parents in Brunswick, near Melbourne, in Australia on 8 November 1881. His real name was Harry Cameron and he soon became enraptured by the world of show business. A visit to the circus at an early age aroused in him a passion for spectacle, shared with Lafayette, which would later lend colour to his most successful years and lead indirectly to his downfall. At first, however, juggling took precedence over magic, following a visit to a local theatre at which the legendary music hall star Paul Cinquevalli was appearing. Cameron's strong physique and steady eye stood him in good stead for the strongman juggling act which he now set out to perfect. There is little doubt that he would ultimately have become an important headliner in the Cinquevalli class had he not become friendly with another Melbourne boy, Victor Martyn. Martyn, later a famous juggler on his own account and father of today's comedy juggler and magician Topper Martyn, had begun as a magician. They soon found themselves teaching each other their respective skills. For the while, however, Cameron persisted with his juggling professionally, settling on Carmo as a stage name and joining a variety company known as Heller's Entertainers, headed by an illusionist,

Professor George Heller. In 1907, together with his wife and assistant, Nellie, he decided to travel to England with Heller. His first great adventure was waiting in the wings.

They set forth from Sydney on 2 February on board the White Star liner, the *Suevic*. On 17 March, their journey virtually complete, a violent storm caused the ship to run aground on rocks off Cornwall's Lizard Point. There was no loss of life, but the vessel was broken in two, making maritime history when her larger half was refloated to Southampton to be refitted with a new prow. Their personal possessions lost, but their props salvaged, the Carmos decided to stay in England, Harry gradually adding more magical content to his juggling repertoire. A special feature, by arrangement with its inventor Servais Le Roy, who had become friendly with Carmo during his Australian tour of 1905, was 'The Devil's Cage', a challenging escape in which the robust showman was imprisoned in the tightest of confinements'. In 1911 Carmo had cause to be thankful to Le Roy again when the Belgian magician loaned him the services of the brilliant Max Sterling to devise and produce a full evening show around his many talents. In the process Carmo became billed as 'The Master Phantasist'. In 1913, now married to his second wife Alma, he repaid his debt to Le Roy by returning to Australia to appear with his juggling

Sadly Carmo's lavish stage spectacle would be economically impossible to take on tour today.

speciality on the Le Roy, Talma and Bosco show. Ironically they travelled on the restructured *Suevic*.

On his return to England Carmo's own show expanded. He had acquired from Le Roy the startling cage transformation of live lion to person as featured by Lafayette in 'The Lion's Bride'. It represented only the beginning of a veritable menagerie which the Australian would gather around him in the next few years, embracing horses, leopards, snakes, an elephant, as well as many smaller animals. He would produce a tiger and vanish a camel. Within a short time he was playing the London Palladium and the principal provincial and Continental theatres, his company numbering some forty people, not to mention the beasts.

Not everything in the Carmo show was on a large scale. He acquired from its inventor Max Sterling the delightful novelty in which a small circle torn from a square of tissue paper, when bounced upon a fan, slowly assumed the shape of an egg, at which Carmo with the élan of the most practised chef would break it with one hand into a dish. He would produce a succession of canaries from his bare hands. Placed in small cages, they were taken into the audience and given away as souvenirs. The label on each cage was an indication of Carmo's showmanship. It stated that those recipients who did not wish to retain their gift from 'The Great Carmo' could exchange it for half-a-crown at the stagedoor after the show. Children got to know of the ploy and would crowd outside the theatre in the hope that they could cadge a bird with which to queue at the stagedoor themselves. Another presentation with a shrewd giveaway angle centred around his 'inexhaustible' wine barrel. Open-ended and obviously empty, this was suspended in mid-air by slender chains from two slim metal stands. After covering both ends with tissue paper, Carmo fitted a small brass tap to the front panel. No less than sixty glasses of port were filled from the almost endless stream that poured forth from the tap. These too were distributed among the audience, before Carmo went on to fill another four large fish bowls from the same mysterious source. Another smaller illusion, revived flamboyantly in more recent years by the exciting Peruvian magician Richiardi, featured an orange, a lemon, an egg and a canary. Each was placed in a separate paper bag. The bags were crushed flat. The cloth covering the table top on which the bags had been placed was pulled away to reveal a thin glass top. All four items had really disappeared! An orange was now produced. This was peeled to reveal a lemon, which in turn disclosed an egg, which when cracked inside the birdcage revealed the canary.

Arguably the most memorable item in his show was the version he acquired of the levitation – one of the most artistic ever produced and recently revived on 'The Paul Daniels Magic Show' by English magician Jeffery Atkins, who has spent a lifetime conscientiously reproducing the lost illusions of magic's past masters. In Carmo's presentation, known as 'The Mummy', the stage revealed an upright sarcophagus. The lid slowly

Carmo in command, every inch a showman.

opened like a drawbridge. First a bat fluttered out, and then a girl, swathed in silk, literally walked forward on the air, rising simultaneously to a position about four feet away from both floor and tomb. After pausing briefly in this position, she would make one-and-a-quarter spins on her own axis, leaving her upright with her right side towards the audience. Tilting backwards to a horizontal position with her face upwards, she gyrated under Carmo's spell without any possible means of support. Carmo passed a hoop over her to prove this, whereupon the girl made a simultaneous quarter-spin and quarter-revolution bringing her to a position facing the audience again but now upside-down! After another pause a further half-revolution brought her upright and able to take the hoop herself with which to skip in mid-air. Handing the hoop back to the magician, she refolded her arms and made a half-spin to bring her face to face with the tomb, into which she now floated back gracefully. No sooner had she reached the sarcophagus than she turned and walked down the sloping lid to take her applause with Carmo. The geometrical complexity of the description, while important for historical accuracy and to underline the sheer impossibility of what happened, does little to convey the breath-taking beauty experienced by those fortunate enough to have seen the Carmo show.

For all the magnificence of such a scene, it was while performing with livestock that Carmo was at his happiest. After the death of Alma in 1927 it was inevitable that his thoughts should return to his first love, the circus, the reason why he had become captivated by show business. His collection of animals increased, while the animals themselves developed their individual skills. There was a Himalayan bear capable of walking backwards on a cylinder, while at Christmas 1927 he lent Baby June, his cycling elephant, to Bertram Mills for his circus at Olympia. The first Carmo Circus opened in Belfast for the summer season the following year. Its success, both artistically and financially, led to his eventual partnership with Bertram Mills in England. The Great Carmo Circus, with backing from Mills, opened in Catford in May 1929, the largest circus under canvas in the United Kingdom since the great days of Lord George Sanger. The overheads, however, of such an operation were enormous. At the end of October, by which time all tenting shows were heading for their winter quarters, Carmo announced that he intended to tour through the winter. He invested £800 in a German heating system to make this plausible. More experienced souls, not least Mills, said he was crazy.

He opened again at Harringay in January. Bad weather kept more seats empty than full, but although losing money fast, he persisted until the tour reached Birmingham in March. There, on the night of the 14th, an unexpected snowstorm caused the big top to cave in, tearing the canvas to shreds and trapping both animals and people under the weight. Fortunately no lives were lost. The tentmakers of England rallied around and four days later Carmo reopened in the full glare of publicity. Exactly one week after the first disaster, the new tent was a blazing inferno. The whole show burned to the ground, the result of panic on the part of the lion trainer's assistant when a Primus stove flared up out of control. Only the heroism of Togare, the lion-trainer himself, saved the livestock from a searing death. Carmo was not present, still at his country estate recovering from the earlier disaster. He rushed to Birmingham, knowing in his heart that his

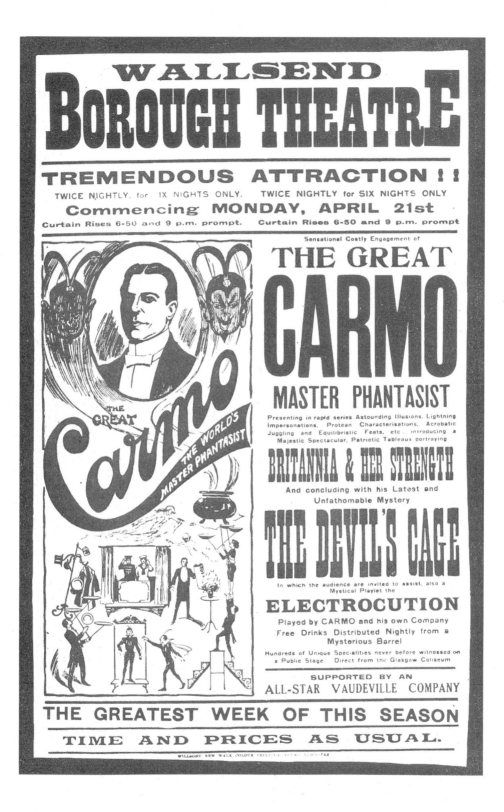

Carmo was equally at home on the music hall stage and in the circus ring.

The GREAT CARMO
The Colossus of Mystery

W. E. BERRY LTD NESFIELD ST. BRADFORD.

days as a big-time showman were over. He ordered yet another tent, even though the last one had not been paid for, let alone insured, but eventually had to concede that the financial liabilities of trying to continue were too great. In an attempt to cut his losses, he did present a smaller circus at the South Shore, Blackpool the following year, but the venue was a naive choice with competition from the rival attractions of the established Blackpool Tower Circus just down the road.

It was ironically at Blackpool Tower Circus during the summer of 1986 that Paul Daniels himself cleverly intertwined the excitement of the sawdust ring with the impossibility of magic in the best Carmo tradition. First fastened into stocks examined by the Mayor of Blackpool and padlocked by the representative of a well-known lock company, Paul was then secured in a sack by circus ringmaster Norman Barrett. A small cage, reminiscent of Carmo's own 'Devil's Cage', containing the sack and Paul, was bolted and raised high above the centre of the ring. Simultaneously, trainer Jim Clubb released seven lions into the larger open cage below. A fuse extending from the small cage to the side of the ring was lit by Norman. Paul had the life-span of this fuse in which to escape before the base of the small cage fell open on a hinge, casting him in the sack to the lions below. As the seconds ticked away, the lions paced restlessly and the fuse grew shorter. It was too late. With a sickening thud the sack plummeted on to the sawdust. An uncertain fear took hold of the audience, but not for long. No one would have been prouder than Carmo himself to see the triumphant Paul Daniels, free of all his shackles, come sliding down seconds later on a rope beneath the cage as the cats scurried out of the ring. As if by way of compensation the Blackpool audience did contain Murray, the distinguished Australian escapologist who topped bills throughout Europe during the 1920s, but never flirted more recklessly with death than on the occasion he escaped from a straitjacket on the actual floor of the lion's cage at Bertram Mills's Circus at Olympia.

In the last years of his life Carmo was reduced to playing fairgrounds and exhibitions, until ENSA, the British entertainment equivalent of America's USO, claimed his services with honour in 1941. He died on 1 August 1944. His greatest achievement had been to combine so happily for a short time the rival attractions of circus and magic, both appealing as they do to our sense of wonder in diametrically opposite ways. Only a handful of magicians have worked with true satisfaction in the ring. The success of the true circus performer depends upon physical strength, daring and realism; that of the magician upon ingenuity, deception and applied psychology. When the acrobat treads the tightrope or flies the trapeze, he provides his own physical counterpoint to the levitation marvels of the illusionist. In the ring what you see is; in the magical arena what you see could never be. Carmo, with his juggling, strongman and wild animal skills, was able to blur the distinction all the way.

13

'It's All Their Own Invention'

A whole book could be written about the inventive process in magic, but equally the whole subject could be summarised on the back of a playing card. The number of distinctly identifiable individual effects in magic is relatively small: production, disappearance, transformation, transposition, penetration, restoration, animation, levitation, time control and omniscience. Each illusion described in these pages can be defined in terms of one or more of these categories, every one of which in its own way sets out to defy a known natural law. The person to devise or discover a new category will become an instant hero among magicians; in the meantime the list presents a perpetual challenge to magic's more creative minds to come up with even more imaginative and, needless to say, baffling variations on the same themes.

As this book reveals, many of the great stage illusionists of the past were inventors as well as entertainers. On the other hand, it is unfair for inventive ability to be considered a prerequisite of the great performer. That argument would expect an actor to write his own plays and the virtuoso instrumentalist to pen his own compositions. Most of the material performed by Paul Daniels in his stage show has its basis among the classic effects of magic, transformed for the occasion as they are by his own distinctive personality. The material required for the television show (when not culled after much research from the exhaustive literature of magic) is more frequently the creative achievement of backstage associates such as Ali Bongo, himself a performer of flair as well as magic's most practical and entertaining ideas man, and Gil Leaney, British magic's foremost technician, with occasional input from Graham Reed, a freelance advertising consultant whose interest in magic extends back to schooldays shared with Paul in Middlesbrough, and others.

It goes without saying that much of the material most frequently performed by magicians is invented by individuals whose names seldom, if ever, appear before the public. Perhaps the most eccentric of these was Guy Jarrett, a wiry, opinionated little man, born in Belmont County, Ohio in 1881, who by the 1920s was in demand as one of the most prolific

Ali Bongo, magic's master of Arabian Nights burlesque.

special-effects men on Broadway. Magicians clamoured to him for original effects, to be set back at first by the seemingly wayward, pipedream nature of his ideas and then most often pleasantly surprised when those brainstorms were turned into reality by his brilliant cunning and mechanical skills.

Jarrett regarded as the greatest of all his illusions 'The 21-Person Cabinet'. The title tells most of the story. From a cabinet barely large enough to hold six chorus girls, three-and-a-half times that number were produced. There was no way for the girls to reach the cabinet secretly – it was isolated on legs away from all scenery – but then there was seemingly nowhere to hide all those people in the cabinet either. More practical to magicians without long line-ups of chorus girls at their beck and call was his development in the area of 'Sawing a Woman'. Whenever you see a magician today – Doug Henning, for example, or the Great Kovari – performing this illusion with a box so small it could not possibly contain more than one girl, and so thin it could not possibly give her scope to move away from the saw, you are watching the result of work pioneered by Jarrett. In 1917, the year before Houdini caused a publicity sensation with his 'Vanishing Elephant' at the New York Hippodrome, it was Jarrett who originated the concept, even though his actual method was not ultimately used, due to a disagreement between himself and Burnside, the producer of the Hippodrome show.

In 1936 he put his tricks and views, often as maniacal as his methods were daring, into a controversial book which soon sold out its 400 copies, each hand-printed and bound by Jarrett himself. When *Jarrett, Magic and Stage Craft, Technical* became more widely accessible, when republished in an annotated edition with notes by modern creative genius Jim Steinmeyer in 1981, it was inevitable that Paul Daniels and his team would be drawn to it in the search for ideas. The result was Paul's intriguing presentation of Jarrett's 'Water Barrel Escape'. Jarrett, with his usual

Gil Leaney, technical genius, with long-time assistant, Frankie.

hyperbole, described it as 'the most ingenious piece of magical apparatus that was ever conceived'. In actual fact, Paul and Gil improved upon the method used, but the effect remained the same, the item more in the nature of a puzzle than an escape or illusion as such. Two barrels were placed one above the other, a table supporting the top one with the lower barrel immediately underneath. The top barrel was filled with water and Paul's son Martin immersed himself in the same, more water being added to overflowing as other assistants clamped the lid on. Almost immediately the bottom barrel was pulled forward and Martin crawled out. The baffling point of the entire presentation, the key to Jarrett's genius, was not the question of how Martin got from the top barrel to the lower one, but how he did so without spilling a drop of water. As Paul verbally underlined the impossibility, so he knocked out the bunghole of the top barrel for the water to gush forth for the entire duration of the closing credits and beyond. Reading between the lines of Jarrett's method, one suspects it is possible that the item was never performed in his own day. It took fifty years for a working showman to realise its possibilities as entertainment, just too late though for its inventor to see his idea put into practice. Jarrett, a health and physical exercise fanatic in his latter days, died at the advanced age of ninety in 1972.

*

In recording his wild ideas for the magicians of his day Jarrett ensured not only that they would be preserved for posterity but that they would stay performed. Unfortunately, others as ingenious have not been so forward-looking. This was the case with inventor and illusionist Henry Roltair. Born in London in 1853, he departed for the New World at an early age, becoming an associate of the great American magician Alexander Herrmann for no less than nine years. He enjoyed a brief spell as a performer in vaudeville himself, but will be remembered as the genius behind the staging of some of the most spectacular illusions ever known, principal attractions at the major fairs and expositions where they were exhibited.

One of his outstanding effects was known as 'Rollo on the Wheel'. In the absence of more concrete information, even today magicians can only guess how it was done. The back of the stage depicted a street scene. Against this view, in full light, Rollo made his entrance on a bicycle. He rode across the stage and then turned, without leaving the view of the audience. As he continued his journey back in the direction whence he came he started to rise higher and higher into the air. All the time he continued to cycle. Turning again he went higher still, until he was some twenty feet above the stage. His mid-air pedalling then became more adventurous as he proceeded to perform loops, figure eights, and every conceivable bicycle manoeuvre. For the finale a series of large hoops mounted on poles were positioned across the stage. Rollo, still on the bicycle, rode in and out of these obstacles with ease.

Roltair took Rollo to spectacular extremes with this floating car.

Perhaps Roltair's greatest achievement was the illusion show, 'The Creation'. He devised this for the St Louis World's Fair of 1904, from which it was subsequently moved to become a permanent exhibit at Dreamland Park on Coney Island. So awe-inspiring was this spectacle that it became the subject of sermons throughout the land. As contemporary stage musicals endeavour increasingly to involve audiences in their own technology, one realises how trivial their efforts are beside those of Roltair. One can do no better than to quote the description that appeared in *Billboard*:

A vast blue dome, one hundred and twenty-two feet high, is one of the spectacular features of the Pike. It is Roltair's tremendous illusion Creation. Creation carries the spectator back to the beginning of time. In a grotesque craft on a canal of water 1,000 feet long the visitor glides backward through twenty centuries, around a dome 150 feet in diameter, ending in the immense shell where a voice repeats the divine commands of Genesis. Out of a cloud of steam the world is peopled with growing nature and living things. A moving panorama of the centuries in plastic and real life is passed en route to the master mechanical denouement. At the first century the passengers leave the boats and enter a Roman temple of that period. Soft music precedes a peal of thunder. The walls of the temple melt away. It is chaos. The visitor is in the midst of the dome, completely enveloped in a cloud of wrack. A voice utters, 'The Lord made the heavens and earth in six days', while darkness surrounds the audience. The voice continues the story of Creation, 'Let there be Light.' It increases until the glare of day reveals the void of clouds about the spectators. 'Let the day appear.' The limitless ocean rolls back, revealing the land. Trees, flowers and shrubs gradually revolve themselves into the Garden of Eden. 'The Lord made two great lights.' The sun and the moon come forth, making day and night effect. 'Let us make man after our image,' says the voice. A spectral form of Adam is seen approaching, reaching the foreground in full light. He reclines on a bed of roses. A rib is seen to leave his body, and take upon itself the form of a beautiful woman. Adam and Eve, and the story of Creation is complete. This is certainly one of the striking features of the Pike; it is also one of the most beautiful exhibitions that the visitor will see. Its massive dome, its artistic waterfalls, front and exquisite interior, will again add to Roltair's fame.

'The Creation' ran at Coney Island until it was destroyed alongside 'Rollo' in the great fire that consumed 'Dreamland' in 1911. Roltair had died the year before in Oklahoma as he came to the end of a vaudeville tour.

In later years, however, the tradition of illusion returned to Coney Island. In 1930 audiences were able to witness another long-forgotten impossibility, the creation of an illusion-builder named St Leon, whose name would disappear down the years as mysteriously as his secrets. His masterpiece was called 'The Broken Butterfly'. The well-lit stage showed a garden scene. In the centre of the lawn, a sculptor was putting the finishing touches to a statue. His work complete, he sat down and fell asleep. As he did so the statue came to life, danced around the artist, and then took up her position again on the grass. The sculptor woke up and walked towards the statue. All the time the lighting of the scene remained constant. Thunder roared in the distance and instantly the statue of the girl visibly appeared to disintegrate into a myriad pieces, spread across the lawn as fragile proof of what had happened. The sculptor then dropped to his knees in prayer, at which – incredibly – the broken pieces appeared to fly back together again. The statue complete and undamaged, the sculptor took her by the hand and together they walked forward to acknowledge the applause. Sadly that is one illusion you will not see performed on 'The Paul Daniels Magic Show'. If it were, the likelihood is that most audiences would dismiss it as a camera trick, in spite of the programme's policy never to use such techniques. Fortunately when 'The Broken Butterfly' was first performed live at Coney Island all those years ago, that is the one solution audiences knew beyond doubt to be inconceivable. Their eyes told them so.

Roltair and St Leon doubtless took advantage of the fact that on permanent sites their illusions did not have to endure the rigours of travelling from town to town, from one vaudeville theatre to the next. In the case of 'The Creation', the building was literally built around the spectacle. Not every illusionist, however, had the luxury of suiting the environment to the method, a problem that became even more drastic as vaudeville theatres closed and magicians, compelled more and more to appear surrounded on cabaret floors, found that they could no longer perform the large-scale magic devised for presentation within a proscenium arch. In magic, though, everything should be possible, and it was left to the brilliant mind of the South African-born illusionist Robert Harbin to take up the challenge in this instance.

✻

Harbin, whose real name was Edward Richard Charles Williams (known affectionately to his friends as Ned), was born in Balfour on 12 February 1909 and emigrated to England in 1929. Originally billed as 'The Sunny South African', he was soon adopted by the British conjuring establishment as their own. One of the last performers to appear at Maskelyne's St George's Hall (where the star magician, Oswald Williams, himself one of magic's most imaginative creators, made him change his name), he became the leading pioneer of magic on television in Britain during the late 1940s and 1950s. Lacking flamboyance as a performer, but possessed of immense personal wit and charm, he cultivated a slightly absent-minded, Professor Branestawm image which perfectly suited his principal enthusiasm in magic – the seemingly endless invention of one new trick after another. Occasionally on stage some detail of a new miracle would not work out as planned and, with a wry, self-deprecating smile, he would move on to something more certain: 'So disheartening when these things don't work.' The audience was immediately on his side. Nevertheless, his writings in books and magazines suggest that he invented more tricks of more kinds with a greater variety of objects than any other magician this century. His greatest achievement, however, was the new approach he brought to stage illusions.

On the conventional theatre stage illusionists had long had access to a whole armoury of secret devices including trap doors, scenic aids, and unseen assistants: on the cabaret floor the hawk-eyed audience have you hemmed in on all sides and the chance of using a trap is out of the question. While others took it for granted that with the demise of variety and vaudeville the era of large-scale magic had passed, Harbin saw the situation as a challenge, grasped the nettle with open palms and triumphantly redefined the scope of the 'stage' illusion. Members of the audience were

The author was honoured to deliver the Magic Circle's Memorial Lecture to commemorate Robert Harbin, the most important British magician between Devant and Daniels.

balanced precariously on chair-backs and themselves sawn in half while totally surrounded by the very people who could vouch that they were not confederates. In 'The Jigsaw Girl' a narrow cabinet with a pretty assistant secured inside was divided vertically and horizontally into four sections, which were then dismantled and opened in turn to show that all four quarters of the girl had conclusively vanished. In cabaret, Harbin would wheel the combination around among the tables for individuals to look closer inside the four sections to satisfy themselves that the disappearance was all he claimed it to be. 'Aunt Matilda's Wardrobe' involved the impossible materialisation of a girl from a skeletal wardrobe frame within a mock-spiritualistic presentation: Harbin would literally pull the wardrobe apart to show it empty. 'The Blades of Opah' enabled a member of the audience to be visibly sliced in two by a pair of blades moving in opposite directions at the same time.

Harbin's greatest single invention was without doubt 'The Zig-Zag Girl'. It sadly became the most copied illusion of all time once Harbin, distressed by the pirating of his miracle by an unscrupulous American, released the authentic secret in a book published in 1970 in an expensive limited edition for private circulation among magicians. However, when first performed on television on 'Sunday Night at the London Palladium' on 21 November 1965, the news spread through the country the following morning as if Everest had been reconquered. There was no way a girl confined to a slim cabinet with her stylised outline in silhouette on the front door could be divided so cleanly into three parts with metal blades and then have her entire centre section slid away from the rest of her body, leaving an obvious gap in its place. All the time her face, a hand, and a foot were in view through holes in their respective sections. At any time they could be touched. There was even a window for her tummy in the centre compartment. Members of the audience could place their fingers against her midriff to find that she still breathed. Fortunately, however many times you see this illusion performed, you are still as baffled as you were the first time, until, if you are a magician, you are told the secret. When you do know, it is one of those few items in magic that becomes even more amazing than when you did not.

Ironically, Harbin himself claimed to have obtained the greatest satisfaction from the method he devised for the classic effect in which he tore up a newspaper and then shook it open to show it completely restored with no torn pieces left. His ingenuity extended to all corners of magic and the very titles of some of his other originations make fascinating reading: 'The Dippy Magnet', 'Experiment 13', 'Through the Fifth Dimension', 'The Assistant's Revenge', 'The Upside-Down Production Box'. He devised all the magical effects for the West End stage version of *The Wizard of Oz* at the Strand Theatre in 1947. The part of Merlin was written into the production for him and very soon afterwards he adopted as his own stage billing 'A Wizard If Ever There Woz'. When he died just one month before his sixty-ninth birthday on 12 January 1978, the countless tributes that came forth from his fellow magicians proved just what an understatement that was. No one in magic has been revered and loved more by his colleagues, both amateur and professional, than Robert Harbin.

Two stages of 'The Zig-Zag Girl', the incomprehensible origination of a master inventor.

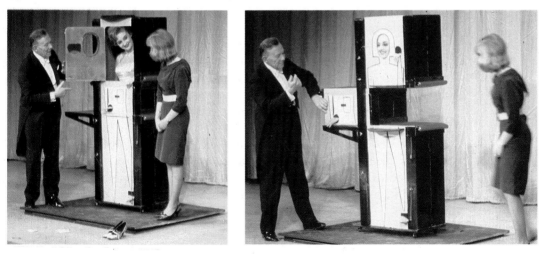

Harbin had a knack of making the news.

*

The tradition of the showman inventor, presenting his own creations to the public more effectively than anyone else could possibly perform them, is most vigorously kept alive today by Germany's leading solo magician, Hans Moretti, born on 24 July 1928 in Bekerow in that part of Poland which became partitioned into Russia after the Nazi–Soviet Pact of 1939. Hans, with his ebullient wife and partner Helga, has made more guest appearances on 'The Paul Daniels Magic Show' than any other performer. One reason for this is the vast number of original presentations which they have at their disposal, each one representing a quantum leap of the imagination which makes the original standard effect on which it is based both unrecognisable and redundant to audiences who have seen both.

Where other magicians still follow the example of Robert-Houdin by balancing their assistants on poles or broomsticks, Moretti uses two paper trees, which the audience sees him tear out of rolled newspapers at the start of the act. The trees are balanced in beer mugs on the floor and Helga has to use a chair to reach the top of them, placing one under her right shoulder, the other under her outstretched left hand. She is subjected to the supposed hypnotic influence, but when it is time for Moretti to remove the tree under her hand to prove this has taken effect, he simply snips through it with a pair of shears. Poised precariously on the single flimsy paper tower, Helga is now tilted to an angle fully 135 degrees from the ground where she remains suspended in the air. At the conclusion of the feat the other support is pruned just as ruthlessly. It is just a paper tree.

Audiences used to seeing magicians plunge swords through their assistants incarcerated in gaudily decorated boxes are taken aback to see the roles reversed in Moretti's presentation of the sword cabinet. This is not the only feature, however, that makes his version unique. The cabinet is no more than a brown manila cardboard box, little more than the size in which one would expect to take home groceries. Before Hans enters, he is totally chained and handcuffed; once inside there is no way he can escape,

Even Robert-Houdin would have been fooled by Moretti's version of his suspension illusion.

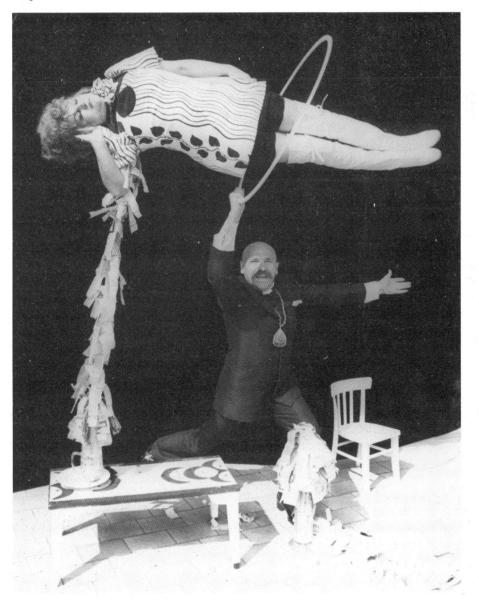

the box perched uncertainly as it is on a small raised table away from all
scenery. No less than sixteen swords are pushed through the box from side
to side; these have all been examined by a committee from the audience;
the committee, not Helga, push them through! When all the swords are in
place there is hardly five inches between any two blades. But the illusion
does not end there. Once Helga has withdrawn the swords, Hans emerges
triumphant. He is now wearing the costume of a clown with full clown
make-up on his face and with a small menagerie of monkey, doves and
chickens perched on his head and shoulders.

Moretti's most exciting presentation is the telepathic version of the game
of 'Russian Roulette' played with not one, but two guns. Ballistics experts
are invited to bring along their own ammunition, live and blank. The
bullets are mixed. In total secrecy they load them haphazardly into the
guns. Since both the live and the blank bullets appear identical there is no
way either they or Hans could know the sequence in either revolver. Next
to Moretti is a screen on which are suspended five plates. In front of each
plate hangs a small metal square. Apparently using only the power of his
mind, Moretti now attempts to sense whether the next bullet to be fired
from either gun will be live or blank. When live, the bullet shatters the
plate, piercing a hole in the metal; when blank, nothing happens, but the

Moretti about to be transfixed by swords in a box impossibly small.

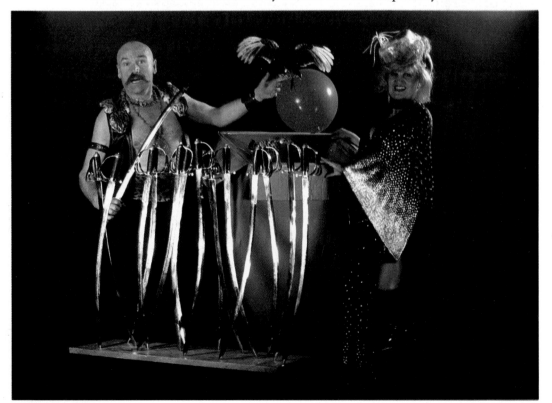

applause is as deafening. Then dramatically, after several shots have passed, he announces that he will play 'Russian Roulette'. Both guns are fired at his head. Both fire blanks.

The courage of the performer defies belief, but there is no way he could know the sequence of the ammunition contained in either gun. It may be a disservice to Moretti even to consider such a feat in the context of magical invention. As with 'The Great Carmo' and Houdini himself, his skills are not confined to magic. His crossbow shooting act is equally hair-raising, relying on precision and skill, not trickery. He performs Houdini's upside-down escape, dangling from a burning rope attached to a helicopter in mid-air, jumping to the ground seconds before the rope breaks. He began as a juggler, but not in the conventional sense, performing suspended from a dental grip in imitation of his boyhood idol, Bert Holt. This genial giant of a wizard is as courageous as he is clever, but he would surely never leave the challenge of the bullets to sheer chance? Or would he?

*

One returns to the Golden Age of stage magic to meet the magician whom many regard as the greatest inventor of conjuring tricks. He was born in Caluire-et-Cuire, a suburb of Lyons, on 18 November 1847, and christened Joseph Buatier; in later years he would become more familiar to audiences as Buatier de Kolta. Originally destined for the priesthood, at fifteen he saw a magician perform and from that moment enthusiasm for his chosen profession waned. He mastered the basic principles of magic and set out as a strolling player, eventually graduating to the leading theatres of Italy and France until, in May 1875, he reached London's Egyptian Hall. De Kolta's 'Disappearing Birdcage', discussed at greater length elsewhere in this book, was first presented in London on that occasion. He later elaborated on the theme of his brainchild with an illusion called 'The Captive's Flight'. This used a much larger cage containing a girl assistant dressed as a canary. De Kolta covered the cage with a cloth. When he whisked the latter away, both girl and cage vanished into the atmosphere.

Unfortunately, eleven years after his London debut, he was prevented from giving the first authentic London performance of his most famous illusion, 'The Vanishing Lady'. He was in too great a demand performing it for enthusiastic Parisian audiences. He first presented 'L'Escamotage en Personne Vivante', to give it its French title, in the offices of the *Figaro* newspaper on 27 April 1886. The illusion instantly became the talking point of both learned society and the theatrical world. Maskelyne soon acquired the rights to its British presentation and, to counteract the imitations which were soon springing up in London music halls, arranged with Buatier's permission for its authorised première at the Egyptian Hall in the capable hands of the staunch Charles Bertram. De Kolta would take over as soon as he could later in the year, but the effect was the same. A

Buatier de Kolta, pioneer inventive genius.

sheet of newspaper was spread on the floor of the stage to preclude the use of traps. A chair was placed in the centre and the lady invited to sit down. A cloth was draped completely over her. All the while the magician continued to converse with the lady. Then, grasping her form through the cloth, he made as if to hurl her into the air. Instantly both cloth and lady disappeared. The illusion involved perfect co-ordination of mechanical ingenuity and dexterity, which makes it all the more remarkable that it became the most imitated of its day. So strong is the effect, however, that it is still performed by major illusionists 100 years later, although no one now attempts the vanish of the cloth, which ironically is more difficult to achieve than that of the lady.

Buatier's distinctive reputation in the field of magical invention is founded as much upon the ingenuity he showed in devising smaller magical effects as in his mastery of full-scale stage illusions. It is easy today to take for granted the manipulative skill with which a magician causes billiard balls to multiply at his fingertips; the flair with which a flagstaff in all its patriotic colours suddenly appears in his hand; the aesthetic appeal of the trick in which flowers, hundreds of them, albeit made of paper, fill to overflowing a paper cornucopia; the tantalising behaviour of handkerchiefs as they pass mysteriously from decanter to decanter or between two previously shown empty soup plates. Whatever the dexterity needed to perform them, all these effects had their technical basis in de Kolta's fertile brain. Like Harbin, he projected a delightful eccentricity in performing them, accentuated in his case by untamed whiskers and ill-fitting dress suit.

It is generally conceded that his greatest creation was his last. A small platform standing on four legs was placed in the centre of the stage. De Kolta then came forward carrying a satchel which he said contained his wife, joking that it saved on transport costs. An assistant was asked to open the bag. All she could see was a die or dice, a small cube about eight inches in dimension. The die was placed on the table. It then visibly expanded in size until it measured some two-and-a-half feet across, completely filling the table top. When the cube was lifted, there was Madame de Kolta sitting cross-legged on a cushion. Like his 'Vanishing Lady', this reversal of the earlier effect defied rational explanation. Behind the scenes the trick represented a miracle of light engineering; with the public it caused another sensation and in September 1903 he accepted an offer to present it at the Eden Musée in New York. From New York he

This contemporary cartoon of de Kolta's memorable illusion omitted one detail –
he also made the cloth disappear.

went to New Orleans where he was suddenly taken ill and died on 7
November. It is the greatest tribute to de Kolta's creativity that, with the
exception of the 'Expanding Die', all his inventions discussed in these
pages are still in performance somewhere in the world today. The technical
intricacy of the die illusion, however, has always intrigued and challenged
Paul Daniels. With a skilled technical team at his disposal, it can only be
time before that too again becomes a reality.

14

Magic for a Special Occasion

The conventional image of the magician at work is one framed by a proscenium arch, a table edge or the television screen. It could be argued, however, that the greatest magic is that which breaks loose from such restraints and that the magician most worthy of the name is the individual who, far from merely acquiring the skills to present the sleights and illusions that constitute his act, has acquired an attitude whereby magic informs his every waking moment whether on stage or off. It is akin to the ability of Groucho to find the right word for any occasion, to the unstudied ability of Astaire to make his every gesture worthy of a choreographer's study. The true magician will read into the right set of circumstances the opportunity to stage, seemingly on the spur of the moment, an apparent miracle, the conditions for which sometimes may never present themselves again.

This capacity for bending the everyday environment to the cause of baffledom is our main concern in this chapter. Few of the miracles described are really capable of presentation in a conventional show. Some of them are once-and-once-only happenings which will never be repeated, but the ingenuity of which deserves a better fate than mere obscurity. Others require less unique circumstances, yet when presented correctly should help to reinforce the impression that the performer is indeed a wizard for all seasons, and not just when his music plays. Other magicians, who study these happenings and translate the thought processes behind them into the situations they meet, will have at their disposal a weapon in the fight for recognition as powerful as the largest stage illusion or the most difficult sleight.

No one understood this basic principle to greater advantage than the great Alexander Herrmann. Born of German parentage in Paris on 11 February 1844, he became America's leading magician during the latter quarter of the last century until his premature death on 17 December 1896. In appearance he looked more Mephistophelean than Mephistopheles, an image that belied his great personal warmth both on- and off-stage. Always, however, his most memorable feats were presented away from the footlights, in that impromptu theatre of legerdemain that he transported with him wherever he went. He would enter a grocery store, select an egg and crack the same, only to reveal to the utter amazement of shopkeeper and customers alike a gold dollar inside. Imagine the dilemma in which this placed the grocer: whether to sell his eggs, for which trade would now never be brisker, or not to sell in the anticipation of untold personal wealth within their shells. Restaurant rolls yielded similar rewards as Herrmann discreetly loaded the unseen coins he had palmed securely in his hand. Such was his skill at making audiences believe what he wanted them to believe that no one ever suspected the simple secret. At his wedding in Manhattan in 1875 Herrmann similarly conjured up a wad of dollar bills from the beard of the Mayor of New York who had conducted the ceremony. On another occasion the whiskers of President Ulysses S. Grant yielded an avalanche of cigars on Herrmann's touch.

There were times when Herrmann was able to turn this flair for extempore magic to more specific personal advantage. On one occasion one of his assistants accused no less than Oscar Hammerstein of coming backstage to spy out the magician's secrets. To defuse the situation, Herrman quick-wittedly broke a diamond-studded locket from his chain and wrapped it in a piece of paper as a gift for Hammerstein. 'Keep it and remember me by it,' he smiled by way of apology. Later when the impresario opened the package in his office, the locket had disappeared. In its place was an old railway ticket.

The heights which Herrmann's chutzpah could reach in this direction were demonstrated in Madrid in 1885 when he was invited by King Alfonso XII of Spain to entertain at the royal palace. After the performance the magician presented the monarch with an Argentinian saddle trimmed with silver, a present so overwhelming that the host begged to be able to pay Herrmann a favour in return. Herrmann was prepared. 'Come to the theatre tomorrow night, and when I call for a spectator to write something on a piece of paper, volunteer to assist me.' The following evening the magician duly requested such assistance, and the King in his turn duly stood up in the royal box. A blank sheet of paper was displayed and given the royal signature for later identification. Herrmann now invoked the spirits to write a message on the same sheet. After a pause he asked the King once more to examine the paper, to check his signature, and then to read out what now was written above it. With a smile on his lips Alfonso proclaimed, 'I will not deny my signature to this document, which appoints Alexander Herrmann prestidigitator to the King of Spain, and, as the spirits have done so, I heartily acquiesce.'

There were occasions when Herrmann's flair for the surprise denouement of a trick produced less happy results. When appearing in Constantinople he was invited on a cruise aboard the royal yacht by the Sultan Abdul Aziz, the ruler of the Ottoman Empire. It was inconceivable to either party that the voyage should come to a close without a display of

The great Alexander Herrmann, a magician for all occasions.

legerdemain. At an appropriate moment, therefore, Herrmann asked the Sultan for the loan of his watch. Taking the priceless timepiece, the magician, without warning of any kind, hurled it into the waves. The atmosphere became tense with embarrassment in spite of the magician's protestations to the Sultan not to worry. He then took a fishing line, cast it overboard, and within a short while landed a catch. When the fish was cut open, the Sultan's watch, unharmed, was discovered inside. But the

"THREE LITTLE MAIDS FROM SCHOOL ARE WE,
WE'S BEEN SO GOOD WE'S GOIN' TO SEE
C. H. Charlton's Mysteries

The special occasion of a magic performance for children was captured in this poster for British illusionist Chris Charlton (1883–1963) by the famous illustrator Mabel Lucie Attwell.

damage had been done. Within days an emissary of the Sultan came to Herrmann with a bag containing 5,000 gold piastres and an envelope carrying the royal seal. Inside was not the medal the magician had hoped to find, but a letter requesting his departure from Constantinople.

On one other occasion the tables were turned on Herrmann. He happened to be sitting alongside the famous humorist, Bill Nye. Herrmann did not know Nye at all and the writer knew the magician only by sight. This did not, however, prevent Herrmann from reaching over to the salad on Nye's plate and extracting a large diamond ring from behind a lettuce leaf. With mock amazement, he rebuked Nye for being so careless with valuables. This time the humorist was ahead of the magician. Calling across to a waitress who had been observing the tableau, he calmly took the jewel and gave it to her with his compliments, 'I'm always leaving things like that around!' Herrmann had to work another kind of magic entirely on the management of the hotel before he could regain possession of the diamond. One thing he gained, however, and never lost from that moment was the friendship of Nye himself.

*

Herrmann's showmanship in turning magic to incidental advantage has been kept alive by a whole parade of conjurors both famous and not so famous. To magicians, John Mulholland was a distinguished performer specialising in lecture circuit and high society bookings on America's East Coast during the middle years of this century, his academic approach to magic leading to contributions to the *Encyclopaedia Britannica* and the editorship of magic's most prestigious journal of those days, *The Sphinx*; to members of the public he was the tall, professional-looking eccentric who could be seen entering the New York subway, dropping his nickel in the turnstile, passing through, then turning round to extract supposedly the same nickel from the ostensibly impregnable fare container.

Horace Spencer was a British performer, a brother of the celebrated painter Stanley Spencer, who earned a precarious living from magic in the 1920s and 1930s. During the summer he would perform for the passengers on one of the pleasure-steamers that travelled the Thames, passing the hat afterwards for remuneration. As they approached a landing stage he would have a card mentally selected, but when this card was looked for in the pack it was no longer there. Spencer would call to a boy fishing from the quay and a quick transaction resulted in the magician buying the fish just caught. The spectator was invited to name the missing card and then to slit open the fish. There, like the Sultan's watch many years before, was the chosen card.

Today Paul continues to bring magic to children through the characters of television's 'Wizbit'.

As unconventional was the Scot, Jardine Ellis, known as the 'Globe-Trotting Magician' and renowned in the early years of this century as an inventor of subtle methods for magicians. Having alerted the press in a particular town to be present, he took great pleasure in entering a café to order tea and currant buns. When he was sure he had someone's attention, he would gesture a teaspoon to stand up and bow to him. It did so. Breaking a bun in two, he placed the two halves on the table in front of him. A moment later the currants started to wriggle out of their resting-places and crawled away from him across the table at his command. The tricks were as incredible as they were silly. The result was lots of local press coverage and a puzzled crowd of onlookers to whom he would sell his secrets at five pounds a time, a vast sum in the early 1920s, on condition that the purchaser did not disclose anything to a soul or use the methods disclosed. After visiting other cafés in the vicinity, Ellis then moved on to another town as anonymously as he had arrived.

No magician had a surer grasp of the publicity value of this kind of sorcery than Max Malini. He was born Max Katz, in Ostrov on the Polish/Austrian border in 1873, and emigrated with his family to New York at a very early age. A squat pug of a man, he represented a paradox among magicians in that he appeared before probably more heads of state than any other wizard in history, in spite of a personality and approach described as brusque and crude and often bordering on the offensive. His career methods were likewise those of a nonconformist. The vaudeville

The likelihood is that the odds would have been on Max Malini and not the Devil!

IT'S A DRAW BETWEEN THE DEVIL AND MALINI !!

Malini favoured court dress for his stage and platform appearances.

houses and music halls that provided platforms for his contemporaries were not for him. Instead he travelled the world ingratiating himself with the managements of the top hotels. As his reputation for performing impromptu miracles for the patrons of a certain hotel increased in the bars and saloons, so the management would concede to him the use of the ballroom for a more conventional show lasting two hours or more. Invariably sold out, this single performance in such a venue would gross Malini at least $1,000 even in the 1920s. And then like Ellis, but at a less parochial level, he would move on.

Malini's full-length concert performance was competent, to say the least, but it was the memory of his extempore magic that stayed etched in the minds of those who experienced it. He was happiest sitting at a bar working to a small select audience. He would borrow a hat beneath which he placed a gold coin. Lifting the hat, he challenged the owner to grab the coin before the hat was replaced. Malini would give the spectator every chance, but eventually, when the man went to grab the coin, it had gone. In its place was a large block of ice. Throughout, Malini's hands stayed dry. The fact that the magician had sometimes been sitting there for an hour before the amazing object appeared only enhanced the effect.

The lengths to which Malini would go to produce a one-off individual miracle are legendary. On one occasion in a tailor's shop in Washington, DC he noticed the name-tag attached to a suit awaiting collection. Max bribed the tailor to sew a playing card secretly inside the lining. No one knows the exact resolution of this ploy, but it is certain that sometime in the future lifespan of the suit the United States Senator whose name Malini had recognised would get the surprise of his life when the magician, having inveigled himself into his presence somehow, conjured a duplicate card freely chosen by the politician into this most impossible of hiding places.

If Malini knew he would be passing a particular way with a friend he would in advance take a card, which had previously been soiled and scrunched up by the heel of his shoe, and discard it face-down in the gutter along the route. While strolling with his friend later he would bring the conversation around to his ability to tell the value of any playing card from the back, no matter what its design. By now, of course, the 'weather-beaten' card would be in sight. More often than not the friend would pounce on this as a challenge, only for Malini to score again.

The most outrageous trick he ever performed took place at a very exclusive dinner party to which he had been invited as a guest. Beforehand he had been able to bribe the kitchen staff to play along with him. Unbelievable as it may sound, Malini had plucked a live turkey, 'hypnotised' it, and arranged the bird in the centre of a platter garnished with the usual trimmings to make it look real. During the meal Malini engineered the conversation around to the subject of resurrection and reincarnation. While he was in full flow the turkey was brought in and set on the table. In the subdued lighting everything appeared in order. One only wishes one could have seen the looks on the diners' faces as the host plunged the carving fork into the bird. The poor creature woke up instantly and scurried off the table, causing nothing short of chaos, panic and probably a cardiac arrest or two. Or so the story goes.

One further story epitomises his style. One of the most impressive feats in his regular show involved finding a series of chosen playing cards by stabbing them with a knife under strict conditions while blindfolded. He once performed this item in the presence of the British Royal family, incurring the displeasure of no less than the Queen. We do not know whether it was Queen Alexandra or Queen Mary, although he certainly performed for both King Edward VII and King George V. Malini had no concern for the surface on which he worked the trick, but the equerry explained to him after the performance that the Queen was upset by the damage he had caused to her fine Louis-Quatorze table. The magician was unabashed and in his gruff broken English said, 'But she can say that the marks were made by the great Malini!' The story defines the unbelievable nerve and impudence of the performer whose slogan was 'You'll Wonder When I'm Coming – You'll Wonder More When I've Gone'. Malini died in Honolulu on 3 October 1942. He had moved in such illustrious circles during a career in which he amassed several fortunes that it is poignant to discover that he died of malnutrition. One wonders still.

*

In more recent years opportunism in magic has been kept alive by Karrell
Fox, the best impersonator of W. C. Fields you will see in years and, as
this is written, the President of the world's largest magical organisation,
the International Brotherhood of Magicians. Fox won his colours in magic
with a unique trick staged for the personal amazement of Henry Ford II.
Anxious in his early years to break into the field of using magic for sales
purposes at industrial shows, he eventually secured an appointment to see
the great man. Ushered into the inner sanctum of his presence, with only
minutes allocated to sell his master plan, Fox launched into his big pitch
and then, to make a point, asked Ford if he could show him some actual
magic. The executive complied, chose the obligatory card, and yawned
ahead to his next appointment. Fox raced to bring the effect to a successful
conclusion, but failed to find the card. Changing the subject quickly to
hide his embarrassment, he found himself gabbling on about Ford's
magnificent garden, the much-publicised pride and joy of a hobby that he
kept on the large balcony outside. Taking pity on the young magician,
the magnate was only too happy to show him around. As they walked
outside Fox paused to ask, 'But tell me, sir, what was the card you
selected?' Ford told him. 'Well, look up there,' replied the magician. Ford
did so. At that moment a skywriting plane flew past writing the name of
the card against the atmosphere. When he had recovered from the shock,
Ford offered Fox the contract that gave him the foothold he craved in the
industrial field. In 1960 he launched 'The Magic World of Ford', the motor
company investing a spectacular three million dollars in a presentation that
travelled the trade-show circuit for several years with up to six units in
operation at any one time. The miracle on Ford's balcony paved the way
for the profitable marriage of magic and merchandising evident at trade
shows throughout the world to this day.

A not dissimilar incident proved a milestone in the early magical life of
Paul Daniels, although he has no direct recollection of exactly what
happened, having to rely upon the first-hand reports of others. He was
aboard a troop ship transporting the Green Howards, the regiment with
which he was serving, across the smooth waters of the Indian Ocean from
a posting in Hong Kong. It was not until half-way through the day
following the performance in question that Paul awakened in the giddy
throes of an almighty hangover, feeling as bad as he had ever felt in his life,
to discover the extreme lengths he had taken to impress the officers in their
mess the night before. He can remember them continually plying him with
drinks, no doubt in an attempt to discover how his tricks worked, and the
gallant acceptance of this high-ranking hospitality by his teetotal self. As
Paul says, you can't really argue with an officer. But he can't remember
performing the trick that was now the talking-point among them. It

Karrell Fox, compulsive jester and creative magician.

transpires that the more drunk he became, the more baffling he became, until eventually he took a pack of cards, had one chosen and returned, and then threw the whole pack against a porthole. All but one card fell, the chosen card sticking against the glass. When the officer helping was asked to take down his card, it was found to be stuck on the *outside* of the porthole. At that point Paul, with a curt 'Sort that one out, you bastards', passed out.

As this was recounted to Paul the following day, he started to feel even more queasy. There are no such things as actual miracles and only one way he could have accomplished the trick described. This would have entailed excusing himself from the officers' company sometime during the evening, going out on deck, and them clambering over the side of the ship to stick a duplicate of the still-to-be-chosen card on the outside of the porthole. He would then have climbed back, gone inside, and continued his performance until he came to the trick in question. No one would notice the card until Paul wanted them to. That is the only way the trick could have been accomplished. The fact that Paul, even when sober, cannot swim and sinks like a stone, in retrospect only enhances the opportunism behind this 'once-in-a-lifetime' effect. That he can personally remember nothing of the performance is the reason why he drinks moderately to this day. Karrell Fox would be the first to credit the New York bandleader and magician Richard Himber, and Paul the American magical genius Bob Hummer, with the two basic premises on which their respective miracles were based. To each, however, must go the credit for taking an idea and using it to maximum advantage at the optimum time, whether sober or not.

Situational magic of this. kind, taking advantage of a non-theatrical environment in which to stage a special trick, was performed to stunning effect in New York in the 1930s. Much consternation was caused in newspaper offices by the alleged antics of a Superman figure spotted in the Harlem district flying around from rooftop to rooftop in a flowing black cloak. Hardened journalists set on the trail of the ghostly flyer readily dismissed the phenomenon as a hoax, but even their scepticism was eventually punctured as more and more members of the public placed themselves on record as witnesses of the phantom. Ironically, upon investigation it was discovered that the magician ultimately responsible was not a conventional stage wizard but the product of another journalist's wild imagination.

Few magicians who trod the boards ever enjoyed the widespread popularity of Mandrake the Magician, whose comic-strip adventures still enjoy a cult following. Such was his appeal in the 1930s that a group of young boys formed a secret society in homage to their idol. His fly-by-night activities were their inspiration. When darkness had overtaken the city two of them would put on identical black cloaks. Hidden in the folds of each garment were two small torches. With the precision of a military operation they would study their terrain. The choice of rooftops was strategically important. One would climb on to a third- or fourth-storey roof adjoining another building whose roof was lower by four or five feet. His partner would position himself at the edge of the roof of another building directly across the street. Then the masquerade was set to commence. The first would-be 'Mandrake' would scream like Frankenstein, holding the lit torches against his forehead to resemble eyes. This seldom failed to attract the attention of a passing pedestrian. When he knew he was being watched he would make the four-feet leap to the lower level still screaming and with much flapping of his cloak, switching off the torches in the process. With split-second timing his colleague would pick up the scream and switch his 'eyes' on. And it did not necessarily stop there. After a further scream, the second boy could jump into the darkness and a third similarly attired member of the society could appear half-way down the street, and so on, *ad infinitum*. People really *did* believe that a man could fly!

*

This link with a fictional magician recalls the close affinity long enjoyed between magicians and writers of the detective story, both setting out as they do to baffle their audience. Clayton Rawson, John Dickson Carr, and

Walter B. Gibson, alias Maxwell Grant, have all proved themselves skilled exponents at both activities, while more than once Agatha Christie has found herself described with justification as 'The Mistress of Misdirection'. Since both the perfect illusion and the perfect crime have to give the same semblance of impossibility, it is not surprising that the skills overlap. Rawson's creation, 'The Great Merlini', was often summoned from the magic shop he managed on Times Square by the New York City Police to solve impossible murders, more often than not demonstrating in the process how the illusionary stratagems of the prestidigitator had been used to commit crimes. Rawson's chief rival was John Dickson Carr, sometimes known by the *nom de plume* Carter Dickson. Their combined speciality was the 'locked room' murder, a term used for a crime committed under a set of circumstances which geographically and chronologically totally defies explanation. The description that follows is not of a crime but of an illusion, performed at the 1952 Convention of The Society of American Magicians in Boston. It is hard to believe when first confronted with its details that it is not one further example of either Rawson's or Carr's devilish ingenuity. In keeping with the theme of this chapter, the miracle in question was not performed on a stage, but in a hotel room accommodating part of a magicians' trade fair. Ken Allen, a prominent dealer in conjuring apparatus, was its brilliant perpetrator.

For all that the casual audience knew otherwise, Allen could have been demonstrating the latest item from his catalogue when he invited two friends to hold up a blanket to conceal him temporarily from view. Seconds later they dropped the cloth and Allen had disappeared. The two friends invited the stunned audience to examine every nook and cranny of the room and its adjoining bathroom. No chair was left unturned, no closet unopened in the search for the evanescent Allen. The room had no windows and the door that led to the hotel corridor had thoughtfully been locked before the trick commenced. Besides, to reach the door Allen would have had to pass through the crowd, which was impossible. When the spectators had admitted defeat, the two assistants held up the blanket again. When it was dropped a second time, Allen walked forward triumphant, knowing that in the eyes of the crowd he now owned the world.

When pressured later to explain what had effected his disappearance Allen could have replied 'a bottle-opener' and left his interrogator even more nonplussed by the truth! The day before he had attempted to open a bottle of beer on a bottle-opener affixed to the cabinet above the wash-basin in the bathroom. When the bottle top refused to budge, Allen pulled even harder and the cabinet came away from the wall. One side, in fact, was hinged curiously to a square opening, the framework and hinges of which were quite invisible from the bathroom. When Allen put his hand through the hole he saw that it opened on to an air shaft extending the complete height of the hotel. It was then that inspiration struck. If he

Paul, at an early moment in his career, with a very special levitation.

cleaned the walls of the shaft and could somehow fix a fastening device to prevent the cabinet being pulled open when people were searching for him, he had here the solution to the ultimate vanish. That he also needed nerves of steel goes without saying. When the time came to stage the illusion his two friends made sure that the blanket gave him sufficient time to enter his unique twentieth-century 'priest's hole'. Once inside the shaft Allen was able to brace the rubber soles of his shoes against the opposite wall as he himself pulled on the fastening device. One slip could have been fatal, which makes the fact that he repeated the illusion several times all the more remarkable.

It is perhaps surprising that there exists little evidence of magical technique being used in the cause of crime detection outside the pages of the mystery writers already mentioned. One gleaming example, however,

Maurice Fogel began as 'The Magical Impressionist' before turning to mind-reading.

does exist of a case in which a magician's quick thinking resulted, if not in the apprehension of the guilty party, at least in the satisfaction of the person wronged. The performer in question was Maurice Fogel, a headliner in British variety during the late 1940s and 1950s. Born on 7 July 1911, in London's East End, he was a warm, ebullient showman whose direct approach to mind-reading made him conceivably Britain's only serious contender to Dunninger at that time. He possessed two qualities even more impressive than his act, namely his generosity and his flair for capitalising magically upon a unique set of circumstances. He once found himself topping a bill which also featured the then little-known Peter Sellers, who, in the years before he became one of England's top screen actors, was a brilliant, but small-time impressionist. Fogel saw his chance. His back to the audience, his nose flat against a massive blackboard that dominated the stage, he challenged anybody to hold up personal possessions which he then described back to them in the most intimate detail. There was no way Fogel could have seen a thing. Nor did he need to, as long as Peter Sellers was happy to stand in the wings with a pair of binoculars and imitate Maurice's emphatic Jewish tones with devastating accuracy.

More relevant, however, was the occasion when he was presenting his one-man show at a theatre somewhere in the Midlands, an event graced by the presence of the mayor and mayoress of the town in question. During the interval the latter retired to the cloakroom where she removed a valuable ring before washing her hands. Returning to the auditorium, she momentarily forgot the ring. When she went back, it had gone. She reported the loss to the manager who consulted Fogel about the possibility of making some form of announcement from the stage. Less resourceful minds would have done just that, but Fogel's approach was far more creative. The curtain rose on the second half and the showman made his appeal. He explained that a crime had been committed and that his ability to read minds told him that the thief was present in the audience. He knew the identity of the culprit, but, to save embarrassment to the theatre and the person from whom the ring had been stolen, announced that during the course of his performance a collection would be made for charity. He showed a small cloth bag which he proposed should be passed among the audience, row by row. Everyone would be expected to place a small coin inside the bag. When it arrived at the guilty party, however, that person would put in the ring. No one would know who that person was. But should the ring not be in the bag at the end of the collection, the police would be called and the identity of the thief revealed to them. Fogel, of course, had no more idea who the culprit was than the mayoress. He had no need to know. When the bag was emptied and the collection counted, the ring shone forth in all its brilliance among the pennies and halfpennies. The story is a perfect example of magical psychology applied to a non-magical problem. It is unlikely, however, that any magician other than Fogel would have arrived at such a singular solution. When he died on 30 October 1981, the world of magic lost a very special member.

The link between magic and crime, both employing deception for their disparate ends, was turned to advantage by the contact mind-readers, Brown, Bishop and Cumberland. A favourite test of all three involved the reconstruction of an imaginary murder. In the absence of the mentalist, one member of the audience would be designated 'corpse' and the dagger, which supposedly implemented the deed, hidden. The showman on his return would first locate the weapon and then go through the action of stabbing the victim. A make-believe culprit could be apprehended with the same technique.

In a recent television show Paul Daniels took the classical 'whodunnit' theme and, working backwards from the premise that the butler *did* do it, used a skilful elimination procedure (recorded as a prediction ahead of the event) to take the servant back to the scene of his crime and the weapon, a free choice from among several. As the butler, Alan Davidson-Lamb, a bona-fide freelance employee of the Royal Family and several Prime Ministers, moved of his own free will between conservatory, kitchen, dining-room, games room, library, bathroom, bedroom, drawing-room and hall in a one-storey, cross-section reconstruction of a country house, so rooms were moved away according to the prediction that resounded from the cassette recorder on the tray in his hands. Amazingly the butler, who was not an accomplice of Paul in any way, always chose to be in a room other than the one to be towed away at any given time. No one was more aghast when at the culmination of the sequence the corpse, a knife in its back, slumped out of an imitation bookcase in the library, the only room to remain. Both library and dagger were announced on the prediction tape that was then given to the butler to take away to satisfy to himself that all was genuine. Throughout the episode Paul stayed at the butler's side; there was no way his voice could have been transmitted through the cassette recorder from an off-camera position. The instructions from Paul to the butler had truthfully been recorded in their entirety several days previously on a single cassette. Paul's own methods, if not the butler's, had proved above suspicion.

*

No mystery presented by Paul has been more vulnerable to criminal action itself than the spectacular disappearance of one million pounds, presented on the occasion of his 1984 Christmas television show. For the most expensive illusion Paul has ever performed part of the studio was converted into a special top-security zone equipped with closed circuit television cameras, pressure pads on the floor to activate alarms, and constant Securicor guard. Under the watchful gaze of Mr Owen Rout, an executive of Barclays Bank from whom the BBC borrowed the money, and Mr Robert Maxwell, the newspaper publisher who had just pioneered million-pound prize bingo in the *Daily Mirror*, the truck transporting the money made a spectacular entry into the studio to the defiant strains of the theme from 'The A Team'. Counted and weighed by Barclays' staff during the afternoon, the cash was not only contained within a heavy metal strong-box with perspex windows in its sides, but that box was bolted in turn within a larger combination safe by a five-foot metal bar padlocked at both ends. The strong-box was removed from the safe, the bar relocked, and the safe closed with two guards remaining one on each side.

When opened, the box revealed more clearly forty bundles of £25,000, each wrapped in regulation blue polythene with white binding strap. Maxwell was asked to choose any one of these. The bundle was opened and verified. One of the ten individual packets within the bundle was then counted on camera by a cashier. There was no doubt that the million pounds was authentic. As Paul explained, one reason for inviting Robert Maxwell had been to give him the opportunity of disclosing in the press anything that was not what Paul made it out to be. The open bundle was now placed back in the box, lid closed, and the whole hoisted over the security zone to be lowered into a heavy-duty perspex container raised above the floor. One added feature of the security zone was now brought into operation. As the alarms were activated by Paul, tear-gas was seen to fill the perspex compartment. At all times one could see under, around and above the money; bona-fide Securicor guards were positioned all around the compound; but when the smoke cleared, the metal box complete with its contents had inexplicably dissolved away.

As Debbie McGee rushed on with a copy of the *Sun* with the dominant headline 'Magician Mislays a Million', Paul made Robert Maxwell admit that he'd been scooped, only to regain Maxwell's allegiance a second later, 'But I've got to tell you, that's the first time that paper's had any news in it.' But if Maxwell was jovial, Rout was agitated. 'What about the money?' Returning to the safe in which the million pounds had been brought into the studio, Paul reopened its front door. There back inside, secured on the metal bolt, the ends of which had been in full view throughout, was the strong-box, the money intact. Taking the loose packet that had been checked originally, Paul indulged a long-held fantasy. The sheer glee on his face, however, as he threw the notes up in the air – 'I've always wanted to do this' – perhaps disguised a tragic disappointment for a more elaborate fantasy. When earlier, before reopening the safe, he had joked to Owen Rout, 'I'm off now to pay for the yacht I ordered', he could, ironically, have been speaking the truth. The first part of the illusion had provided the perfect cover for the most ingenious heist of all time; this in spite of the elaborate security operation carried out behind the scenes to safeguard the actual money, right down to an instruction to everyone working on the show never to mention the million pounds beforehand but to use the code-phrase 'baby elephant' whenever referring to the illusion.

The concept of magically transporting a million pounds from one part of the studio to another originated in the fertile mind of Los Angeles magician, Dick Zimmerman. As Paul has explained, however, had the money not been set to return to the safe, it would have been technically easy from a magical point of view to have switched in a duplicate strong-box at an opportune moment prior to the recording. From such a box with a detachable base, an accomplice of Paul's concealed in the trolley could easily have removed the forty bundles as it was transported from the studio counting area to the security zone. As soon as the trolley was off-stage, Paul's staff could have whisked the actual million pounds away from the premises while the strong-box with the million pounds – or more accurately, a camouflage of blue polythene – supposedly still visible through its glass windows was being hoisted into the perspex box. In other words, the trick would now become the illusion of the vanishing strong-box and by the time the bank officials went to reclaim the money from its secret destination – all objects that vanish have to arrive somewhere – it would have been too late.

There was all the time in the world. As Paul explained on air, this was the one trick that he had never rehearsed because the bank had not made the money available until the recording. Therefore taking more time to raise and lower the strong-box into the security zone would have been perfectly acceptable. Weights placed in the box beforehand would have reinforced the illusion that the money was still there. All the security men involved in the operation had their eyes glued to the box throughout. It would have been a breach of their contract to have been looking elsewhere.

Albert Le Bas, about to turn a boy into a 'human gasometer'!

The getaway would have been the easiest in the world. The climax of recovering the money on air prevented Paul from succumbing to temptation, but even as a publicity ploy it would have been marvellous, the heist happening in full view of the audience and recorded. And yet in spite of that, no one would have seen the money go.

*

There must be space for one last example of 'magic for a special occasion'. If an Oscar were to be awarded to one magician for rising to that occasion when challenged in an impromptu situation, it would surely go to the Irish wizard Albert Le Bas, a fast-rising star in his own country when he met an early death at the age of forty-four in September 1972. His stage repertoire, like Paul's, was essentially that of the conventional magician's small magic, made larger by a personality that lit up the eyes and warmed the hearts of audiences who had seen it all before.

On the occasion in question he was travelling to an engagement by train. Four or five other people were sharing the carriage with him. There was no corridor. Conversation eventually revealed that he was a magician and he soon found himself performing some simple tricks for the young daughter of one of the passengers. It was not difficult for Le Bas to tell from her expression that she was not impressed. Deciding to put the magic away, he was suddenly stopped in his tracks when the girl glared at him and asked, 'If you're a magician, why don't you make the train go backwards?' At a time when other magicians would have given anything for a hole to appear in the floor, Le Bas kept both his cool and his charm and within two minutes had, like a genie, made the child's wish come true.

He first explained that in order to perform magic that spectacular he had to cast a spell. For this he would need the young girl's help. Taking his handkerchief he folded it bandage-fashion and blindfolded her. Placing his hands securely on her shoulders he then slowly turned her around four or five times. While this was taking place, he silently beckoned to everyone else in the carriage to change their seats and move their luggage from one side to the other so that their new positions represented a mirror-image of what had gone before. Then he carefully untied the blindfold and told the girl to open her eyes. When she looked out of the window, wonder blossomed on her face. As far as she could tell the train was now travelling in the opposite direction. If Le Bas's whole magical career had been restricted to that one afternoon in a musty train carriage he would still deserve the special place he holds in Magic's Hall of Fame.

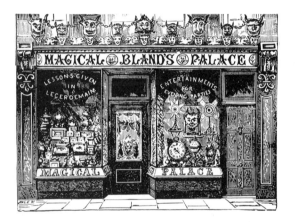

15

The Ziegfelds of Magic

With the possible exception of David Devant, no past master of illusion is spoken of with greater affection by those who saw him perform than Harry Blackstone, the fourth in a continuous progression of grand showmen to dominate American stages with a full evening mystery show from the middle of the last century. Alexander Herrmann, Harry Kellar and Howard Thurston had each in turn been accepted by the American public as the reigning monarch of magic, but it is unlikely that any of them achieved more widespread national popularity than the performer who could accurately boast, 'When I'm on stage, an elephant can walk on unnoticed.'

Apart from his innate personal magnetism, Blackstone's advantage was his canny use of the burgeoning media industry. At the height of his fame in the early 1940s, he joined the company of Superman, Batman, and Flash Gordon as the comic strip hero of his own comic book. *Super Magic Comics*, *Super Magician Comics*, *Master Magician Comics* and *Blackstone, the Magician Detective* (written on the magician's behalf by the prolific pulp writer, Walter B. Gibson, himself a magician of distinction) enabled thousands of American children who had never set foot inside a theatre to follow the exploits of the snowy-haired wonder-worker. So successful were these adventures that in 1944 a radio show, 'Blackstone, the Magician Detective', reached the airwaves. No less than seventy-eight episodes were broadcast. As television came into its stride, Blackstone was alert to the promotional advantages even a single appearance could bring. Inevitably he appeared on variety programmes and NBC's 'Tonight' show, but more significantly in line with his special status he received the accolade of a 'Person to Person' interview by the distinguished broadcaster Ed Murrow, as well as the surprise of being the subject of Ralph Edwards's original 'This Is Your Life'. Al Capp even included 'Whackstone', an obvious spoof of the illusionist, in his celebrated daily syndicated comic strip 'Li'l Abner'.

As he allowed himself to be promoted by areas of the media which had not existed before, Blackstone also realised the need to keep his

Harry Blackstone Senior, about to win a friend for life.

performance in pace with modern times. Whereas Thurston, who preceded him, had represented the quintessence of dignity and decorum on stage, Blackstone ensured that he was never taken seriously for too long. Harry Blackstone Junior, the great American magician of today, has described his father's approach. 'My dad performed each show as if he'd just thought up a new game in which he and the audience must participate.' The past masters of magic had made a big feature of including small red imps on their lavishly illustrated posters as evidence of their Mephistophelean connections. In Blackstone's case the only place for imps was in his humour.

He wore conventional white tie and tails, but often added a large white cowboy hat set at a rakish angle for eccentric effect, especially when

Blackstone knew how to capitalise on Hallowe'en – all the year round!

sawing through a lady with a full-size circular saw. 'I shall cut a little lady in two – so help me!' When he caused a horse to disappear, he was left with the saddle between his legs. One moment he would present his awe-inspiring version of the levitation, the next he would explain in a warm sonorous voice to the children in his audience, 'And boys and girls when you go out into the lobby you will meet a man called "Big Hearted Jim" and he will give you all a box of magic, but I want you to be big-hearted in return and make sure that you give him something back, like a quarter.' No magician ever represented Middle America with more telling effect; he was the con man and the farm hand, Wild Bill Hickock and Mark Twain all rolled into one.

Blackstone's real name was Harry Boughton. He was born on 27 September 1885 in Chicago where his father owned a flower shop. Boughton was shortened to Bouton when in 1910 as the magical straight man he formed a short-lived comedy act entitled 'Straight and Crooked Magic' with his brother Pete attired in white-face and baggy pants. Pete Bouton would in time become as important behind the scenes of the full evening Blackstone show as his brother was on stage. Meanwhile Harry would tour under a succession of different names before arriving at the one that would become a household word in North America. Martini, the Great Stanley, Francisco, Harry Careejo, Mr Quick, C. Porter Newton,

Opposite, Harry Kellar (1849–1922), master American illusionist of his own day who enthused about the young Blackstone to Houdini.

LeRoy Boughton, Beaumont the Great, and Fredrik the Great all had their passing moments of glory until 7 January 1918 at the Grand Opera in Tiffin, Ohio when the name Blackstone made its debut, anti-German feeling against 'Fredrik' having brought about the now-permanent change. In later years the magician would variously explain away the inspiration behind 'Blackstone' as his grandmother's maiden name, the sign of the famous Blackstone Hotel in Chicago, and a hoarding advertising Blackstone cigars. According to the magician's first wife, Inez Nourse, the latter is correct, the location of the hoarding Wappokineta, Ohio. Blackstone's sense of humour, however, was such that it was difficult to know when he was kidding or not. With his tongue fixed firmly in his cheek, he would tell far-fetched tales off-stage of his adventures as a spy in Bulgaria, his exploits as a brain surgeon in the Congo, and his time as a Cornell undergraduate. His charm was immense and people believed, even when he added to his autograph:

> May you live as long as you want
> And never want as long as you live
> And live ten years longer than I
> And I shall never die.

Blackstone's original interest in magic had been aroused at McVicker's

Blackstone (*second from left*) welcomes a contingent of British magicians to the USA. On his right is Cardini. Goodliffe wields the guillotine.

Theatre, Chicago in 1897 when he watched a performance of the great Harry Kellar. In 1920 Kellar himself, living in retirement in Los Angeles, would write to his friend Houdini:

> You asked me in your letter if I saw Blackstone. Yes, I went to his show three times and enjoyed it very much. Blackstone is an artist of a very high order. He is my ideal of a great magician. He works clean, his illusions are presented in a masterly way, and he impresses his audience with the idea that he is a wonder-worker. All in all it is the best magic show I have seen in many years. He will get there.

In time the show Kellar saw would grow in scale and spectacle and Blackstone justifiably became known as 'The Ziegfeld of Magic'.

His 'Show of 1001 Wonders' employed as many as thirty assistants and required two ninety-foot railway baggage cars to carry the 189 theatrical crates of equipment. The show was full of spectacular illusions, but it also contained more genuinely effective intimate magic than any other touring mystery show. Very often illusionists will employ smaller tricks to cover delays as larger props are set behind the curtain. Even today people jest about the Blackstone show, whether of father or son, that the larger props are set backstage to cover the delays while the magician is performing in front, but in fact the joke is testimony to their mutual skill, on a par with that of Devant and Daniels in Britain, at investing material with the power of a personality that would still be able to fill a theatre with no props at all.

Nevertheless the Blackstone show transported audiences through the whole spectrum of what was possible in large-scale sorcery. When the whirling blade of his lumber saw tore into the flesh of a hypnotised face-down assistant, it was not only seen to cut into her bare midriff, but also to sever a solid wooden plank placed beneath her. As she came forward apparently none the worse for wear at the conclusion of the experiment, Blackstone would wink and assure the more squeamish members of the audience that they could now take their hands from their eyes. They would certainly need to keep their eyes open extra wide to appreciate the grandeur and impossibility on a fully lit stage away from all scenery of 'The Levitation of the Princess Karnac', a version of Maskelyne's original illusion handed down to Blackstone with improvements by Kellar. Many of American magic's most informed connoisseurs have regarded the Blackstone presentation of this illusion as being as near to a miracle as they ever saw, its sheer simplicity as the sleeping princess rose slowly on an apparent cushion of air, in order for a hoop to be passed completely over her, achieving in Blackstone's hands a mystical quality beyond mere hocus-pocus.

The show also contained several less conventional ideas. Car tyres were called into the service of a magical illusion for the first time. A girl climbed into a tube formed by several tyres arranged on end and side by side in a

Blackstone assumed a
Daliesque appearance in
this publicity caricature.

rack. One by one the tyres were rolled across the stage to be stacked in a tower. Slowly it became clear that the girl had disappeared, but when a rope was lowered into the tower, up she came. In another sequence the narrow cabinet in which twenty-four rods are pushed through an assistant became transformed into one with twenty-four long neon tubes all glowing as the penetration took place. Common sense dictated that while you could bend or disconnect metal rods, you could not bend or disconnect tubular glass bulbs with an electric current running through them. Blackstone had 'The Great Leon' to thank for this item.

In 'The Bridal Chamber' an entire bedroom scene complete with bride and her maid was conjured from nowhere within a simple curtained framework. Nor was Blackstone content to stand back and make the magic happen, being only too happy to involve himself in an illusion. In 'The Mystery of Delhi', or 'A Fantasy Based on the Famous Sepoy Mutiny', he was lashed to the mouth of a cannon, disintegrating in a cloud of smoke as the weapon was fired. Within seconds the bearded Indian who perpetrated the execution removed his disguise to reveal himself as Blackstone. His most successful sequence along these lines was entitled 'Who Wears the Whiskers?' In May 1913, the reporter for the *Daily Tribune*, Gary, Indiana reported the miracle as follows:

The concluding feat sent the audience home wondering. Bouton, dressed in a slouch-hat, unfurls a large flag and holds it in front of him. His assistant, disguised in long whiskers, a robe and a large hat pulled down over his face, fires at the flag. It drops and only a puff of smoke behind it shows where the magician had been. Immediately afterwards from the wings comes a huge bear who bows and removes his head disclosing the assistant, while the magician stands pistol in hand on the spot where the assistant fired at the flag. The effect is astonishing and the audience is still speculating upon the deception.

In later years the sequence became more streamlined, the flag dropping to reveal the bear in place of the magician. The bear and Mr Whiskers, as he became known, went into a dance together as the tempo of the music increased. Suddenly the dance stopped, Mr Whiskers tearing away his disguise. It was Blackstone, whom the audience had assumed to be dressed as the bear. The illusion always closed the show for one reason: it always stopped it.

As long as he had an audience at hand, the magic still continued for Harry Blackstone off-stage. A favourite ruse involved going into a restaurant to order a coffee and two doughnuts, 'one plain and one chocolate'. The waitress had scarcely turned away from delivering the order when Blackstone would call after her, 'I'm sorry, miss, but what doughnuts did I order?' 'One plain and one chocolate,' replied the girl, staring in disbelief at the plain doughnut and cinnamon doughnut on the plate in front of her. Sheepishly taking away the plate to rectify the mistake, she no sooner brought the replacement order and turned to go than Blackstone asked the question a second time, 'I'm sorry, miss, but . . .' Her mouth dropped as she turned to see two chocolate doughnuts on the plate she had just brought. He would keep this up several times before his true identity became known to the waitress. One trusts she would never find out about his visit to the doughnut shop on his way to the restaurant where he bought a selection of different doughnuts which he pinned in a bag inside the lining of his suit.

An equally unconventional trick of Blackstone's involved bringing a dead house-fly back to life. Harry would explain that the fly was really in a state of suspended animation. He placed it on a sheet of paper and covered it with salt poured from a salt cellar. Within a short while it would fly away. It would be unfair to reveal the exact condition of the fly, but people did believe that the magician could in all seriousness bring the dead back to life. One of his greatest frustrations was that the trick was too small even for *him* to present on a stage. He made attempts at magnifying it for the theatre audience, but without success.

Perhaps the most important trick Blackstone performed in his entire career was not a trick at all in the accepted sense of the word, but nevertheless it perfectly demonstrates the quick thinking required by a magician when something goes wrong on stage. Nothing could have been more disastrous than what might have happened during the matinée at the

Lincoln Theatre in Decatur, Illinois on 2 September 1942. Blackstone was on stage entertaining a capacity audience of 3,200 people when Ted Banks, his stage manager, quietly walked out and whispered to him that the building next door was on fire and that the theatre was itself in jeopardy. Blackstone had never been ruffled on stage and he was not going to start now. Walking forward to the footlights he announced that his latest illusion was so grand, so spectacular that it could not be performed on an ordinary theatre stage. As a special surprise he would perform it that afternoon outdoors. Row by row to his precise instructions the audience filed out in orderly fashion in anticipation of seeing the biggest trick in the history of magic. Fortunately the fire was brought under control and the theatre itself left intact. The following day Ted Banks died of a heart attack attributed to the exertions of the emergency. There can be no doubt that but for the cool command of a master magician the consequences could have been even more tragic.

Blackstone himself would live to the age of eighty, retiring to the environs of the Magic Castle in Hollywood, California where he died in 1965. For many years he had made a base in the small town of Colon, Michigan, where every summer he returned with his company to refurbish the show and experiment with possible new miracles for the season ahead. Today the main street of Colon bears his name and the island on the small lake where he had his house and workshop is known as Blackstone Island. One of the rooms at the Magic Castle is named after him. He had come to full prominence with the death of Thurston in 1936 in the trough of the Depression years, and succeeded in bringing to the travelling magic show a glamour, verve, and lightness of touch that corresponded to the escapism which in its real-life dreariness the mass American public had come to expect from the Hollywood Dream. Fifty years later magic through television commands even wider attention from the public, but those essential qualities brought by Blackstone to the conventional practice of 'hey presto' are still held in esteem. It is today reassuring that the man who can justifiably lay claim to the billing 'America's Premier Prestidigitator' is still a Harry Blackstone, the son of the original, born on 30 June 1934 at Three Rivers, Michigan, not far from Blackstone Island.

It would be wrong to assume that Blackstone simply inherited his father's show. There was a considerable hiatus between the latter's retirement and the debut of his son's own full evening production. The economic restrictions of touring in the 1960s and 1970s led Harry to develop an act for the nightclub circuit with occasional forays into television. But the idea of reviving his father's show became a crusade within him. Escalating prices and restrictive union agreements could have proved prohibitive, but Harry, with his wife Gay, persisted against the odds. Painstaking research was needed to reconstruct old illusions and new ones were added. Gradually a new show evolved. On its inaugural tour it played in 156 cities across the United States before opening on Broadway

at the Majestic Theatre on 13 May 1980, where it ran for five months, becoming the longest-running pure magic show ever to appear on the Great White Way. At the time the musical *Barnum* was playing at the St James's Theatre directly across West 44th Street, prompting the distinguished drama critic, Brendan Gill, to write in the *New Yorker*, 'And if it turns out that there's less Barnum in *Barnum* than there is in

Overleaf, the 'Indian Rope Trick' and the 'Vanishing Camel' were both featured in this typical Blackstone extravaganza.

BIGGEST
NECROMANTIC
EXPOSITION
ON EARTH

BLACK

with every good wish
Col. Harry Blackstone
12-21-1959

ORIENTAL NIGHTS

BLACKSTONE'S TENF
SUCH AS RIVALS THE R
METAMORPHOSES OUTBIDS TH
THE ENCHANTED CAMEL—THE P

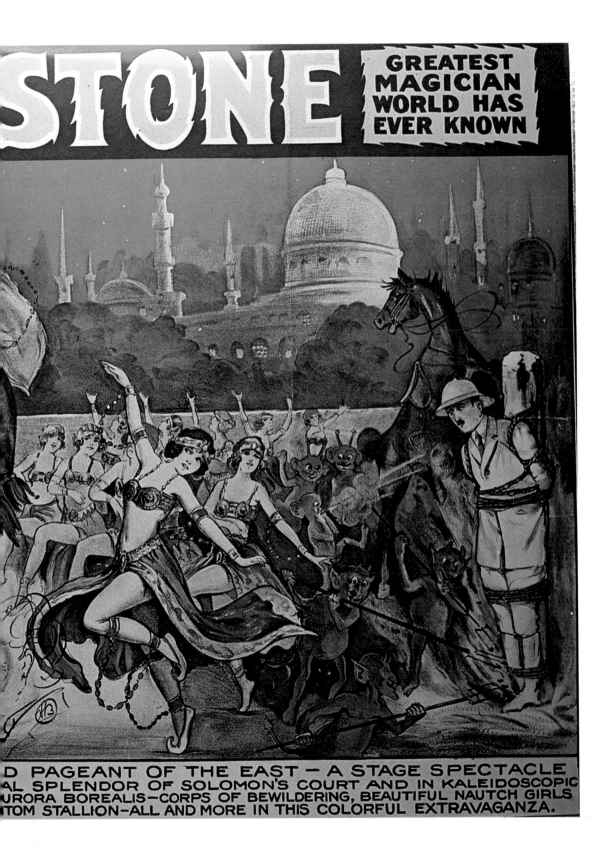

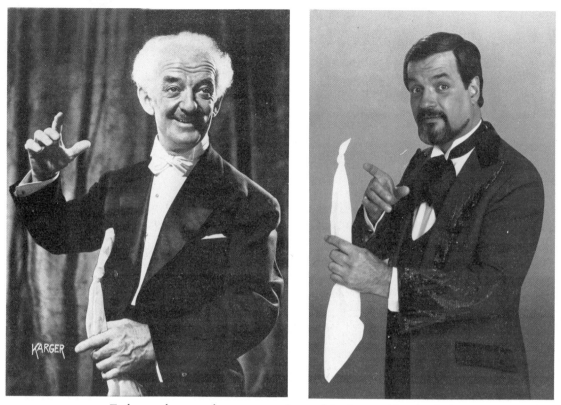

Father and son and two generations of 'a ghost with muscles'.

"*Blackstone!*" – well, that's show biz for you.' In so doing he was paying a double compliment to father and son, hitting the nerve of what made the older man successful and what the younger one was now intent on translating into his own show – an unashamed flair for carnival razzmatazz that struck a chord in the heart of every true American.

If the record of the smaller magic presented in the show of Blackstone Senior appeared to be glossed over, that is only because it represents the nucleus of the repertoire of his son. When today's Blackstone causes a canary in a cage to vanish from the hands of a stageful of children or to whisk off the shirt of a spectator as the climax to 'The Committee' – a skilled combination of pickpocketing and audience participation in which for most of the time the hands of the performer are tied securely behind his back – it is hard to imagine that such tricks were performed with more powerful presence and more telling effect for the audience of his father's day.

No Blackstone show has ever been complete without a performance of 'The Dancing Handkerchief', a miracle first taught to Blackstone Senior by the magician John Grdina after Harry had seen it performed by the theatrical spirit medium Anna Eva Fay. The handkerchief, borrowed from a member of the audience, is tied at one corner with a simple knot to represent the head of 'a real live ghost with muscles'. In the magician's hands it becomes rigid as steel one moment, as wobbly as jelly the next. One is not sure who is teasing whom. When the magician points one way, the handkerchief points the other. But there is no way a magician can allow himself to be humiliated by a handkerchief. He throws it down on the ground and just in time traps it with his foot. Still a free corner squirms as if to get away. He smacks again and again with the heel of his hand. Still it springs back up. He smacks it harder, 'Aaah – killed it!' But no sooner has the cotton corpse been tucked inside his jacket than it comes to life again. Balancing the handkerchief upright on the floor, Blackstone demands 'a little dance music, maestro', whereupon the ghost cavorts and shimmies and performs the best version of the soft shoe shuffle you will ever see a piece of cloth perform in your life. Harry picks up the handkerchief to return it to the audience, but it continues to wriggle and squirm in his hands right up until the moment it is in its owner's care. Then it returns to the humdrum existence of a simple square of white fabric. For four enchanted minutes the magician has transported the audience to a hey-diddle-diddle world where conceivably cows might just jump over the moon.

That carefree nursery world is never far away during the performance of another Blackstone classic. In this the initial production of a rabbit is incidental. Mystery gives way to sheer joy as Harry Junior, like his father before him, offers to give away the rabbit to the first boy or girl to shout 'Aye'. Amid the uproar of unanimous assent, one boy or girl is coaxed on to the stage. The dialogue that follows is a skilfully constructed chain of cautionary advice delivered with a warmth and firmness that is never allowed to become maudlin, pompous, or patronising. The child is made to promise that it will give the rabbit a home, food and water, and a name, but that it will never lift a bunny by its ears as in the cartoon: 'You will promise me, even if you become President.' The pet is wrapped in a newspaper for the child to take back to its seat, but the child has scarcely turned to leave the stage before Blackstone has voiced his suspicion that it has squeezed the parcel too tight, so tight that the rabbit has changed into a box of chocolate candies. The paper is opened, the rabbit has gone, and the candy cleverly becomes its own cue for caution. 'If anybody you don't know well offers you a piece of candy, take it home and offer a piece to Dad and if he lives through it, then you can eat it!' The child's disappointment that it must return without the pet is offset by the promise of a story. As the story unfolds – a tale about a magician and a rabbit and a theatre – it slowly dawns on the child that he or she, no less, is the central character: who else has recently squeezed a rabbit into a box of candy? This tale too carries its own contribution to the good behaviour code, namely that things thrown down should be picked up, like newspapers, for example. Crumpling the discarded newspaper in his hands, the magician in the story moulds the shape of a rabbit. Fitting the actions to the words, Blackstone notices a real live bunny materialise between the paper ears. The audience can relax at last and the child leaves the stage with both the candy and the rabbit. The tradition of giving away a rabbit at each performance became a trademark of the full-length Blackstone show. Only one child would go away from the theatre with a new furry friend, but this one item alone ensured that everyone else left possessed of wonder and enchantment, their generosity of spirit recharged. Everything was right with the world.

It is hard to imagine two magicians more dissimilar in appearance and background than the formal Harry Blackstone, steeped in his father's tradition, and the casual, self-taught Paul Daniels. And yet Blackstone's style represents the closest approximation in America today to that of Daniels. He too possesses a rapier-sharp sense of repartee, the ability to transcend relatively simple material with the power of personality, and the knack of making every single member of the audience feel personally involved in his performance. Not surprisingly, respect and friendship are mutual between the two men. Blackstone has made several appearances on 'The Paul Daniels Magic Show', re-creating his father's 'Buzz Saw' illusion as well as performing the handkerchief, birdcage, and light bulb sequences with his own special élan. While no formal copyright exists in the area of magicians and their material, it is acknowledged throughout the world of magic that the Blackstone presentations of these items are sacrosanct to the family name. When Paul Daniels was asked hypothetically which of all the tricks in the repertoires of the world's magicians he would most like to perform should such ethics not exist, it is not surprising that of his first three choices two were from the Blackstone repertoire, namely the rabbit sequence and the levitation of the light bulb.

One has to save the detail about Blackstone's light bulb illusion until last. In Paul's opinion it is the best levitation of an inanimate object he has ever seen or is likely to see, but even that is an understatement. The effect is simplicity itself. A bulb unscrewed from a table lamp remains alight with no apparent source for the electricity it is burning. When Blackstone lets go, it stays suspended in the air. A hoop passed around it in every direction proves that there are no extraneous means of support. To further emphasise the impossibility Blackstone walks into the audience, where he allows the bulb to be passed from one person to another for scrutiny. The last person is told to let go and the audience audibly gasps as it first rises, then hovers twelve inches above the hand that has just examined it. Blackstone returns to the stage. Still the lighted bulb floats. Then, addressing a distant part of the auditorium, he adds, 'Perhaps you over there would like to see it too', at which the bulb soars from his hand over the heads of the audience. Coming to a stop inches away from the bewildered gaze of another spectator, it remains momentarily suspended, turning a mystery into the closest thing to a miracle in modern magic, before returning to

Opposite, a dream came true on Broadway when Harry Blackstone reinterpreted his father's show within his own style.

Blackstone's hands to be replaced in the table lamp from which it was first taken.

Of all the illusions in the current show of today's Blackstone, it is the one of which Blackstone Senior would be most proud. He never achieved the journey of the light bulb over the audience, but when his son announces at the beginning of the item, 'I want to show you something that you will remember for the longest day you live', it is this single moment above-any other that ensures that you will. The illusion is complete, the heritage secure.

16

The Enigma of Chung Ling Soo

No Chinese magician ever attained greater fame or prestige than the legendary Chung Ling Soo. His real name was William Ellsworth Robinson, and he was born, probably of Scottish parentage, in New York on 2 April 1861. Apprenticeship as an illusion-builder to American performers as prominent as Harry Kellar and Alexander Herrmann led to his being invited to fulfil a short engagement at the *Folies Bergère* in Paris in direct imitation of the authentic Ching Ling Foo, a sensation at the time as the first individual Chinese magician to achieve popularity with Western audiences. Robinson adopted the name Hop Sing Loo, which was soon changed to Chung Ling Soo, meaning 'very good luck', and within a short time the 'impostor' had gained such ground on the original that a challenge of authenticity issued by Foo was won by Robinson, albeit by default when the challenger failed to appear, possibly daunted by Robinson's superior magical skills. Soon Ching Ling Foo imitators were no more; Chung Ling Soo had taken his place as the rage of the copyists.

One of his most thought-provoking mysteries was named 'Aerial Fishing'. Standing at the very front of the stage he would take a long rod and attach to the hook at the end of the line a small piece of worm as bait. By his side one of his assistants would be holding a large glass bowl of water. Soo would commence to wave the line over the heads of the audience. His gaze already suggested that he could see something there in the atmosphere that more ordinary mortals could not. Then he would suddenly whip the rod upwards. Instantly a goldfish would appear glistening at the end of the line. Swinging the fish in towards himself, he would detach it with care and drop it into the water where the audience could see it swimming around. When they had convinced themselves that the fish was genuine and alive, Soo would slowly repeat the whole procedure. In this way he would catch as many as six fish out of thin air.

Few tricks have created such a sensation with the media. The reporter writing in the *News of the World* on 9 April 1905 was typical of the lengths to which journalists, as well as rival magicians, would go in order to satisfy themselves, wrongly, that they knew the secret:

Left, William Ellsworth Robinson in his pre-Soo days and (*above*) Ching Ling Foo who started it all.

Anyone may know how Chung does the goldfish trick but it does not follow that, having been told, one can do it. The hook is a powerful magnet, and if one could examine the goldfish caught, one would detect pieces of metal attached to the bodies of the finny captives. The live goldfish repose in little Suee Seen's sleeve, and when a more than usually skilful cast brings the magnetic bait for a second into the interior of the girl's sleeve, a catch has at once been effected, and the fish is seen dangling and wriggling in the air at the end of the line.

The journalist need not in fact have exercised his imagination so strenuously. Soo had already patented the illusion, and the official explanation is accessible to all. Whatever explanations the press published, however, had little effect on his audiences. As far as they were concerned, Chung Ling Soo really did catch fish out of the air.

The original version of the trick had, in fact, been invented by Professor Mingus, a magician from New Jersey, but until Soo introduced it to London audiences it had attracted little attention. It subsequently became identified as Soo's personal miracle throughout the world. When theatre critics today discuss it in the context of the folk traditions of China, Robinson must be having the last laugh. They are unconsciously

Chung Ling Soo's pantomimic skills made him a great all-round entertainer.

acknowledging the greatest illusion he ever performed, namely the skilful way in which he lived up to the identity of his *alter ego* from the moment he shaved his head to don his first pigtail on 17 May 1900.

A master of the art of mime, Soo never spoke on stage, even though he often gave marathon performances of two hours duration. Off-stage in public he would continue to wear his Chinese make-up and spoke only 'Chinese', accommodating reporters through the 'interpretations' of his stage manager, Frank Kametaro. In 1908 he did allow the first edition of the *Liverpool Theatrical News* to publish a story regarding his true identity, mainly as a ploy to clear his name from any accusations that might be levelled against a member of the race that had committed the atrocities of the Boxer Rebellion. The story went unnoticed. The public did not want to know, probably dismissing it all as a hoax. In the eyes of the public Soo continued to live up to his publicity as 'A Gift from the Gods to Mortals on Earth to Amuse and Mystify', while in retrospect Robinson sedately earned his title as the all-time Emperor of inscrutability.

His full evening show built to a visual spectacle, 'The Dream of Wealth', which no magician since has attempted to emulate. It began modestly enough with Soo pouring a jug of milk into a small trinket box which he then proceeded to warm over a spirit lamp. As the magician tipped open the box on to a tray a shower of silver coins poured forth. They would not stop. Within a short time the whole stage was inundated with this glittering, metallic rain. When Soo looked to check that the box was at last empty, a piece of paper fluttered down. It had to be a bank note. It was, the first of many five-pound notes that similarly cascaded out of the shallow metal container in his hands. As his assistants rushed to gather them in baskets, two lines were attached to something else in the box. When they were pulled, a huge silk replica of a 1,000-pound note appeared, covering the entire back of the stage. In an instant, this was whisked away to reveal hanging centre-stage a giant golden sovereign. As it swung from above, triangular sections opened from its rim, transforming it into a gleaming sun, inside which resided the goddess Fortune pouring out another seemingly endless shower of golden coins from the cornucopia in her hand. Soo stepped forward resplendent in full black-silk Mandarin costume to take his applause. The curtain slowly fell, but rose again the instant it touched the stage. Soo stood there still, in identical hat and gown, except now dressed entirely in white.

It is ironic, in view of the genuine artistry of his characterisation, that today Soo is best remembered for the macabre circumstances of his death during a performance of the bullet-catching trick at London's Wood Green Empire on the night of 23 March 1918. Few illusions have captured the popular imagination as excitingly as this dangerous feat; none has claimed more victims among its practitioners. The first record of the trick appeared in a treatise entitled 'Theatre of God's Judgments' by the Reverend Thomas Beard as long ago as 1597, the performer being a

resident of Lorraine by the name of Coulen who 'would suffer har-
quebusses or pistols to be shot at him and catch the bullets in his hand
without receiving any hurt'. He survived the trick, but was killed by an
angry servant who subsequently struck him with the pistol.

However, of all the tragedies associated with the gun trick, none has
exercised the minds of magicians as much as that involving Chung Ling
Soo. The suburban London music hall was packed for the second
performance on that Saturday in 1918. In a prominent position on the
programme was the item described as 'Condemned to Death by the Boxers
– Defying their Bullets'. It is fair to ask why Soo, with his flair for visual
spectacle, should have featured the bullet trick at all, but this billing
contains the clue. There still lingered indignation in Britain against China
as a result of the Boxer Rebellion of 1900. Diplomats and missionaries
alike had been attacked and slain in the violent outburst of fanatical
nationalism which the Boxers represented. Order was restored to Peking
by an expeditionary force, but anti-Boxer feeling persisted. Soo had been
in a dilemma. He could neither afford to lose the glamour and mystique of
his Chinese identity, nor run the risk of bad personal feeling. He therefore
fabricated a press story that claimed he belonged to a group which was
friendly to foreigners and that this was why he had been forced to leave
China after being captured by the Boxers themselves. Condemned by
them to death by firing squad, he escaped through a supernatural power
that enabled him to render bullets harmless. He was prepared to duplicate
what happened on stage. With the episode described in this way over the
years, the inscrutable publicist was able to turn a potentially serious
political problem to his advantage.

The start of the presentation was predictable enough. An assistant
invited two members of the audience – on the night in question, two
discharged British Tommies – on stage to inspect a pair of old-fashioned,
muzzle-loading rifles. Under their scrutiny, Soo ignited a small amount of
black powder on a tray to prove it was gunpowder, while Suee Seen asked
two further members of the audience to select two round lead bullets from
a box and to mark them secretly with a knife for later identification. These
were brought back to the stage in a cup and tipped into the hands of the
original volunteers. Soo poured a charge of gunpowder into the barrels,
followed by wads to keep the powder compressed, finally ramming home
the marked bullets. The soldiers handed the loaded rifles to Dan Crowley
and Jack Grossman, two of Soo's assistants dressed as Boxer marksmen,
and were sent back to their seats. Soo moved solemnly to the right-hand
side of the stage facing the audience and, holding a Willow-patterned plate
in which to catch the bullets at arm's length in front of his chest, gave an
imperceptible nod to his chief assistant to signal that he was ready. The
latter issued the command to fire. Two shots rang out. The illusionist
staggered and fell. Applause, always at first tentative to greet this item,
gradually gave way to the hesitant silence that says all is not as it should be.

Overleaf, 'A Gift from the Gods', quite simply Paul Daniels's favourite poster.

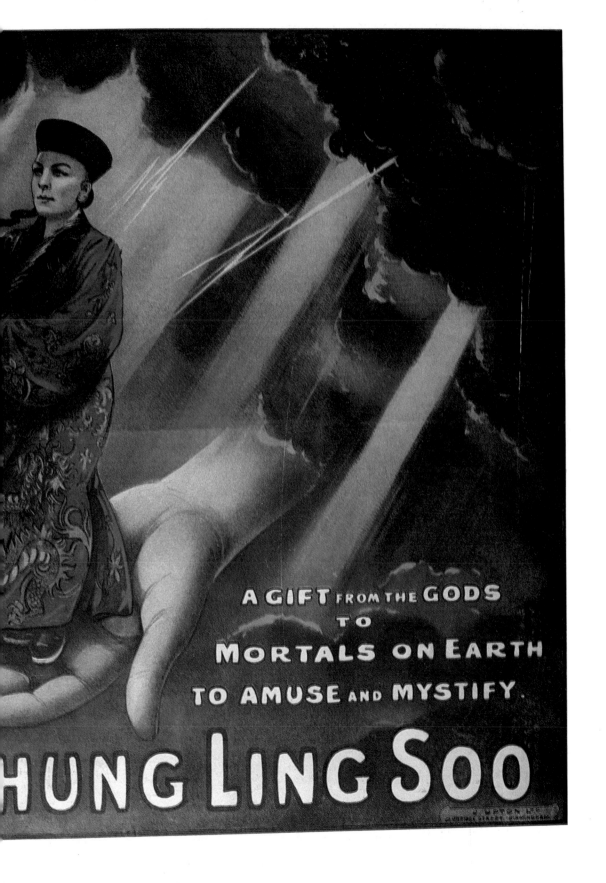

The curtain was rung down. With a theatre drape to absorb the blood, Soo was rushed to Wood Green Cottage Hospital where at 5 a.m. the following morning he died. A single bullet had transfixed his right lung. The inquest that followed registered the verdict 'death from misadventure'. Robert Churchill, the famous gun expert, testified to years of corrosion in one of the guns, brought about by the continual preparation required by Soo to make the trick possible in the first place. Suicide and murder had both been taken into account at the hearing. The day before Soo had summarily settled all his accounts; but, in fairness, he was just about to embark on an overseas tour. His marriage to Suee Seen was known to be unhappy, his attentions transferred to another woman. Rumour and theories would persist, but ultimately conscientious study of the evidence can only endorse the original verdict.

No one could possibly have been aware at the time that over half a century later Britain's foremost magician of the day, not born at the time of Soo's death, would re-create Soo's presentation of the bullet trick with none other than one of the original marksmen firing the rifle. The circumstances under which this came about are remarkable in themselves. Attending a Magic Circle concert in the company of two neighbours, June and Peter du Bosky, Clifford Davis, a journalist and magician, could not believe his ears when in the interval June casually mentioned, 'You know, my father shot Chung Ling Soo.' It happened that her father, Jack Grossman, then a sprightly eighty-one years of age, was alive and well and living in Sheffield. A meeting between Davis and Grossman led to the eventual restaging of the Soo bullet-catching for television in November 1982, with Paul Daniels in the robes of Soo's Chinese mandarin and Grossman, the only marksman on this revised occasion, at the trigger. In the audience was Hector Robinson, the 73-year-old son of the great illusionist, only eight years old at the time of his father's tragedy. Although he had seen his father perform many times at matinées, he had never seen him attempt to catch the bullets: Soo thought it unsuitable for the children who were a staple part of his matinée audiences. It was an eerie experience for both men. Soo had died because one of the gimmicked muskets which he used had developed a flaw. The musket featured by Paul Daniels, while similar in appearance, was a rare 1880 specimen from the BBC's own armoury. An assurance had to be given that it would not be tampered with: through the genius of magical craftsman Gil Leaney at no point in the proceedings was that promise broken. And Paul still caught the bullet. As he said at the time, 'It's the most exciting show I've ever done. There isn't a magician in the world who wouldn't give his right arm to be doing this.' Had Leaney been in Soo's original employ, the tragedy might never have happened.

Grossman had been on Soo's staff for eighteen months at the time of the accident and had never told his story except for the evidence he had been required to give at the coroner's court. On the programme, when inter-

Quelques-unes des Trucs présentés par CHUNG-LING-SOO à l'Alhambra.

A comprehensive record of Soo's repertoire at the Paris Alhambra, 1912.

What other magicians conjured from a hat, Soo produced from a cauldron.

Above, Soo's stage set for 'Defying the Bullets' in all its military splendour.
Below, Paul about to re-create Soo's most dangerous exploit with Jack Grossman.

viewed by Paul Daniels, he conveyed a number of details which were not given at the inquest. On their way home together a few days before Soo died, the older man had confided to his assistant that there were times when he would have been happier earning five pounds a week as an un-known performer than the £500 he could then command on a percentage basis. He explained how he was suffering from the after-effects of dysentery acquired on a foreign tour. A tense atmosphere off-stage between himself and Suee Seen, the real-life Mrs Olive or 'Dot' Robinson, who – while openly living with another member of the company – refused Soo a divorce to live with the Englishwoman he loved and by whom he now had three children, contributed to his general unhappiness. Grossman claimed that Soo's contract with Stoll Theatres, the principal music hall circuit, stipulated that he wear a bullet-proof vest whenever he performed 'Defying the Bullets'. On the night in question this was left in the dressing-room. Over the years Grossman had had ample time in which to formulate his own verdict: 'Murder? I don't think so. But from what I saw of Soo and from what he told me before he died, it *could* have been suicide.'

In retrospect it is difficult to believe that Grossman's recall had not become distorted over the years. As Hector Robinson has since been at pains to point out, the matter of the bullet-proof vest was not brought up at the inquest, as it surely would have been had such a clause existed in Soo's contract. Even less credible is the fact that a man of Soo's fifty-seven years would have been prepared to discuss his intimate marital problems with an extremely junior employee no more than seventeen years of age. Had suicide figured in Soo's plans, there is surely no way he would choose such a fantastically chancy method. At the inquest both Grossman and Crowley were asked where they were supposed to aim their guns. They replied, 'In the general direction of Mr Soo.' The possibility of a fatal wound, as distinct from being maimed for life, in such circumstances, would have been remote. Ultimately all the more sensational theories must stand refuted by the expert evidence given at the inquest by Robert Churchill and the precise nature of the malfunction of the gun in question, a flaw caused by gradual wear and not by malice aforethought. If any criticism can be levelled against Soo himself it is no more than that of carelessness born of ignorance.

Since the television reconstruction, Grossman himself has died. Whatever his theories, even he never knew the answer to the ultimate puzzle: no one knows to this day whose weapon actually shot Soo. After the accident both muskets were taken away by the police. At the inquest Crowley recalled that on the night in question his gun kicked much harder than usual against his shoulder. One can only surmise. For all the controversy surrounding both the original incident and the reconstruction, it is hard to believe that Grossman, an alert, down-to-earth man in his advanced years, was a seeker of sensation or publicity. If only for that, it is reassuring to think that he was not the one who fired the fatal bullet.

17

Houdini – the Magician as Mythical Figure

More attention has been lavished upon Houdini than any other entertainer of the vaudeville era. Even though he has been dead for more than sixty years, he is still today the subject of mass media concern, on a level with Chaplin in the movies and Sherlock Holmes in literature. In recent years a musical, an opera, as well as several films have been added to the countless books and articles written about him. To study the man and his life is soon to realise that the groundwork for such attention was laid by the performer himself, living as he did in morbid fear of the thought of obscurity in his own lifetime and taking extreme measures to avoid the same. His success outlasted its need, to an extent even he would find impossible to believe.

He was born Ehrich Weiss, the son of a Rabbi, not in Appleton, Wisconsin, on 6 April 1874, as he always claimed, but in Budapest, Hungary, thirteen days earlier. It would have been too neat a coincidence for his birthday to coincide with that of a later colleague, Paul Daniels himself, who was born on 6 April 1938. The proof that their lives do not match in this respect is the register of the Budapest Israelitic Cult-Parish Council which actually shows Houdini's date of birth as 24 March. It is possible that his parents contrived the later date in order for their child to be brought up an American citizen, but even so it is unlikely that the family arrived in the New World much before May. Quite feasibly confusion arose through the disparity between the Gregorian and Jewish calendars and the difficulties of communicating with non-Hungarian-speaking immigration officials on entry.

Amid the poverty of his early years he became captivated by magic, not least by the memoirs of the pioneering Robert-Houdin. So impressed was he that by the time he was seventeen he had already added an 'i' to the master's last name and was calling himself Houdini. A short, muscular individual, he had developed a powerful physique, proving himself to be a capable swimmer and diver. In the years to come magic and athleticism would complement each other in a way he could never have foreseen. As Harry Houdini (his first name was a variant of 'Ehrie', a childhood nickname), he slowly grafted his way in the company of his younger

The most penetrating gaze in show-business history.

brother Theo from dime museums and sideshows to the 1893 Chicago World's Fair. Within a short time he had married Wilhelmina Beatrice Rahner, a tiny brunette singer, known always as Bess, and developed an act with her, the central feature of which was an adaptation of the basic Maskelyne trunk mystery. Houdini christened his version 'Metamorphosis', an apt description in view of the rapid substitution that followed. He began with a detail overlooked by the many performers who have since re-created the effect. He would have his wrists tied together behind his back, then, taking a coat borrowed from a member of the audience, step within a small curtained cabinet. Seconds later he would appear wearing the jacket,

Long before Houdini entered the world of escapology he adopted a less dangerous speciality.

but with his wrists still tied. His wrists having been examined, Houdini –
still wearing the coat – would now be secured within an examined sack;

which in turn was locked inside the trunk. The trunk was positioned just inside the curtained enclosure. Bess would explain what was to happen. 'I will step into the cabinet and clap my hands three times – then notice the effect.' She did so, and less than three seconds later Houdini stepped out. When the trunk and the sack – both apparently untampered-with – were opened, it was Bess who now wore the jacket, her hands tied behind her. The lightning speed of the change and the emphasis on the restraints involved gave Houdini two strong selling-points. The trick still astounds today, particularly in the act of 'The Pendragons', themselves physical culture experts and stunt performers as well as magicians, and therefore spiritual heirs to Houdini in more ways than one.

It was at this time that Houdini developed his fascination for handcuffs, eventually substituting them for the rope used to secure his wrists within the sack. He had hopes for a whole act based on handcuff escapes, but theatre managers at first refused to see any glamour in such an idea. Long before Houdini's time, an Australian by the name of Godfrey had presented in America a challenge act of this kind, in which local police chiefs and locksmiths were invited to bring their own handcuffs with which to secure the performer on stage. Gradually Houdini applied the showmanship born of necessity and ambition, offering rewards of rising value to anyone who could handcuff him so that he could not escape. Study and dedication made his knowledge in this area encyclopaedic. No matter what pattern or age the handcuffs in question, Houdini would succeed where rival 'handcuff kings' succumbed. He was still a small-time

Houdini could not resist the challenge of the stocks on a visit to Ashton-under-Lyne, Lancashire in April 1909.

Harry with his beloved Bess.

sideshow attraction, but by the time he made it big theatrically in Europe at the turn of the century he was offering £100 to anyone who succeeded in 'fixing' him with their own fetters, this in addition to a $5,000 world challenge whereby he would forfeit the same to anyone who could duplicate his escapes from handcuffs and leg irons under test conditions:

> That is to strip stark naked, be thoroughly searched, mouth sealed up, making it impossible to conceal keys, springs, or lock pickers, and in that state escape from all fetters that may be locked or laced on arms, legs, or body.

As the wording of the challenge implies, Houdini now included straitjackets within his scope. On a visit to a mental institution in New Brunswick, Canada, in 1896, he had observed an inmate struggling within such a restraint. Obtaining a regulation garment from the physician, he took it home to analyse its construction and after a week of arduous practice was ready to present an escape from the leather and canvas tunic on stage. Today, because of Houdini and virtually every escape artist since, audiences tend to associate straitjackets with escapologists first and their more serious purpose second. In Houdini's time they had a grimmer, more realistic connotation, which greatly enhanced the dramatic effect Houdini was able to achieve. The item would not come completely into its own, however, until much later in his career when Houdini had the chance to present the illusion outdoors, suspended upside-down by his ankles from a rope attached to the cornice of a tall building. It became one of his most memorable publicity stunts, always concluding with the straitjacket falling and the showman taking a bow upside-down in the air.

Houdini did not come within real reach of stardom until March 1899. He was appearing in a small hall at St Paul, Minnesota. After the show a short, stocky man with a German accent approached him, anxious to know whether Houdini could escape from *any* manacles. Houdini replied that the restraints did not exist from which he could not free himself. The man was Martin Beck, the famous booker for the Orpheum Vaudeville circuit. He wasted no time in testing the brash young showman's claim and immediately offered him a contract on condition that he played down the magic in his act in favour of the handcuff escapes. Houdini's original instinct had been confirmed, at the same time as a more significant escape had been set in motion. Houdini and Bess were about to break out of the small time.

Beck's professional intuition about the act proved correct. Houdini was a sensation in vaudeville, but after a year became restless for a wider challenge and decided to try his luck in England. He arrived without a contract in his pocket and approached the manager of London's prestigious Alhambra music hall for work. He was treated with indifference, until Houdini explained that he was going to take the manager of the rival Empire Theatre with him to Scotland Yard to see a full demonstration of his special talent. The result was that the Alhambra manager escorted the escape artist to police headquarters himself. 'I think this fellow is crazy – lock him up for a while,' the impresario remarked to the inspector in charge, who obliged by handcuffing Houdini around a pole. This feature of the restraint seemed unusual to the escapologist. 'This is the way we lock 'em up over here,' explained the officer. 'And this is the way we get out of them in America,' replied Houdini, freeing himself in an instant. The following week he opened at the Alhambra. It was July 1900. Within a year he was the top music hall attraction in Europe.

Houdini's flair for challenge and the unusual kept his name constantly in the eye of the wider newspaper-reading public. On 17 March 1904, for example, his showmanship was put to the supreme test at a special matinée held at the London Hippodrome in answer to a challenge from the *Daily Mirror*, then the *Daily Illustrated Mirror*. If ever proof were needed of the skill and ingenuity required to perform his handcuff act, this was the occasion. Representatives of the newspaper claimed they had found a Birmingham blacksmith who had devised a special pair of handcuffs which no mortal could pick. So cunning was its mechanism that it had taken five years to construct, with six sets of locks and nine tumblers in each cuff.

The formidable manacles were clamped to his wrists and at 3.15 p.m. he entered his cabinet. After twenty-two minutes he emerged to look at the cuffs in the better light of the footlights. Thirteen minutes later he requested a cushion for his sore knees. This was handed to him inside the cabinet. Twenty minutes later he emerged exhausted to ask for the cuffs to be temporarily removed so that he could take off his coat. This request was denied, on the grounds that he had not so far seen the unlocking process. In full view of the audience he then removed a penknife from his waistcoat pocket, opened it with great difficulty between his teeth and, turning his jacket inside-out over his head, proceeded to shred it to ribbons. This characteristic display of determination and dexterity brought cheers from the audience. Again he entered the cabinet. At long last, after a total of seventy minutes, he emerged free. In all that time the orchestra had played on relentlessly, the tension in the auditorium simmering to near boiling point. Exultant, Houdini held up the handcuffs. As a mighty roar went up from the crowd, tears were rolling down his cheeks. Amid the pandemonium, Houdini was raised shoulder-high by the committee on stage. Many are the theories as to how he met the challenge, not least that the Birmingham blacksmith had approached the press at Houdini's instigation. But the methods are as nothing compared with the skill, flair

Houdini gave vaudeville audiences triple value for money at the end of his career.

and dramatic insight with which he could capture the imagination of the public, raising an audience to near hysteria with, in effect, a minimum of action over such a protracted length of time.

Once Houdini got into his stride, there was no limit to the number of unique restraints he was prepared to tackle. In Russia, he escaped from a Siberian Transport Cell, a heavily armoured van used to transport prisoners; in Holland, from the sail of a windmill, even though the sail broke; in London, from the manacles that had restrained Comte de Lorge in the Bastille for fifteen years; in Washington, DC from the cell on 'Murderers' Row' that held Charles J. Guiteau, the assassin of President Garfield. On this last occasion, he not only freed himself, but also opened the doors to all the other cells, told the prisoners to change places, and then relocked them in their new homes, all without the authorities' knowledge. He escaped underwater from a fully weighted regulation diving suit after the headpiece had been padlocked to the shoulders and the air supply cut off. He was nailed, handcuffed and leg-ironed inside a packing case weighted down with 200 pounds of lead and thrown overboard into the murky deep: fifty-seven seconds later he reappeared at the surface.

In addition to the more statutory ladders, chairs, railway lines, coffins, safes, and milk churns to which he was tied or confined, there were other restraints that took on sublimely surrealistic overtones in this context: jumbo-size paper bags; zinc-lined piano cases; a gigantic lace-up football made by a local sports goods manufacturer; a plate-glass box made by the Pittsburgh Glass Company; even a colossal sausage skin. Without doubt the most bizarre escape of his life was performed in Boston in 1911 when, manacled again, he was laced and chained inside the embalmed body of a 'sea-monster' weighing seven tons – a cross between a whale and an octopus – that had been beached near Cape Cod. On this occasion the arsenical fumes from the taxidermist's preservation fluid proved to be a far greater challenge than the swirling waters of the East River. Houdini declared he would never try a similar escape again. But however esoteric the imprisonment, the conclusion was always the same. Whatever he escaped from, the object itself was never damaged or physically altered in the process. This enables one to see why he regarded the seemingly simple paper bag escape as one of the most difficult.

No performer ever had a more secure grasp of showmanship. In later life he would describe the circumstances in which he first realised that: 'The public seek drama. Give them a hint of danger, perhaps of death, and you will have them packing in to see you.' Once, under pressure in his early days to get to a particular engagement in time, he arrived at a railway station without sufficient funds for his fare. He offered to leave his luggage as security, but the stationmaster refused to give him a ticket. He was at his wits' end when inspiration struck. Flinging himself down on to the track, he declared at the top of his voice, 'I will not move from here until I am allowed to board the train.' Not only did he eventually get his ticket but,

Opposite, one of his more unusual restraints, revived with great effect in recent years by the Amazing Randi.

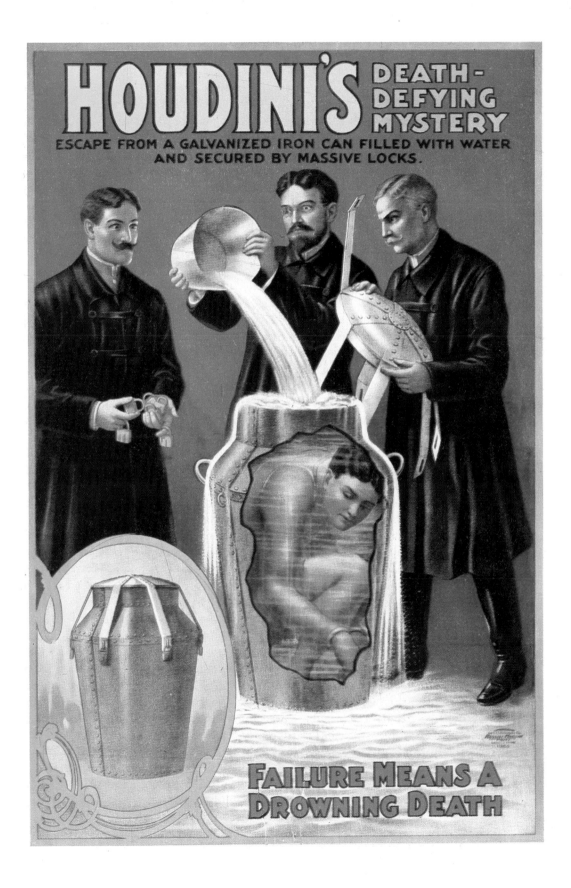

before that, a crowd of spectators. From this simple incident sprang the philosophy that informed his entire career.

It was a foregone conclusion that when the new medium of the movies was ready, Houdini would attempt to translate this outlook to celluloid. He was not entirely successful: the realism his escapes carried in real life became diluted within the artificial confines of a dramatic plot, however great the pains he took to emphasise that all his feats were still performed by himself, without the aid of double or stuntman, even those like transferring from one plane to another in mid-air which had no obvious magic or escapology link. However, films such as *The Grim Game*, *Terror Island*, *The Man from Beyond* and *Haldane of the Secret Service* played their own part in making Houdini the most recognisable name in magic.

So great was his fame that by 1920 his name had even been honoured by inclusion – as a verb, 'to houdinize', meaning 'to escape' – in Funk and Wagnall's celebrated dictionary. George Bernard Shaw once said that the three most famous people, real or imaginary, were Jesus Christ, Sherlock Holmes and Houdini. Almost half a century after his death, when E. L. Doctorow penned his celebrated novel *Ragtime*, Houdini was included alongside Henry Ford and Sigmund Freud in the small handful of celebrities whose lives were used to throw into focus the author's bitter and perceptive view of early twentieth-century America. In spite of these accolades, however, even today magicians discuss disparagingly his relative merit as a magician as distinct from escape artist, contending that the former was not the equal of the latter. One wonders if away from commercial considerations Houdini ever really distinguished between the two. He knew deception was needed in both cases. He once defined showmanship as follows, 'The secret of showmanship consists not of what you really do, but of what the mystery-loving public thinks you do.' Well, the public really thought he did materialise through solid walls, even if it failed to believe that he, or anyone else for that matter, could actually make an elephant disappear. The fact that the public believed his escapes was as great a compliment to his instinctive grasp of illusion and stagecraft as that accorded to any performer in this book.

There was one illusion in his repertoire that successfully balanced the probable with the impossible. It was introduced by P. T. Selbit at Maskelyne's St George's Hall in June 1914, where it caused an immediate sensation. Sidney Josolyne, a lesser London performer, instantly claimed the effect as his own invention. Whereas Selbit had caused a girl to walk through a brick wall, Josolyne had caused her to penetrate a metal plate. Houdini, knowing a good thing when he saw it, bought the American rights from Josolyne, but rather cheekily incorporated the brick wall of the Selbit presentation. Within a month it was the hit of his programme at Hammerstein's Roof Garden in New York, now all the more sensational because Houdini himself passed through the wall. He was the one conceivable person who just might be physically able to do so.

In the Houdini version, as in Selbit's, the audience first saw a team of bricklayers erect a wall about nine feet high on a steel beam on rollers only two inches above the stage. A large canvas cloth was stretched over the floor and members of the audience asked to stand on its corners. A rug was in turn placed over the centre of the canvas and the wall moved into position at right-angles to the front of the stage. There were obviously no traps in either canvas or rug to enable anyone to pass beneath the wall. Nor were there any traps in the wall itself: its solidity could be tested with hammers. Two small three-fold screens were then placed on opposite sides of the wall. Houdini went behind one shouting, 'Here I am', then, 'Now I'm going', to be followed finally a few seconds later by, 'Now I'm on the other side.' When the screens were removed, this was the case. And yet he could not have climbed over or walked around behind the wall since a committee from the audience surrounded the whole proceedings. Everything could be examined. There was no way Houdini could have got from one side of the solid structure to the other, unless he was actually able to walk through a solid brick wall! As his publicity declared, he made 'The Impossible Possible'.

The plot has an engaging simplicity that was bound to capture the imagination of Paul Daniels. Anxious to preserve every single condition of impossibility, how could he prove even more conclusively that there was no actual route through the wall? Paul's answer was to get members of the audience to build a wall not of bricks, but of free-standing china mugs – literally a 'Great Wall of China'. If as many as one was removed, the whole lot would come crashing down. All the other conditions were the same, except that small tunnels replaced the larger screens, while the impossibility of Paul passing under the wall was emphasised even further by the typically solid concrete of the television studio floor. As Houdini had done before him, Paul literally melted through. The great escapologist, however, had not had the eventual satisfaction of being able to dislodge one mug and send the whole wall crashing to the floor in smithereens, proof that with such a precarious structure all the obvious solutions were out of the question. Never has a magician's face shown greater relish than Paul's at that moment.

Of all the items performed by Paul Daniels on stage and television, the one that has most captured the spirit of Houdini must be the sequence filmed on the British Grand Prix motor racing circuit at Silverstone. Chained and manacled as Houdini had been so many times before, Paul too was tied in a sack and then nailed into a wooden packing case. A crane manoeuvred the crate into the most vulnerable position in the centre of the track at the same time as three-times world motor racing champion, Jackie Stewart, driving a specially developed RS 200, started a lap of the three-mile course, the challenge being for Paul to escape before Jackie, travelling at 160 m.p.h., crashed into the box. Paul's only contact with the outside world in case of emergency was a red flag with which he could

Paul at Silverstone, with Mike Smith and Jackie Stewart, about to face the most shattering moment of his career.

signal through a hole in the crate. The suspense that must have hung over many a Houdini crowd as the escapologist still showed no sign of extricating himself from the restraint of the moment, lived again in the Buckinghamshire countryside as Stewart drove at relentless speed around the course. With a quarter of a mile to go there was still no sign of Paul Daniels; with less than a hundred yards the flag appeared, too late for Stewart to avert a direct collision, sending a cascade of splinters into the air. The crowd, not least commentator Mike Smith, was choked with emotion. They could make out the remains of the red sack beneath the car. It screeches to a halt. Jackie Stewart emerges. He takes off his helmet. It's Paul Daniels. Where then is Jackie Stewart? He's driving the crane! Houdini would have approved. The best elements of the traditional escape and his beloved 'metamorphosis' illusion had been combined to produce one thrilling sequence that no one who witnessed it, least of all Mike Smith, will ever forget.

Traditionally, the most dangerous of all Houdini's regular stage escapes was the upside-down restraint known as the 'Chinese Water Torture Cell'. When it was first suggested to Paul Daniels that he might perform this on television, the initial reply was not the expected negative born of fear and an inability to swim, but the resigned admission of a true professional that if he were going to perform the feat in the requisite bathing costume, he must first cultivate a body tan! In the end his son Martin risked a watery end, if only because of the need dictated by television for an informed presenter to place the item in its full historical context – and who better for that than Paul? It has been suggested that in the future the tables might be turned, with Martin securing his father inside the cell. In the meantime this is the place to remind ourselves of the impact Houdini made with this spectacular item. He first exhibited it publicly during an engagement with the famous Circus Busch in Germany in 1912. A thoroughly examined, metal-lined, mahogany tank with a plate-glass front was filled with water. A metal cage was lowered within, this to contain Houdini should the glass have to be broken and the water made to escape. Houdini's ankles were now secured in heavy stocks encased in a metal frame and his whole body first hoisted up and then, amid much splashing, lowered head first into the water. The top of the tank was padlocked without delay and a curtained canopy pulled around the whole structure. Assistants stood by with axes in case of the worst. Mournfully the orchestra played 'The Diver', while the audience held its breath to bursting-point to see if it could survive as long as Houdini. The impossibility of anyone obtaining extra air in that inverted position had already been pointed out. In fact he issued a $1,000 reward to anyone who could prove otherwise. Two minutes later the curtains parted and Houdini, dripping with water and exhaustion, shambled out on to the stage. As always, the tank was sealed as securely as when it first went out of view behind the canopy.

One of the great myths of Houdini's legend, perpetrated by the 1953 film of his name starring Tony Curtis in the title role, is that Houdini actually lost his life in the first 'unsuccessful' attempt to perform his escape from the 'Chinese Water Torture Cell'. In fact the item had been a regular and always successful feature in his repertoire for no less than fourteen years when he died on 31 October 1926. The circumstances leading to his death are more grotesque. While playing Montreal on 22 October, he received a visit backstage from some students from McGill University. Casually one of them, J. Gordon Whitehead, asked the performer if it was correct that he could withstand blows to his stomach without discomfort. Houdini replied that he could indeed, whereupon the student asked for permission to aim some experimental punches. Before Houdini had time to brace himself, Whitehead delivered four heavy blows against his midriff. His two colleagues thought Whitehead had gone berserk and all three departed swiftly. That night Houdini continued to perform in spite of increasing abdominal pain. When he reached the next town, Detroit, acute appendicitis was diagnosed, but he made the vain and fatal mistake of playing one last performance to a full house before being rushed, but only· at the insistence of an hysterical Bess, to hospital. He was operated upon immediately, but peritonitis had already set in. He died a week later,

Few escapes contributed more to the myth of Houdini than the ordeal of the 'Chinese Water Torture'.

appropriately on Hallowe'en, the date when traditionally the spirits are released from their bonds to wander at large on earth.

In the months and years to come many attempts were made to establish spiritual contact with Houdini himself. In the last years of his life he had become an ardent adversary of fraudulent spirit mediums: indeed, his final full evening show comprised one-third devoted to escapes, one-third to more conventional magic, and one-third to the exposure of the methods used by unscrupulous mediums. He made it clear that he respected genuine believers, but equally so that he had never met a genuine medium, which was not to say that such a person did not exist. Before he died, it is likely that he made a pact with Bess that if he should die before her he would attempt to make contact from the spirit world. On the tenth anniversary of his death, Bess held her last public seance. Since then many magicians and psychic investigators have taken her commitment upon themselves, but Houdini, for all the resilience and self-assurance, resourcefulness and drive within his worldly self, has still not made his incontrovertible presence known. His admirers today must be content with the knowledge that whenever he underwent one of his more dangerous escapes, he was enacting a symbolic ritual of death and rebirth. His countless triumphs doubtless heightened expectation that he could one day set himself free from the bonds of death itself, but here even Houdini proved powerless. Many years previously Osiris, the ancient Egyptian god of death and resurrection, had been nailed within a box, sealed with molten lead, and cast into the Nile. Houdini simply redefined the ritual in the context of the American Dream, conveying a message of hope and optimism to the people of his own day.

The March 1913 issue of *The Magicians' Monthly*, a popular journal of the conjuring profession, contained a vivid account of Houdini on stage written by a spectator invited to act as a committeeman in his presentation of the 'Chinese Water Torture Cell':

If ever there was a born fighter, Houdini is one! There is a suggestion of the great Napoleon about his head and the carriage of his body. 'You in front,' he seems to say, 'which of you are my friends and which my enemies? Which believe in me and which do not? But it matters little. I am what I am; I do what I say I do. It is Harry Houdini who stands before you.' The man has personality. The mere sight of him stirs you. There is an electric feeling in the air. And when he speaks, the grip he already has on you grows tighter. As the words, well chosen, deliberate, full of meaning, come forcefully from his lips, you listen as to a master.

It is worth being reminded of what these words convey. Hero, symbol, legend he undoubtedly became, but first and foremost he was quite simply a very great performer.

18

Myth or Magic?

The world of myth and legend and the world of stage magic are inextricably linked, both standing for the triumph of the possible over the impossible and awakening in the individual a sense of wonder in relation to the universe, at once mundane and mysterious, in which he lives. Houdini's own mythical status is due in no small measure to the fact that he was able to enact the role of wonder-worker upon the wider, non-theatrical stage of the universe itself, his most publicised escapes being played against a real live backdrop of the world's most spectacular rivers, skyscrapers and bridges. It is not surprising, therefore, that when in 1985 BBC Television bestowed upon 'The Paul Daniels Magic Show' the financial facility to record sequences on location away from the studio, the programme should look to legend and mythology for major inspiration.

Several of Paul's more adventurous excursions into escapology away from the restrictions of a studio have already been chronicled. It is doubtful, though, if any would have flattered Houdini himself more than Paul's portrayal of 'Robin Hoodini', the myth of the noble outlaw confirming that of the 'Handcuff King'. This hybrid of two legendary characters, separated in history by possibly seven centuries, was conceived as a pastiche of the early television series in which Richard Greene portrayed the hero of Sherwood Forest. In actual fact, Robin Hoodini, with his special method of robbing from the rich to give to the poor by the simple expedient of appropriately rigging his 'Olde Bunco Boothe', at first owed more to Paul Daniels than to either of the legends. Only when Paul was detained by the Sheriff of Nottingham, played with dastardly relish by the celebrated actor Lionel Jeffries, did the spirit of Harry Houdini assert itself. Shackled to a target before the precision gaze of a long line of archers, Paul could not possibly extricate himself. Eventually the arrows piercing his corpse, which is delivered to the sheriff at a funereal pace by Little John and Friar Tuck, are conclusive proof that he has not escaped. But the Sheriff knows naught of Hoodini. No sooner is the body found to be made of straw than Friar Tuck, involved for all to see in tying Robin to

Left, Debbie McGee made a magical Maid Marian for Paul's Robin Hoodini. *Right*, Ali Bongo portrayed Merlin when Paul re-created the magic of the Camelot legend.

the target in the first place, throws back his cowl to reveal – Hoodini!

Paul Daniels was not the first magician to play Robin Hood. It was the portrayal of this role by Jasper Maskelyne, the grandson of John Nevil, in a village amateur pantomime that persuaded his family that he must pursue his agricultural apprenticeship no longer – his personality and flair would be far better employed in keeping the name of Maskelyne ablaze on theatrical marquees. In time Jasper would retire from the stage, emigrate to Kenya, and return to his beloved farming, but not before he had proved himself to be possibly the most illustrious performer among all his grandfather's offspring. In the same way Paul was not the first magician to address himself to the challenge presented by Arthurian legend and the reputation of the wizard Merlin. In 1983 Doug Henning portrayed the magician as his younger self in the Broadway musical called simply *Merlin*. Henning met the challenge magnificently, but was restricted by the four walls of the Mark Hellinger Theatre. Paul Daniels, for one performance only, had the breathtaking natural splendour of Tintagel Castle in Cornwall, Arthur's reputed birthplace, as a backcloth, while below – as if for magical inspiration – the waves crashed into the cave in which legend says Merlin lived.

The wizard's most celebrated feat had been to secure the accession of the young Arthur to the throne by assembling all the contenders when King

Uther Pendragon died. Only Arthur was able to pull the glittering sword, Excalibur, from the stone anvil and thus claim the monarchy for himself. Without attempting to portray Merlin in any way, Paul was content to stage-manage a ceremony in which five swords petrified into five stones arranged symbolically at the five points of a pentagram were seen to defeat the strength of five of Cornwall's strongest men. A young boy was then given the chance to pull any of those swords from its stone. The one he chose came away as compliantly as had Arthur's all those years before. Amid cheers from the crowd – 'I bet Prince Charles is worried,' joked Paul – the boy was hailed King for a day. For the second time in history thanks were due to Merlin, but no sooner had the boy caught sight of the actual figure of the wizard surveying the scene from a battlement than the magician disappeared. There was one thing left to do. Climbing the rampart overlooking the cave, Paul, as Arthur had ordered Sir Bedivere to do long ago, hurled the sword into the water. With an eerie dignity the hand that caught it slowly emerged above the waves, the blade glinting in the sun. Seconds after the completion of filming, a Royal Naval rescue launch turned into the cove in response to reports of strange happenings. It was as if some supernatural agency were intent on bringing Paul Daniels and the entire crew back to reality with a bump, if not actually puncturing the whole legend of Arthur, Merlin and Tintagel. The dinghy, you see, was a pneumatic one!

At the opposite end of the British Isles another watery location with supernatural overtones claimed Paul Daniels's attention. Few legends have had such a consistent hold upon the British imagination as that of the Loch Ness Monster. The size of the loch, approximately twenty-four miles long and 750 feet deep, gives it a capacity almost twice the size of the entire North Sea. You could immerse the whole human race in Loch Ness three times over and still lose them. Such statistics would appear to have room to accommodate a mystery or two. With this in mind Paul Daniels embarked upon the most extraordinary expedition in magical history. In the 1930s the illusionist P. T. Selbit had responded to a challenge from Bertram Mills Circus. Mills was offering £20,000 to anyone who could produce the monster which, for insurance reasons, had been defined on behalf of the Circus by two fellows of the Royal Zoological Society as 'an animal and/or reptile and/or fish either hitherto unknown or believed to be extinct, measuring not less than twenty feet in length or weighing not less than one thousand pounds'. Selbit's plan had been to stage a 'Disappearance of the Loch Ness Monster' nightly, but this would have involved using a fake, something Mills would not sanction whatever the publicity value. Selbit's consolation was that if he did not collect the reward, nobody else did either. To this day it stands, a fact that led Paul to thinking that the monster may exist at a spectral level like the village of Brigadoon, invisible most of the time and manifesting itself only occasionally.

And so one sunny June day, in the company of Scottish actor Fulton

Mackay and Tony Harmsworth, the curator of the Loch Ness Monster Exhibition, both present as independent witnesses to see fair play, Paul went fishing. In the centre of the loch various objects were consigned to the clear centre compartment of an oversized fishing float, all of them valid as possible bait with which to attract Nessie: a large egg found on the shore that morning; a picture of Robert Redford (Nessie is believed to be female, after all); a bowl of porridge and a spoon; a transistor radio without the batteries; and a hip flask full to the brim with whisky. The actor and the curator were both invited to mark any object at random with their signature on labels. The whole device was lowered over the side of the boat on to the surface of the dark, peat-coloured water. At no point did the clear section go out of sight of cameras or committee. Then the disturbance came. An angler fishing in the distance capsized. A trail of bubbles surged towards the float. It was rapidly hauled back on board. One by one the objects were checked. The signatures were intact, but that was all: the hip flask was empty; the radio now played – 'Does this prove that Nessie is radioactive?'; the porridge had been eaten; the spoon was bent; the black and white photograph of Robert Redford blushed pink; and the egg had

Nessie lurks behind Paul in the gloom of Loch Ness.

hatched in its incubator into a squirming mass of baby monsters. Tongue-in-cheek and with superb entertainment value Paul had proved his thesis in circumstances as stringent as those of any of the experiments performed in the studio 'Under Laboratory Conditions'. But he had not reckoned that Nessie would leave her calling card in lieu of the bait attached beneath the float. The physical nature of the message 'You can't catch me! – Nessie' should have warned him that if his theory was correct, this might well be the day when Nessie appeared. Fulton Mackay was the first to see her. Paul was still sceptical, dismissing the actor's sighting over his shoulder as an old pantomime joke. Until, that is, he looked himself. 'Full steam ahead!' The chase was on!

Of all the illusions in magic none has attained a more mythical status than the 'Indian Rope Trick'. In that respect it is conjuring's own Loch Ness Monster, having for many years been at the centre of a controversy that questions its very existence. Many stage magicians – not least Devant, Goldin, Thurston, Hertz and Blackstone – have presented approximations of the effect in the controlled circumstances of a theatre stage. Ironically, however, it was never performed by the most prestigious Indian magician of modern times, Sorcar (1913–71), who relied almost exclusively on magical principles developed in the West, when not cutting off and then restoring a slither of flesh from the tongue of a member of his audience! Maybe Sorcar, so close to the tradition that inspired the legend, was more sensitive than most to the shortcomings that would exist between what was possible theatrically and the sheer impossibility of the original which, to be worthy of its reputation, had to be performed outdoors where there was little opportunity to use stage chicanery.

The first eyewitness account of the 'Indian Rope Trick' was that of Abu Abdullah Mohammed, the Arab theologian, also known as Ibn Batuta, 'The Traveller'. The manuscript in which he recorded his journeys was completed in 1355, although not translated into English until early in the nineteenth century. He placed the performance of the miracle at Hangchau in China, although recent evidence that he may never have reached that country suggests that he may have seen it in India after all. He does state that the time was the hottest season of the year, the place the middle of the courtyard or garden of a palace:

> I was entertained by the Emir in his own home in a most splendid manner. At the banquet were present the Khan's jugglers, the chief of whom was ordered to show some of his wonders. He then took a wooden sphere, in which there were holes, and in these long straps, and threw it up into the air till it went out of sight, as I myself witnessed, while the strap remained in his hand. He then commanded one of his disciples to take hold of, and ascend by this strap, which he did until he also went out of sight. His master then called him three times, but no answer came; he then took a knife in his hand, apparently in anger, laid

hold of the strap and also went quite out of sight. He then threw the
hand of the boy upon the ground, then his foot, then his other hand,
then his other foot, then his body, then his head. He then came down,
panting for breath, and his clothes stained with blood. The juggler then
took the limbs of the boy and applied them one to another; he then
stamped upon them, and it stood up complete and erect. I was
astonished, and was seized in consequence by a palpitation at the heart;
but they gave me some drink and I recovered.

Over the years the detail of what is supposed to happen has become
stylised. When Paul Daniels was presented with a recording schedule that
took him outdoors, the challenge of re-creating the 'Indian Rope Trick' in
this stylised form became too great to resist. Accordingly, in the grounds
of Longleat viewers saw Paul charm one end of an otherwise limp rope
twelve feet off the ground where it hovered in the breeze. An Indian boy,
magically produced from a cobalt blue shawl, was commanded to climb.
Upon reaching the summit he disappeared in a burst of flame, at the same
time as his clothes fell to the ground. Paul, with a dagger clenched between
his teeth, ascended the rope in pursuit. As he brandished the weapon the
dismembered pieces of the boy's body plummeted gruesomely out of the
atmosphere to the ground below. Paul came down. Delicately he returned
the corpse and the clothes to the basket. This was covered with the original
blue shawl. Slowly a form materialised beneath. It was the boy. As
magician and child took their bow, the rope collapsed, inanimate once
more. No butchery had taken place. A twin had not been used. To all
intents and purposes the 'Indian Rope Trick' had taken place according to
legend.

But had it? Paul was well aware that his presentation, while the first in
recorded history to be performed in full detail al fresco by a Western
magician, embraced the subtle application of theatrical methods to the
outdoor environment, methods inconsistent with so many hearsay
versions of the effect, not least the need to wait for nightfall to perform an
illusion often associated with blazing sunlight. Over the years many
rewards had been offered for the performance of the trick under such
conditions, not least by the Magic Circle, John Nevil Maskelyne, Houdini,
Bertram Mills, and Edward VIII, then Prince of Wales. No Western
magician had ever seen it for himself. It had remained a chimera, the trick
that had always been seen by somebody else, but never by the person you
were speaking to at the time. And yet something, however basic, must
have happened to give rise to a legend so potent. In this context the most
remarkable aspect of that night at Longleat was not Paul's performance at
all, but a chain of events that began before the recording commenced and
did not conclude until six days later in a hospital 443 miles away, as the
crow flies, in Inverness.

To add colour and authenticity to the Longleat setting a small Indian

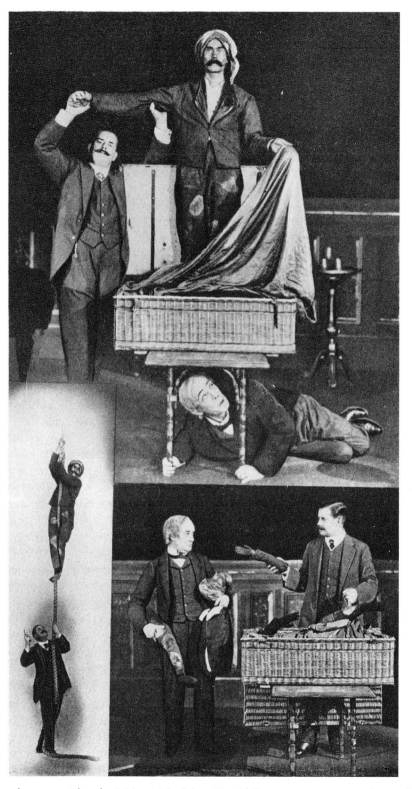

An early attempt by the Master Magician, David Devant, to re-create the 'Indian Rope Trick' on stage.

orchestra had been booked to play through the performance. Its leader was Shambhu Gupta, a one-time research chemist whose marriage to the sitar player Pumita Gupta led to his own professional involvement in re-creating the traditional music of his native land. Until he arrived at Longleat he had no idea of what exactly was required of himself and his colleagues other than to participate in 'The Paul Daniels Magic Show'. No sooner had Paul explained to him that they were to accompany a performance of the 'Indian Rope Trick' than he exclaimed, 'Oh, I've seen that.' He then proceeded to recall his experience as a boy in the Rajasthan district of India, where every autumn at festival time strolling players would come round to the schools to entertain, usually on the playing field. On the occasion in question the itinerant magician took from a sack a heavy coil of rope and placed it upon the ground. He then started to play a snake-charmer's flute and the rope began to rise into the air until it was hovering erect with the lower end about three feet from the ground. He asked a boy to grab that end and pull, but the rope would not come back. Then something seemed to go amiss. The rope started to go higher and higher, the boy still holding the end of the rope with both hands and screaming. Suddenly the screams stopped. Both the boy and the rope had disappeared. The magician, a fine actor into the bargain, gave a show of great pain and anxiety, claiming that someone evil in the crowd had compromised his control of the trick and that he had lost his son as a result. On the verge of tears himself, he carried the crowd as far as he could emotionally before admitting that there was a way to bring back the boy. A great offering had to be made to a particular god. This required travelling to the Himalayas to engage in intense prayer, but without money that was impossible. If he could now make a sincere promise that he would go, then the boy would come back. Here was religion's answer to the post-dated cheque. Everyone in the crowd threw their coins into a sheet. When the pile could grow no higher, slowly and mysteriously the vertical rope descended, the boy still holding the end. The magician bowed. The rope fell in a coil and was returned to its sack. As Mr Gupta explained, he had always had an inquisitive mind and could generally work things out for himself by questioning a particular situation. But he had never managed to understand how this trick was achieved. He had not described the full traditional version of the mystery. However, without any reason to boast, to exaggerate, or to latch on to a publicity bandwagon of any kind, he had offered a spontaneous description of what *he* had *seen*, not what somebody else who knew somebody else had seen.

Both elated and surprised by the circumstances of this account, Paul turned his attention to the performance of the traditional illusion. Unfortunately during the recording he suffered serious burns when the flash from a handful of gunpowder thrown into a blazing bowl shot right up his arm. He was rushed to hospital and the recording re-scheduled. In the early hours of the following morning he was discharged with

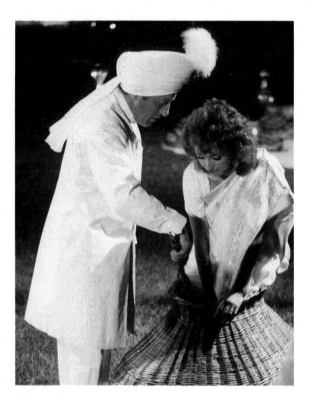

Debbie McGee helps Paul test the basket for his outdoor version of the 'Indian Rope Trick'.

permission to continue working, on the understanding that he report to a hospital each day for the surgical dressing to be renewed. Later that same week, after an arduous day filming on Loch Ness, he realised that he had so far not kept his promise for that day. It was eleven o'clock at night when he eventually strolled into Inverness Hospital to be greeted by Dr Singh, the Casualty Officer, who wanted to know the background to the accident. Paul mentioned the 'Indian Rope Trick'. Without knowing his response could well induce apoplexy in the magician, the doctor replied, 'Oh, I've seen that.'

Miraculously it transpired that he too had spent his boyhood in Rajasthan. Again it was the autumn festival season. Again a gypsy magician came to the school. But there the similarities ceased. On this occasion the illusion was performed indoors, in the school gymnasium. The magician called the attention of the audience to the climbing ropes hanging from the rafters. He went into a rage of stomping and stamping, chanting mantras at the top of his voice. When the audience looked up a second time, the tops of the ropes were detached eighteen inches from the rafters. The opposite ends were still not touching the floor, so he called several people, not from the crowd but members of his troupe, to hold on to them. He too had a flute, the playing of which occasioned the serpentine swaying of the tops of the ropes in unison. When the crowd looked down, the people holding the ropes had disappeared.

Opposite, the legendary illusion in all its splendour.

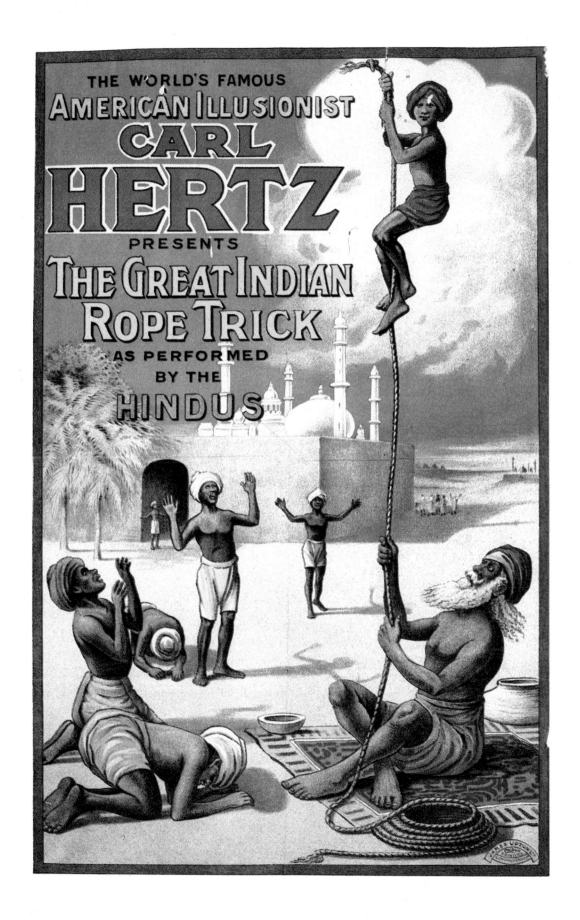

It is not difficult to imagine either episode. The oscillation of the ropes at one end would have provided ample misdirection to effect the exit of the people who supposedly vanished. The boy in the first report was obviously an accomplice. It is not unreasonable to suppose that from simpler effects like these the legend of a more spectacular happening grew, exaggerated and embroidered upon in the telling. Who knows exactly what Ibn Batuta saw? The Arab had a readership to satisfy. Besides, there has always been an honest tendency in magical audiences to distort the simplicity of what impresses them most. But how can one explain the circumstances in which a master magician received within a single week otherwise elusive eye-witness corroboration of the same phenomenon from differing sources based at opposite ends of the British Isles? It was as if Paul's accident had been predestined, the Inverness account ultimately transforming possible scepticism towards the first report into more resigned acceptance the second time around. The next stop must be Rajasthan. It might mean missing Hallowe'en.

19

Epilogue

Throughout its long history magic has known no greater aficionado than Orson Welles, who could list the levitation of Lucille Ball and the sawing into halves of Marlene Dietrich alongside his weightier cinematic achievements such as *Citizen Kane*. So important was magic in his life that shortly before he died he admitted, 'I'd be proud to be known as a great magician, though I never will be.' It was also Welles who said that any entertainment only ever succeeds because it corresponds with a particular moment in time. On this basis it is not difficult to find reasons for the upsurge in the interest in magic over the last decade. At a time when the ordinary citizen has come to acknowledge grudgingly that he is the constant dupe of bureaucracy and big business, he is more than happy to welcome into his life one legitimate fraud that can produce nothing but wonder. Paul Daniels sees the trend as part of a revolt against an entertainment system where the technology has tended to overshadow the performer. He is amazed how many young people there are in his audiences, and sees their enthusiasm as the natural reaction of a public seduced by the marketing hype of the recording industry and in the process cheated of a form of live entertainment it did not even realise was there.

Magic is fortunate in that for all the advanced technology available to magicians, methods simply not existing fifty years ago, that technology has never been allowed to overshadow the magician himself. The human contact between wonder-worker and his audience is still the most important asset magic has. No magician in the world today exploits the sheer humanity of this situation more engagingly than Paul Daniels, and nowhere is this more evident than in his presentation of the 'Chinese Rings', that trick in which solid steel bands melt through one another to link and unlink with no possible clue to a solution. However, it is here that Paul does give the clue to his own success. Having given two separate rings to a small girl coaxed from the audience, he proceeds with his lesson in magic. Holding something invisible between his finger and thumb, he hands it to her. 'Do you know what that is? It's called confidence.

Confidence is the most magical thing in the world. Once you've got that, you know, you can do anything. Yes. Swallow it.' Disbelievingly she does and to her amazement the rings link. 'And then, if you remember that you swallowed a little bit of confidence and that you stood in front of all these people and you just left it, that confidence will grow until one day, if you want to, you will be able to stand on a big stage like this all by yourself and you will be able to say, "My name is Jane. I am the world's greatest magician – er, second greatest magician." You will be able to join solid steel rings together like this and twiddle them all the way round; you'll be able to throw them up together and when they come down they'll be in a big long chain. And then when you feel like it you'll be able to knit one, purl two, and get one off, and then you'll get hold of another one and be able to take the second one off, and before you know where you are you will be back to where you started with one, two, three, four separate steel rings.'

The lesson is complete. The audience is beguiled by the charm of the situation, Paul playing Jiminy Cricket to the child's Pinocchio. But beneath the fairy story runs a subtext. Here is the story of Paul's success, a story in which positive thinking and hard conviction in oneself as performer play the principal parts.

It is hard to know what there is left for Paul to achieve as a magician. There are many tricks still to be performed, many ideas still to be explored, but none represents the ultimate challenge which his status dictates. The American Jerry Andrus, a legendary inventor of magic, once said, 'Every magician is looking for a trick that requires no deception.' Maybe that should be Paul's goal? Maybe it is possible to levitate yourself over the Grand Canyon without using camera trickery? Maybe the 'Indian Rope Trick' is waiting to be discovered and re-created in all its simple authenticity? Maybe . . . ? Magic is quite the most exciting of all the theatre arts, because it knows no ultimate limit.

Acknowledgments

The thanks of Paul Daniels and myself are due to many people for the part they have played in the completion of this volume. Especially I should like to place on record the help, encouragement, and/or inspiration received from: Jeffery Atkins, Will Ayling, Harry and Gay Blackstone, Ali Bongo, Jorgen Börsch, Peter Börsch, Marie Carlton, Mike Caveney, Caz, Maureen Christopher, the late Milbourne Christopher, the late Sidney W. Clarke, Malcolm Clay, Leslie Cole, Duncan Cooper, James Crossini, Nancy and Hughie Daniels, Sandy Davidson, Clifford Davis, Professor Edwin A. Dawes, David Drummond, Colin Fay, Charles Garland, John Gaughan, Marion Grimshaw, James Hagy, Ricky Jay, George Jenness, Peter Lane, Bill and Irene Larsen, Milt Larsen, Brian Lead, Gil Leaney, Tina Lenert, Debbie McGee, Billy Marsh, Jay Marshall, John Kennedy Melling, Hans and Helga Moretti, Mervyn O'Horan, Johnny and Winnie Paul, Peter Pit, David Price, Graham Reed, Charles and Regina Reynolds, John Salisse CBE, Neil Shand, Siegfried and Roy, Don Stacey, Harry Stanley, Paul Stone, Robert and Valerie Swadling, Joyce Waldeck, Donald and Betty Wallace, Bob Warans, Alan Wesencraft, Francis White, Mac Wilson, Karl-Heinz Ziethen.

For detailed information without which this record would not be complete I extend special gratitude to: Owen Griffiths on Buatier de Kolta; Bayard Grimshaw on Carmo; John Alexander McKinven on Roltair; Ben Robinson on the history of the Bullet-catch; Hector Robinson on his father, Chung Ling Soo; Jim Steinmeyer on Jarrett; Peter Warlock on P. T. Selbit; and Christopher Woodward on Maurice Fogel. More generally, I personally can never underestimate the help given and knowledge shared by Bayard Grimshaw and Peter Warlock. Their joint knowledge of magical matters is unsurpassed. I am honoured to be able to write in their shadow.

Over the years many people have contributed to make 'The Paul Daniels Magic Show' a success on television. It would be impossible to list every single name, but I would like to place on record the more recent technical efforts of Stuart Brisdon and Andy Lazell in making the impossible

possible; the precise and patient skills over many years of our editor John Sillitto, a wizard of another kind; and the enduring support of Bill Cotton, Michael Grade, James Moir, and Tony James at an executive level. Likewise worthy of special emphasis are the talents behind the scenes of this book itself: Anthony Colwell and Mandy Greenfield editorially, Ian Craig and Rowan Seymour for the design, and not least Tom Maschler for his initial impetus and total faith in the project throughout.

All the illustrations are derived from the personal collection of the author and/or the individual contemporary performers depicted, with the exception of those on the following pages: BBC Enterprises: 160, 251 bottom; the Milbourne Christopher Collection: 21 bottom, 167, 261; the Circus Fans Association: 182, 184; the Edwin A. Dawes Collection: 178; Irving Desfor and the American Museum of Magic, Marshall, Michigan, USA: 18, 96, 225; David Drummond, Pleasures of Past Times: 30 left, 33 left, 59, 67, 143, 202, 242 left; David Edwards: 13, 85, 131 right; the Peter Lane Collection: 161 left, 175, 176, 179 left, 233; Bill Larsen, the Magic Castle: 94 bottom, 97 right; Andy Lazell: 264 right, 269 left, 276; Jay Marshall: 46, 49, 227; John Alexander McKinven: 193; John Salisse, CBE: 121; Madame Tussaud's: 65; Mac Wilson, the Magic Circle: 69, 107, 119, 126, 127, 132/3, 141, 197, 222, 226, 251 top, 277; Christopher Woodward: 218 left; and Paul Daniels: 23 right, 52 right, 72, 84, 94 top, 110, 111, 163, 166, 171, 179 right, 203, 208, 209, 217, 234/5, 243, 246/7, 249, 250, 255, 264 left, and 271. It is the belief of both the publishers and myself that all necessary permissions have been obtained with reference to copyright material, both illustrative and quoted. However, should there be any omissions in this respect, we apologise and shall be pleased to make the appropriate acknowledgments in future editions.

Not least I have to thank my wife Susanna, and daughters Genevieve and Madeleine: without their loving tolerance *Paul Daniels and the Story of Magic* could not have been told.

London, July 1987   JOHN FISHER

Index

Figures in italics refer to illustrations